Deception

The last few decades of the 20th century demonstrated a greater awareness of the psychological significance of adolescent development. Research moved away from the earlier emphasis on adolescents' negative characteristics. As the new millennium progresses, psychology now takes a more positive view of adolescent development. Research looks at the tasks and challenges within the developmental progress of young people in society, with regards to cultural and technological innovations, their close relationships and the links across generations. This series reflects these changes by presenting up-to-date research findings in various aspects of adolescent development. It is intended for researchers on adolescence and will also be of interest to parents and practitioners.

Deception

A Young Person's Life Skill?

Rachel Taylor and Lynsey Gozna

Psychology Press
Taylor & Francis Group

HOVE AND NEW YORK

First published 2011
by Psychology Press
27 Church Road, Hove, East Sussex BN3 2FA

Simultaneously published in the USA and Canada
by Psychology Press
270 Madison Avenue, New York, NY 10016

*Psychology Press is an imprint of the Taylor & Francis Group, an
Informa business*

© 2011 Psychology Press

Typeset in Times by Garfield Morgan, Swansea, West Glamorgan
Printed and bound in Great Britain by TJ International Ltd,
Padstow, Cornwall
Cover design by Jim Wilkie

This publication has been produced with paper manufactured to strict
environmental standards and with pulp derived from sustainable
forests.

British Library Cataloguing in Publication Data
A catalogue record for this book is available from the British Library

Library of Congress Cataloging in Publication Data
Taylor, Rachel, 1974-
    Deception : a young person's life skill? / Rachel Taylor and Lynsey
Gozna.
        p. cm.
    Includes bibliographical references and index.
    ISBN 978-1-84169-876-2 (hb : alk. paper) 1. Deception in
adolescence. 2. Truthfulness and falsehood in adolescence.
3. Deception–Social aspects. I. Gozna, Lynsey, 1974- II. Title.
    BF724.3.T78T39 2010
    155.5'18–dc22
                                                          2010027861

ISBN: 978-1-84169-876-2 (hbk only)

Contents

Series preface

In the eyes of the mass media and in the minds of many adults, adolescents are often portrayed in largely negative terms, focusing on features such as their noisy and exuberant social behaviour, teenage gangs and their often violent, anti-social activities, teenage pregnancy, drinking, smoking drug-taking, anti-school attitudes and disagreements with parents.

Such portrayals are painted as if they were typical of what most, if not all, adolescents do, and, accordingly, regarded as a justification for adult society to consider the teenage years as a problem period in human development and adolescents as a problem for society.

For much of the 20th century, this popular, stereotypic picture was supported by what was written by social scientists in books and other publications, which presented adolescence as a period of "storm and stress". Adolescence was seen as a period of turbulence, inner turmoil and confusion, characterised by conflicts with parents, teachers and other authority figures.

Over the last three decades of the 20th century important theoretical changes began to emerge. Psychologists began to question the "storm and stress" perspective and to provide evidence that this developmental pattern was neither a typical nor a necessary part of adolescence. In parallel with this, a less problem-centred approach to thinking about adolescence began to emerge: an approach that emphasized processes of change and adjustment which young people undergo in responding to the varied tasks and transitions they face. An increasing number of books and articles on adolescence began to appear which differed markedly from earlier publications in emphasis and orientation. In contrast to the clinical perspective, this new work was based on a more empirical approach and focused upon a variety of different aspects of adolescent development. Further, longitudinal assessments over large time spans basically support the idea of a more gradual change leading to an overall positive outcome. Such publications stimulated further interest in adolescence as an area of study and in doing so started a process which led on to the emergence of research on adolescence as one of the most active fields in developmental psychological research. As a result, discussion of many aspects of adolescence has become a prominent feature of developmental conferences and scientific journals in Europe and elsewhere.

However, times change. The early years of the new millennium have seen technological innovations, global risks from terrorism and demographic shifts occurring in most countries of the world. For example, there are now as many people over the age of sixty-five years as there are teenagers in most of the world's societies. Macrosocial changes such as growing up in a context of ethnic diversity and living in single-parent families are increasingly experienced by adolescents in Western industrialized countries.

Further, as the new millennium advances psychology now takes a more positive view of human development, seeing changes and transitions as challenges within the developmental progress of young people, in society generally, *vis-à-vis* cultural and technological innovations and in relation to other generations.

The European Association for Research on Adolescence (EARA) is an organization which aims to promote and conduct high quality fundamental and applied research on all aspects of adolescent development. Its founder and then President, the late Sandy Jackson, devoted much of his professional life to advancing these aims. Before his death in 2003, he initiated a co-operation with Psychology Press to start this series, "Studies in Adolescent Development", and commissioned and published two books during his editorship. We, the current editors, are grateful for Sandy's vision and trust that we can progress the academic and practitioner interest in adolescence as an area of scholarly study which he initiated.

The present series aims to respond to the recent shifts in the social and ecological environment of adolescents and in the new theoretical perspectives within the social sciences, by providing a range of books, each of which deals in depth with an aspect of current interest within the field of adolescent development.

The co-editors delineate a number of broad topics that require significant attention and invite academics, researchers and practitioners to submit book proposals. Each proposal is carefully evaluated by the co-editors for selection in the series. Hence, each book is written by a chosen expert (or experts) in a specific aspect of adolescence and sets out to provide either a clear picture of the research endeavours which are currently serving to extend the boundaries of our knowledge and understanding of the field, or an insightful theoretical perspective of adolescent development.

Each book in the series represents a step towards the fulfilment of this aim. The European Association for Research on Adolescence is grateful to Psychology Press for all that it has done in developing and promoting the series and for assisting EARA in extending knowledge and understanding of the many aspects of adolescent development in a rapidly changing and challenging world.

Professors Leo B. Hendry, Marion Kloep & Inge Seiffge-Krenke
Series Editors

Acknowledgements

Writing this book has been a significant process for both of us and there are a number of people we would like to thank. Given that we are both in different institutions, there are some people we would like to acknowledge separately and some whom we would like to recognize jointly. First in this latter group are Professors Leo Hendry, Marion Kloep and Inge Seiffge-Krenke, the Series Editors for the Studies in Adolescent Development series. Thanks to them for inviting us to submit a proposal for this series and for their feedback throughout the writing process (in particular, thanks to Marion and Leo for their detailed and constructive comments on the first draft). Second we would like to thank Lucy Kennedy, Tara Stebnicky, Sharla Plant and all at Psychology Press who provided editorial support during the writing process. We would like to acknowledge all the students, school pupils, offenders, and other young people who generously gave us their time and their stories as part of the research and all of the teachers, police officers, prison and probation staff and other practitioners who assisted with access and other research support. We would jointly like to thank the four reviewers who took the time to read and provide extremely helpful feedback on the first draft. And finally, to all those who have lied to us! Whether you were detected or not, you have enriched our understanding and insight into deception. As mentioned above, there are some people we wish to thank separately.

Rachel would like to thank

Marion Kloep and Leo Hendry – this time for the numerous debates and supportive conversations on the train which really helped me to refine my thinking.

Particular thanks need to go to Peter Mayer for facilitating clear time to write this book and for supporting me throughout the planning and writing process. This book would definitely not have happened without you. Also I want to say thanks to Peter for generating a great title – and for other flashes of creativity too numerous to mention.

Advice, feedback, encouragement and occasionally conversational distractions were forthcoming from all of the Psychology team at Glamorgan, but I would particularly like to recognize Ian Stuart-Hamilton, Bev John, Martin Graff, Jane Prince and Paul Nash who provided all of the above plus chocolate when required.

Outside of Glamorgan, my family plus friends including Joan Carter, Lesley Stockton, Miranda Horvath, Richard Howell-Jones, Brandon Renaud, Sonia Jones and Josephine Chen-Wilson listened to extensive waffling about the book and provided constructive (and, in some cases extremely "honest"!) suggestions. Thanks to all.

Finally, Hugh Wagner started me off on my academic journey, taught me a number of life lessons and was always happy to talk about the football (even if it was the wrong team!). Sadly Hugh died in 2007 so I cannot say thank you in person. However, this book is for him and I hope he would have approved.

Lynsey would like to thank

Julian Boon, for your support, insight and intellect and for all the discussions and debates over the years about what truly is 'psychological psychology', and Sarah and Ruairidh who have taught me a great deal about young life, mischief-making and downright fibs, albeit thinking they were getting away with it!

Sebastian Teicher, friend, colleague and long-suffering student of deception, whose integrity is second to none and whose knowledge of empirical and real world research in this field has been invaluable in the development of my thoughts when writing this book. The insight I gained about the first accounts of young suspects in police interviews was hugely enhanced through our discussions.

Hannah Gray, who developed with me her knowledge of the offending and deceptive side of youth and the challenge of emerging personalities and associated interpersonal interactions. Lessons that will not be forgotten!

Miranda Horvath, Margaret Wilson and Jennifer Brown – my alive but departed colleagues from the University of Surrey who have supported me and continue to support me in my academic and extra-curricular endeavours.

Aldert Vrij and Ray Bull – for introducing me to the wonders, complexities and challenges of deception and for inspiring me to find innovative and real-world ways of tackling them.

To my Mum and sister Michelle who supported me throughout the writing of this book and in so doing learned more than they cared to know about my own experience of deception during adolescence! For Mum, the lyrics "leave a light on for me" have a whole new meaning! And to Dad, who no doubt would have found the thought of me writing a book rather amusing. I'll send you a signed copy!

Introduction

This volume covers deception in adolescence, defined for this purpose as between the ages of 10 and 21. It considers both published research and new data. Some of the published research has been produced by other people and some by us and is from a wide range of topic areas. However, all can be drawn upon to answer three basic questions:

1. What predicts deception choice and deception success in adolescence and how can this be explained as a developmental process?
2. What strategies should parents and practitioners use for detecting adolescents' deceptions and for effective intergenerational communication?
3. What is the value of applying a holistic, flexible and skills-based approach to understanding all communication, not just deception?

In this book we consider deceptive and truthful communications as just that, communication. We recognize that not all communications are straightforwardly truthful or deceptive and that there is a large grey area in between these two extremes. Therefore we will be arguing that it is not possible to understand adolescent deception without understanding adolescent truthtelling and the ground in between these two points. Also, while not all adolescents are engaged in risky or negative behaviour, and examples of "positive" deceptions are provided in Chapter 3, it is recognized that young people will generally come to the attention of practitioners when they have committed offences or are engaged in some other form of risky behaviour. Therefore one of the key aims of the book is to provide a reference point for practitioners by providing tips and encouraging a flexible approach to deception detection. As part of this, reference will be made to dynamic systems perspectives and to developmental psychological approaches to demonstrate how these can add to practitioners' understanding of young people.

Chapter 1 elaborates our perspective, illustrates the problems associated with using traditional approaches to deceptive behaviour and introduces the rationale for applying a developmental systems approach to the understanding of all types of communication, true and false. Chapter 1 also includes information about the challenges facing academic researchers into deception and practitioners working with young people and considers how a dynamic systems approach can help to address these issues. We then consider the developmental challenge model (Hendry & Kloep, 2002; Kloep & Hendry, in press) in more detail and explain the factors that might influence adolescent communications. This is taken further in Chapter 2, where hypotheses about the roles of biological, social, cognitive and structural factors in adolescent communication choice and communication success are presented. Chapter 2 is necessarily selective and focuses on the main features associated with adolescent deception, rather than providing an exhaustive list. Predictions are generated about how certain resources could address different deception challenges. These are then discussed in more detail in Chapters 3 to 5.

Chapter 3 focuses on those lies told in an interpersonal context and presents new data in the form of interviews and focus groups with adolescents in non-forensic settings. Interviewees were asked to generate definitions of deception and discuss non-prototypical examples before indicating under what circumstances they thought lying was more (and less) acceptable. Once this was discussed, participants were asked to describe situations where they would be more or less likely to choose deception as a strategy, what alternative strategies would be adopted and why, and to cite examples of when deceptions had been successful or unsuccessful. All interviews and focus groups were then transcribed and subjected to inductive thematic analysis (Braun & Clarke, 2006). Data from these interviews and the associated themes are presented here. As part of this discussion, practitioner (parent/teacher) and developmental perspectives are presented for four different case studies. These give concrete examples of how both approaches can provide a strong contribution to our understanding of young people.

Chapter 4 considers communication behaviour of an offender or a young person at risk of offending, including deception choice and deception success of persistent young offenders (PYOs) as evidenced by the use of case studies. As well as the case studies with PYOs, published observational research by the second author clearly illustrates the way that these strategies and tactics can be applied in police interviews. Similarities and differences are evident between the strategies used by young suspects in police interviews and non-offending young people as discussed in Chapter 3 and these are highlighted and discussed. Chapter 4 also considers the importance of maintaining reputation and how this can influence offenders' choice of communication and ends with a discussion of the role of young offenders' perceptions of masculinity. This clearly illustrates the different worldviews that young offenders may hold compared to practitioners and highlights the importance of understanding the client's perspective.

While Chapter 4 considers young people who have committed offences or are in contact with the police in some way, Chapter 5 broadens the scope of communication to consider young people who might not have yet committed offences but are "at risk" in some way. Specifically this chapter focuses on psychopathology, deception and offending and explores characteristic of conduct disorder, personality disorders, adolescent narcissism and psychopathy. All of these conditions have been linked to deception by extensive research and understanding the specific communication challenges presented by such individuals is necessary for practitioners.

In Chapter 6, the focus shifts to detection of young people's lies. Here communication recommendations are given for practitioners dealing with young people as well as some information on detecting adolescents' lies. The holistic and flexible approach is emphasized here and this is strengthened by presenting the second author's conceptualization of chameleon offending (Gozna & Boon, 2010; Gozna, Teicher, & Boon, 2010). This provides a strong framework to understand patterns of interpersonal interaction that may be particularly challenging for practitioners. Finally, Chapter 7 returns to the model and provides a summary of how this has been developed and where future research should be focused. Given the novelty of the approaches used here, it is in this final chapter that we can provide signposts for future directions.

1 The development of deceptive communication

Deceptive communication is an everyday, lifelong and complex process. It can occur in a range of different settings, in relationships between strangers, friends, partners and family members and can be perpetrated by all age groups. We can think, for example, of the five year old pretending that she has not eaten a chocolate cake (despite the evidence of the chocolate around the side of her mouth), the father who tells his toddler to be good "or there will be no visit from Father Christmas" and the teenager who claims to be "studying" at a friend's house while really getting dressed up to go to the pub. We can also think of the banker being investigated for irregular trading, the pensioner who has been arrested for suspected shop-lifting and the teenager who is being interviewed after being caught driving too fast in a stolen car. Given that there is such a range of potential deception situations, each based on a different relationship between the deceiver and target and each driven by a different outcome or motive, how can we make sense of these different types of deception?

One way to address this would be to generate some hard and fast general rules that are applied rigidly to each deception situation. While these might not be perfect, surely we would then be able to account for most lies that people tell – at least if the rules were general enough. Surely this would be right? After all, this is what most people claim to do in everyday life, don't they? Research on beliefs about liars' behaviour suggests that we hold general perceptions about what liars do and these are generally consistent right across the world (Global Deception Research Team, 2006). However, when it comes to research on the actual behaviour exhibited by liars (e.g. DePaulo, Lindsay, Malone, Muhlenbruck, Charlton, & Cooper, 2003) the picture is much less clear. In fact, the cues that distinguish a liar from a truthteller are influenced by the relationship to the target, the amount of planning involved and the motive or goal of the lie itself. Therefore, we clearly should be addressing the full range of deceptive communication, including goals, relationships, background and the age of the liar. In this present volume, we consider one period of the lifecourse – adolescence – and examine how the processes of deceptive communication can develop.

Therefore this book considers when and why adolescents choose to lie, how successful they are, and how their deceptions may be uncovered by adults and by members of their peer group. It includes information about adolescents from a range of life circumstances: those from apparently stable family backgrounds who achieve highly at school; those who come from chaotic family environments, or have conduct or personality disorders; and those who find themselves in situations where they are "forced into" lying to get out of trouble or to support a friend. However, the main argument of this book is that it is not possible to consider deception in isolation of wider actions and therefore we propose a holistic approach to understanding and interpreting such behaviours. Deceptive communications can differ in the amount of deception required to be successful and some interactions will contain more truthful than deceptive content. Therefore, considering deception without addressing truthtelling is artificial and unrealistic – it is not possible to approach this area without considering the grey areas that exist between the truth and the lie. Similarly, an interaction between two people only makes sense if we understand that both people come to that interaction with a set of preconceived ideas, goals and motives, all of which will potentially influence the process. Hence, to understand these deceptions we need to consider the wider context in which they occur. This is important for parents, academics and practitioners as a contextual approach can provide solutions to the challenges faced by those involved in detecting deceit. In the next section, some of these challenges will be defined. However, first definitions of deception and adolescence will be presented to ensure that you have a clear sense of what is referred to when these terms are used and the approach and perspective we are taking throughout this book.

DEFINING ADOLESCENCE

"Adolescence" is defined for the purposes of the current book as being a period of life between 10 and 21 years of age and we choose this definition for several reasons:

1   It generally includes young people who have attained the age of criminal responsibility (i.e. those who are considered to be responsible for their actions and are subject to some form of sanction by the criminal justice system). Currently in England and Wales, the age of criminal responsibility is 10 years old, although children under 12 do not receive custodial sentences unless they commit a serious offence, the type for which an adult could receive at least 14 years' imprisonment (Youth Justice Board, 2009). Additionally, offenders between 18 and 21 years of age who receive custodial sentences are detained in young offenders institutions or segregated sections of adult prisons and are also dealt with differently by the criminal justice system (Prison Service, 2009a, 2009b).

2. Such a definition covers all of the so-called "teenage years" as the terms "teenager" and "adolescent" are, at least for many people, used interchangeably. As young people in the UK are increasingly remaining in the family home for longer (in the UK, 58% of men and 39% of women aged 20–24 still lived at home with their parents in 2006 compared to 50% and 32% respectively in 1991; ONS, 2007), issues associated with the establishment of autonomy could apply equally well to those of 19 or 20 years of age, traditionally regarded as adults in western society.

3 As adolescence is a time of transition, one where we move from those methods of deceiving which are appropriate for childhood to deception strategies used by adults, such a range allows for consideration of these changes. Changes in the power relationship in the home, the responsibility for action in the educational and justice systems and the perceptions of adolescents held by adults in a range of settings are just some of the features of this transitional period.

DEFINING DECEPTION

The generally accepted definitions of deception in the field are those of Vrij (2008, p. 15), who presents deception as: "a successful or unsuccessful deliberate attempt, without forewarning, to create in another a belief which the communicator considers to be untrue"; and Ekman (2001, p. 41) who refers specifically to lying as: ". . . a deliberate choice to mislead a target without giving any notification of the intent to do so. There are two major forms of lying: concealment . . . and falsification."

Both of these definitions include elements of intentionality on the part of the deceiver, unawareness of the deception on the part of the target and a change in belief or understanding. Neither requires deception to be successful. This apparent straightforwardness, however, includes a huge range of different behaviours such as outright untruthful accounts, distortions of the truth and concealment of certain facts. The purposes for which we tell lies also vary greatly and can include deceptions to make ourselves appear better, to protect others, to gain some form of material advantage and to avoid punishment. A diary study on everyday lying conducted by DePaulo and colleagues (DePaulo, Kashy, Kirkendol, Wyer, & Epstein, 1996) identified all of these as being important goals in everyday deceptive interactions. We can also mislead others through verbal and non-verbal means, in face-to-face or mediated interactions and with or without the collusion and support of third parties. Therefore, although definitions of deception are themselves generally accepted within the field, the communication behaviours referred to in these definitions are extremely varied and can often be both complex and sophisticated. In fact, deception is only one of a potential series of communication strategies and choices. Adolescents (and adults) will often choose truthful communication or partial deception even when this does not appear entirely advantageous to the immediate goal;

often because the immediate goal may not be as salient as a long-term aim. This means that deception presents a number of different challenges, both from an academic and a practice point of view. These will now be considered.

CHALLENGES FOR ACADEMIC DECEPTION RESEARCH

Psychological approaches to deceptive behaviour are designed to explain why lies fail and the types of behaviour that liars show. Broadly speaking, lies are expected to fail for two sorts of reasons: due to emotional arousal (and associated overcontrol) and cognitive load (e.g. Ekman, 2001; Vrij, 2004). The act of lying is expected to be emotionally arousing because of the assumption that the act of deceit will result in feelings of guilt, fear of being caught or "duping delight" (the excitement associated with a success-ful deception). These approaches to deception are, however, based on a view of the deceiver as reacting to situations rather than making conscious strategic choices to present themself in the best possible light. There is support from recent research towards a consideration of strategy and self-presentation (e.g. Hartwig, Granhag, & Strömwall, 2007) rather than a reliance on specific cues to deception, particularly in light of the most recent large-scale meta-analysis (DePaulo *et al.*, 2003). However, there is further requirement for research to identify the true benefits of these approaches.

Additionally, while there is some attempt to consider how the deceiver and the target of the deceit may be connected (e.g. lies towards friends vs. strangers), the complexity and dynamic nature of these interactions are still poorly understood. Previous attempts to consider the interactive nature of deception (e.g. Buller & Burgoon, 1996) have not met with unqualified success (e.g. DePaulo, Ansfield, & Bell, 1996) and, while some progress has been made in understanding deception through computer-mediated com-munication (e.g. Carlson, George, Burgoon, Adkins, & White, 2004), the process of everyday and forensic deceptions is still unclear.

Finally, ecological validity has been a challenge for much of the academic research that is largely reliant on samples of university students, although some studies do include older adults either from lay (e.g.Vrij, Akehurst, Brown, & Mann, 2006) or practitioner groups (e.g. Vrij, Mann, Robbins, & Robinson, 2006). These latter studies often explore differences between groups in terms of detection, arguing that training or practitioner experi-ence is important in these cases. As will be discussed in the next section, questions need to be raised about the generalizability of such research into the real-world context. However, a more fundamental question arises that is of particular relevance to this book. There is an assumption in the majority of this research that, aside from gender, occupational, personality, or limited situational variables (usually manipulated in isolation of one another), all deceivers from the teenage years upwards are broadly similar in their abilities. In other words, there is no consideration of development occurring across the lifespan in terms of deception strategy adopted or the choice to deceive or tell the truth in a particular situation. Given that experience of different kinds, either in terms of relational familiarity (e.g. McCornack & Levine, 1990a, 1990b) or practitioner experience (e.g. Vrij *et al.*, 2006) is considered to be relevant, it is surprising that such an assumption should be adopted. After all, development of cognitive and social abilities such as reading ability, abstract reasoning and communication in intimate relationships does not stop when a child reaches adolescence; instead it continues through the lifespan. Therefore, is there any reason why the choice and ability to deceive should stop developing between adolescence and adulthood?

There are, of course, some exceptions to this general pattern, with researchers having asked young people about the types of lies they tell and the reasons for doing so (Arnett-Jensen, Arnett, Feldman, & Cauffman, 2004; Perkins & Turiel, 2007). Additionally, likelihood of lying has been linked to parental relationships and adolescent personality (e.g Engels, Finkenhauer, & van Kooten, 2006). However, the assumption in the majority of this literature has been that deception is a negative or problematic behaviour, and as such the functional or adaptive nature of deceptive communication has not been fully considered. Additionally, very little focus has been given to the way that adolescents successfully communicate untruthfully. Understanding this as well as the different motives for adolescents' lies ultimately has the potential to assist the field of academic deception research and enable a broader perspective on the context of deception as a whole to be taken.

CHALLENGES FOR PRACTITIONERS

As well as the challenges faced by academic researchers, those who work with young people face especially challenging issues relating to their decision making and interactions. Such challenges apply to a greater degree when a young person displays challenging behaviour or deception but are also relevant to teachers and parents whose children have engaged in moderate functional/adaptive deception. The first challenge is to consider the young person's presentation in context – to take a holistic approach which is tailored to the individual in question. This context should include information about the young person's background, presence of any disorder (e.g. personality or conduct disorder), their previous experience with the target and any other evidence or information relating to the issues in question. It requires both an understanding of the behaviours being displayed and the motives that underpin such behaviour as well as an appreciation of the origin of such motives. Taking this holistic approach can provide insight into the source of the presentation and the presentation style itself. This is especially relevant and is a key feature of the chameleon presentations addressed in Chapter 6, but is also useful for interpreting the interpersonal lies discussed in Chapter 3.

As well as understanding the "whole person", a further challenge facing practitioners is to communicate effectively with the young person they are speaking with. Communicating with someone who has, for example, been let down by significant adults on multiple occasions in the past is likely to present particular problems with trust. However, equally challenging could be the young person who appears compliant but refuses to acknowledge that there might be a problem with their behaviour. Therefore, flexible communication methods are vital for parents, teachers and other practitioners for them to respond effectively to a range of challenging interactions. This is particularly the case when a young person presents complex and challenging behaviour that contains some components of deception and some truthful information and there is no way of "objectively" verifying the information given. In this case the practitioner may be faced with managing difficult behaviour as well as obtaining information most relevant to the goal of the interview. In the world of politics, such challenges are illustrated by politicians' responses to direct questioning which can result in evasion and equivocation (Bull, 2006). Such strategies to avoid responding fully to a question can be adopted as easily by young people and some of these will be evident in the case examples in Chapters 3 to 5.

A final challenge for those in practice, and one which is related to the challenge of effective communication, is that of effective response. Again here the practitioner needs to ensure that the objective of the interview is attained and that they maintain objectivity throughout their interaction. One factor that can be beneficial is to understand why it is that adolescents lie. Hence this is one of the key aims of the book – being addressed in Chapters 3 to 5. However, as part of this practitioners need to be aware of their own expectations of the young person they are interviewing and how past exposure and experience can both help and hinder our subsequent interactions. We know from research in social cognition that people's preconceptions can influence the way that they interpret ambiguous information (e.g. Wilkowski, Robinson, Gordon, & Troop-Gordon, 2007), the types of questions they ask or even the way that interactions are remembered. Further, research on implicit social cognition suggests that these expectations have an influence even though we may not be aware of it (e.g. Knowles, Lowery, & Schaumberg, 2010).

Therefore, a lack of insight into their own expectations can be counterproductive and impede a successful interaction between a young person and the practitioner. This is especially relevant when the lies told are functional and adaptive and the interpersonal presentations designed to achieve a goal that is irrelevant to the interaction occurring. An excessively negative or defensive response to such an interaction by a practitioner might be just what the interviewee is seeking, as this will confirm their view of themselves or of how they are seen by adults. Similarly, as will be seen in the next chapter, young people can experience strong feelings of unfairness or injustice when they are accused of something they have not actually done, and this can negatively influence the relationship that they have with the accuser in question. Negative reactions have also been illustrated in the reporting of the policing of youth in certain communities where the perceived unjustified, unlawful, or excessive use of the UK police's stop and search powers has caused resentment amongst those singled out and is often the subject of criticism from media and political parties. In such instances, young people report they are being stopped a disproportionate amount compared with other members of their community, although the number of occasions when the police were correct to stop an individual is less well reported. This may lead to young people perceiving that such powers are inappropriate and therefore they may be harder to convince about their being used. For example, Porter and Hirsch's "Liberty Central" blog (2 September, 2009) described an event at Salisbury's arts centre where children took part in dance and rap activities designed to "explain" the stop and search powers. These were perceived by the organizers as a means of establishing higher levels of community engagement and citizenship within the group of young people involved. However, the organizers may in fact be "imposing" their view of acceptable childhood on to the group. This view certainly appears shared by Porter and Tirsch and their post entitled "Drilling Compliance into Children" raises questions about the necessity and legitimacy of such actions. Similarly the UK comedian Mark Thomas has produced a "handy downloadable card" for people who might be subject to illegal searches. This card warns police officers that "I pledge to waste your time if you decide to waste mine" (Guardian, 10 February, 2009). Although a flippant response towards the professional activities of the police, such criticisms reflect an issue of particular relevance to practitioners, namely when correctly to assume deception and when to accept a young person's assertions that they are innocent. After all, if your decisions are being "judged" and "held accountable" not just to line managers but also to those in the media and general populations, the task of weighing up a young person's presentation becomes far less abstract. While there are no easy answers, the content of this book has been written in order to assist those in practice in making the best decisions possible.

THE CONTRIBUTION OF A DEVELOPMENTAL APPROACH

In the previous two sections, some issues were identified for academic deception research and for practice. One of the main arguments in this book is that a developmental approach, and specifically a dynamic systems approach, provides a necessary holistic perspective which both academics and practitioners can adopt to strengthen their understanding of credibility assessment in interpersonal presentations. This is because a dynamic systems approach:

- regulates development through connections between all levels of the system (from the individual's physiology to wider societal factors such as political systems). These connections are dynamic and can work in both directions
- presents individuals and the surrounding system as being capable of change
- considers interaction between those working in different disciplines as being vital for a full understanding of development
- allows for the possibility of "constraint" within the system
- rejects simple dichotomous distinctions (Lerner, 2006).

Hence, when we consider the credibility of adolescents' presentations and take a dynamic systems approach (one which shares the characteristics outlined by Lerner above), it is possible to see how a young offender's conviction for assault could curtail any criminal or non-criminal activity on release, or how the economic instability of a region could lead an 11 year old to become silent and withdrawn due to worry about a parent being made redundant. It is also possible within a dynamic systems approach to understand a 15-year-old girl who has been lying to parents in order to go to the pub at least twice a week for 6 months, hanging around with a "bad crowd" and neglecting schoolwork but who ultimately graduates from university at 23 years with a Masters degree with distinction. Finally, the approach enables insight into the young person who leaves the house with the statement "Mum, I'm going to Lucy's house to study" which is interpreted as a literal truth but ultimately presents an incomplete communication (i.e. that's where I'm going, but what I don't tell you is that my boyfriend is also going to be there). Therefore this approach is holistic and flexible and provides insights into prosocial and antisocial behaviour to benefit both practitioners and academics.

The next section will consider in more detail how this approach can be applied. First, there will be a consideration of process theories in general – including research on developmental trajectories. Then dynamic systems approaches will be discussed in more detail. Finally, a specific systems approach – the developmental challenge model – will be presented as a means of addressing the questions of young people's communication choices and associated outcomes.

PROCESS THEORIES OF DEVELOPMENT

Developmental trajectories

Lifespan approaches and those that consider the process by which development occurs have already been applied to related areas of adolescent development. In line with "criminal career approaches" in criminology (e.g. Farrington, 2003), researchers working in the area of delinquency have long been interested in offending trajectories and differences between those who persist in and those who desist from offending. For example, Moffitt (1997) identified two groups of adolescent offenders, those who engaged in "adolescence-limited" offending and those who were "life-course persistent". The proposition of two very different offending groups, each accompanied by different aetiologies and explanatory frameworks, provides a powerful explanation for the peak of offending behaviour that occurs in adolescence.

According to Moffit (1997), the increase in prevalence and incidence during adolescence compared to other periods in the life course is not just because of a small group of adolescents increasing their offending rates but because many other adolescents will temporarily engage in offending behaviour. It is therefore difficult to distinguish between those whose offending is "adolescence limited" versus those who become prolific and embark on criminal careers. However, there is a potential difficulty in labelling young people as delinquent because this brings with it a host of associated perceptions from society and in some cases could result in individuals becoming resigned to the fact that they will always been viewed as "criminal".

Moffitt argues that life-course persistent offending may stem from a variety of factors including problematic parental relationships, a failure to learn prosocial or appropriate approaches to social situations and a series of decisions which "close off" opportunities to escape from this antisocial behaviour. Dynamic systems approaches argue that degrees of freedom may be constrained by life choices and engagement in antisocial actions which could be indicative of a lack of social sensitivity and poor impulse control. Huesmann, Eron, Lefkowitz, and Walder (1984) examined aggressive behaviour in three generations of participants as well as exploring stability in aggressive behaviour from ages 8 to 30. While some stability in levels of aggression was observed across the age range from 8 to 30, a much greater stability was seen in the comparisons between children, parents, and grandparents – those who were aggressive had aggressive grandparents and parents. This spread of aggressivity across the generations is an interesting outcome and highlights the extent to which certain behaviours can become an acceptable part of a family perspective.

As well as these purported environmental factors, Moffitt argues that life-course persistent offending may be associated with levels of psychopathology such as child conduct disorder and psychopathy. Antisocial Personality Disorder (APD) may also be associated with life-course persistent offending because individuals with APD are easily frustrated, highly impulsive and have little regard for others' perspectives or feelings. It is clear, therefore, that this group has a cluster of associated problems which may impact on their ability or decision to change their trajectory.

In contrast to life-course persistent offenders, Moffitt (1997) identifies adolescence-limited offending behaviour. Moffit argues that this is motivated by a desire for autonomy, a perception that those already involved in offending do not suffer from the same constraints and hence a degree of social mimicry. This is then reinforced by the apparent material benefits associated with crime such as access to clothes, cars or high-end electrical equipment. Alternatively, this could be reinforced through the social interaction associated with being in a delinquent peer group, or by a requirement to maintain a reputation that has been acquired. This is reinforced by evidence suggesting that life-course persistent delinquent youth actually play more of a part in mainstream peer groups (Elliott & Menard, 1996), in contrast to their marginalization during early childhood (Coie, Belding, & Underwood, 1988) and in adulthood. However, this group of offenders desists from offending for a range of reasons including: the acknowledgement and identification of the negative consequences associated with prolific offending; experiencing the reality of the criminal justice system (e.g. being sent to a young offenders institution); being a victim of crime; or having access to a positive trajectory. This may be because personality disorders and cognitive limitations are less linked to adolescence limited offending or because this group has already had opportunities to develop a repertoire of prosocial behaviours. However, young offenders who have emerging characteristics of psychopathy have the potential to readily turn their focus towards positive goals depending on their levels of impulsivity and associated behaviours.

Adopting this theoretical perspective, Livingston, Stewart, Allard, and Ogilvie (2008) examined data across a six-year period for an offending cohort of over 4000 young people in Australia. Three distinct offending trajectories were identified in their sample; a group of "early peaking-moderate" offenders, a group of "late onset-moderate offenders" and a group of chronic offenders. In this sample, chronic offenders were more likely to be male and members of indigenous populations than either of the other two groups and were twice as likely to have an adult court appearance as either of the two remaining offending groups. This suggests the importance of examining a range of factors and taking a life-course approach. Features shared by other systems approaches such as the ecological approach are discussed next.

Bronfenbrenner's ecological approach

Bronfenbrenner's ecological approach (e.g. Bronfenbrenner, 1979) does not conceptualize development as a series of qualitatively distinct stages. Rather, the process by which development occurs, as a result of an "evolving interaction" (p. 3) between the person and the environment, is elaborated and discussed. This person–environment interaction is considered at different levels of analysis and hence comprises different settings, as well as the interactions between them. As Bronfenbrenner (1979, p. 3) states: "the ecological environment is conceived as a set of nested structures, each inside the next, like a set of Russian dolls."

The first level, the *micro-system*, comprises the individual within their immediate setting (such as school, family). This is followed by the *exo-system*, a term which refers to the wider context of development, and the *macro-system* which is wider still and comprises societal features and cultural norms. Additionally, this model involves dynamic interactions between different micro-systems, these being called *meso-systems*. For example, a 15 year old's decision to lie to his parents about going to the pub on a particular night might depend on:

- his relationship with his parents (micro-system)
- the parents' relationship with each other (a micro-system for the parents, an exo-system for the 15 year old)
- society's definitions of where it is acceptable for a 15 year old to be (the macro-system).

The interaction between the adolescent–parent relationship and the parent–parent relationship would in this example be the meso-system. Although not applied to the study of deception before this, this model has a distinct advantage in terms of the interpretation and understanding of deceptive behaviour, in that it allows for dynamic interactions between multiple factors and acknowledges the communication as clearly grounded in the link between two micro-systems, namely the meso-system. However, this model alone does not allow us to elaborate the underlying mechanisms which predict deception choice and deception success. It is therefore necessary to draw on another approach to fully understand this and the developmental challenge model is crucial here due to fully elaborating the relationship between different levels of the system and explaining how these can be applied to a particular goal.

The developmental challenge model

Hendry and Kloep's (2002) developmental challenge model has three components: the resource pool, the pool of potential tasks and the task–resource interaction. The fundamental argument is that development occurs through the successful completion of appropriately challenging tasks. The "resource pool" is unique to each individual and comprises a combination of biological dispositions, social resources, skills, self-efficacy and structural features. This pool of potential resources is then applied to meeting specific challenges and the key is that the resources an individual possesses at a particular time are appropriate to meet the challenges presented. The outcome of the task is explained below in terms of the challenge presented and the resources available to an individual:

- If the task is appropriately challenging and is dealt with successfully, development occurs.
- If resources are not sufficient to meet the tasks and this state of affairs persists over time it is likely that some form of decay will occur.
- If tasks are not appropriately challenging then it is possible that an individual will stagnate – a distinction being made between contented or unhappy stagnation.

Choosing deception as a way of communicating is one potential means of meeting the challenges of a specific situation and this choice itself will depend on the resources available (and the person's accurate assessment of them). Having made the choice to deceive, success at carrying this out will further depend on the amount of resources available and their match to the requirements of a particular deception task.

Although unique to each individual it is possible to make some general-izations about the types of elements most appropriate for specific tasks and a "deception resource pool" is presented in the following section. Like Bronfenbrenner, Hendry and Kloep (2002) present a dynamic system, something evolving as a result of each successfully met challenge, and this allows for the incorporation of feedback and an indication of how the feedback will impact on future development. Hendry and Kloep's con-sideration of normative and non-normative shifts (those which do or do not happen to most people at a certain stage in life) is important here as, for adolescents, "trying on" new identities and acquiring autonomy are vital developmental processes but may not always occur as part of normative events.

Additionally, societal definitions of what is normative and non-normative will likely strongly impact on the way that these challenges are presented and hence directly on deception choice and deception success. Finally, the range of elements that constitute the resource pool and the range of potential tasks faced by developing individuals seem to address some of the issues of interactional and strategic complexity missing in contemporary models of deception research.

Revised developmental challenge model

The revised developmental challenge model as applied to deception continues to take a systemic life-course approach to human development. As with the developmental challenge model presented by Hendry and Kloep (2002), the revised model takes a multidimensional "systemic" process approach to development. This is in contrast to traditional stage theories, or even to simple linear processes of development. Where this revised model does depart from the original, however, is in the emphasis on the role of "open systems", thus removing the boundaries between the individual and the larger systems in which he or she may be embedded.

As Kloep and Hendry (in press) point out, open systems constantly receive a flow of information, energy and resources. This means that the individual's state may be modified as a result of changes in the wider system. For example, someone who stands up in front of a group of their peers to give a presentation may begin their speech with a sense of nerves, may become more confident as they see part of the audience nodding and smiling, but may experience a temporary dip in confidence as their boss walks into the room.

In other situations, known as attractor states, the system might appear stable for certain periods of time but then change as a result of an accumulation of information, energy and resources. For example, someone might happily work for an insurance company for 15 years (an attractor state or a state of equilibrium) but then may decide to return to university to study for a higher degree as a result of a seemingly unconnected event (their parents retiring and moving to Spain). If this person were interviewed in more depth about the decision, they may talk about "realizing that life is worth living" and also cite their partner's feelings of being undervalued in his or her job, a health scare they themselves received last year and their children moving to secondary school. Therefore the move out of the attractor state was not the one event but an accumulation of energy. This explains how the same person could take a decision to lie in one interaction with a target and a decision to be truthful in another interaction with the same person. For example, a 12 year old could decide to lie to their parents about studying at a friend's house on Monday but tell the truth about going to a party on the Friday. Or the same 12 year old could successfully lie about why they were late for school one week but not get away with a lie about why their homework was not done. The revised model also considers the dynamic nature of deceptive communication – this evolving as a result of the interaction between deceiver, detector and deception situation (each bringing features to the communication process). Finally, the notion of attractor states could provide a useful explanatory mechanism for adolescents who retain "childlike" approaches to deceptive communication, who transfer successful lying to more risky deception situations or who persist with unsuccessful communication strategies even in the face of obvious disbelief.

THE DECEPTION RESOURCE POOL AND TASK–RESOURCE INTERACTION

The main problem faced by academic deception research is that even contemporary communication models of deceptive behaviour do not fully account for the processes involved in the detection of deception. These models make a useful attempt to consider the process of deception as a dynamic one, to integrate deceiver and detector perspectives and incorporate the idea of feedback to both parties. However, there is little consideration of how the feedback mechanisms are used to actually change the antecedents of the next deceptive encounter either between these two parties or between one of them and another person. Further, these models are designed to account for deceptive behaviour which is already occurring and do not fully consider the processes underpinning the choice of deception as one of a series of strategies. This is where the developmental challenge model of Hendry and Kloep (2002) plays a key role in understanding how development may occur successfully, rather than leading to stagnation or decay, and how this will impact on future interactions. It further provides us with an opportunity to explore how people choose deception as an appropriate strategy to meet the communication task presented to them. After all, if an individual does not have sufficient resources to lie success-fully, he or she may perceive that honesty is the best policy. However, on the other hand, this may not be the case and some examples where indi-viduals persist in lying will be seen in later chapters.

While the rest of the book explores these issues, the rest of this chapter highlights some key features from the "deception resource pool" (Figure 1.1). Some of the components are those suggested by Hendry and Kloep, while others have been included because of their specific relevance to deception. All aspects of the resource pool can operate independently or interact with one another depending on the communication task require-ments. It should also be noted that the deception resource pool will be likely to contain similar elements regardless of age, although the amount of individual resources and the adequacy of matching resources to tasks may, however, vary as a function of age. For example, the accumulation of experience across a range of social interactions throughout life may increase the social skills resource available. As can be seen from Figure 1.1, these fall into five different categories:

Biological factors	**Skills**	**Structural resources**
Personality, intelligence (including emotional intelligence), attractiveness, facial features, physiological arousal experiences and facial feedback on emotion, emotional and behavioural disorders	Basic skills, theory of mind, social skills, cognitive skills (memory, language, attention, logic), meta-skills, moral reasoning	(NB: all may have direct effects or be mediated by other people's perceptions) Age, gender, race, class

Self-efficacy	**Social resources**
Self-efficacy appraisals, prior deception success, prior deception failure, feedback on failed deceptions, locus of control	Network size, network quality, identification with ingroup, presence of outgroup, trust and attachment in close relationships

Figure 1.1 The deception resource pool.

For each category, some of the most salient examples have been selected to provide an overview of the range of relevant factors under consideration and are reviewed in the next chapter. As will be seen from this information, factors predicting adolescent deception are extremely diverse and may affect the deception process in a number of different ways. However, it is not possible to summarize the myriad of these in this book and this is why we have included the most salient elements. More detail on the deception resource pool can be seen in Gozna and Taylor (2011) where a larger range of potential resources is presented along with further detail about how these could apply to deception choice and deception success.

CHAPTER SUMMARY

Despite over 40 years of academic deception research, there are many gaps to address. One of the biggest is the failure adequately to address the question of deception as a process where individuals could develop successful (or even unsuccessful strategies) over the course of their lifetimes. There has also been a problem with the ecological validity of many research studies that limit the knowledge which can be applied to real world settings. Further, challenges have been identified for those who are working with young people, specifically in terms of taking a holistic and flexible approach as well as communicating effectively to achieve the goals of a particular interaction. Both the academic gaps and the practical challenges may be addressed by the application of a developmental approach, specifically a dynamic systems perspective. This perspective, which explicitly considers the interrelationships between an individual's personal characteristics and the wider interpersonal or situational factors, can provide the broad, flexible overview that both practitioners and academics in this field may be seeking. An example of a dynamic systems approach which could apply to both deception choice and deception success is then presented. The developmental challenge model (e.g. Hendry and Kloep, 2002) presents development as occurring through successful completion of a series of challenges; successful completion happening when an individual has sufficient resources to address the challenge presented. These resources could fit into five different categories and examples of these are presented in the next chapter.

2 Factors influencing adolescent communication

At the end of the previous chapter we presented a dynamic systems model that considered the fit between resources and challenges as being necessary for development. A "pool of resources" that might apply to a young person's choice of deception or truth as a communication strategy was then developed. This "resource pool" was also linked to their likely success at deceit. In this chapter, we present some examples of each type of resource which have been chosen to provide the reader with some of the most salient influences on adolescent communication. These are divided into the five categories presented at the end of Chapter 1.

BIOLOGICAL FACTORS

Included here, following Hendry and Kloep (2002), are characteristics that may have a biological component such as personality and intelligence. A range of personality variables could be included here. Private and public self-consciousness (Fenigstein, Scheier, & Buss, 1975), Machiavellianism (Christie & Geis, 1970), "acting" (Riggio, 1986) and social adroitness (Kashy & DePaulo, 1996) have all been associated with persistence in deception or deception success (e.g. Johnson, Maio, & Smith-McLallen, 2005; Riggio, 1986; Vrij & Holland, 1998).

Riggio's (1986) paper presents a seven-dimensional model of social skills that outlines the key role for social and emotional expressivity in deceptive presentation. Later research conducted by Riggio and colleagues indicated support for this model in terms of deception ability. High levels of extraversion and emotional expressivity were associated with deception success (Riggio, Salinas, & Tucker, 1988; Riggio, Tucker, & Throckmorton, 1987; Riggio, Tucker, & Widaman, 1987) and this suggests a high level of interpersonal awareness is necessary for successful deception. Similarly, Vrij and Holland (1998) found variables associated with emotional expressivity were positively correlated with persistence in lying for their undergraduate sample. They gave students a 13-question interview as well as a number of personality scales, including self-monitoring, public and private self-consciousness and social expressivity scales. Students who were high in private self-consciousness were less likely to persist in lying, felt more anxious and less credible and experienced higher levels of guilt and cognitive load. In contrast, those who were high in social expressivity variables such as "acting" and emotional expressivity felt more comfortable lying, believed they were less detectable and persisted in lying for longer. This research was supported by Gozna (2002) in studies focusing on individual differences in the ability to deceive. While this would suggest that deception ability may be predicted by individual difference variables, the nature of these relationships suggests lying is actually a matter of social skills and interpersonal experiences rather than personality traits.

Johnson *et al.* (2005) asked undergraduate students (aged 19 to 25 years old) to present three short segments of behaviour – giving truthful biographical information, "faking good" and "faking bad" – and then to complete two personality questionnaires: the Schizotypal Personality Questionnaire (SPQ; Raine, 1991) and the Self-Consciousness Scale (SCS; Fenigstein *et al.*, 1975). While results did not indicate any effects on deception ability for the SPQ or the Public subscale of the SCS, there were significant correlations with deception ability and the Private subscale of the Self-Consciousness Scale. Individuals who were higher in private self-awareness were better deceivers, supporting that private self-consciousness is associated with an awareness of others' minds.

When turning to intelligence, it should be noted that not all deceptive situations require high levels of intelligence for successful completion. However, in complex deceptions there is a consideration of cognitive load associated, particularly in the face of contradictory information presenting itself. Emotional intelligence (Mayer, Salovey, & Caruso, 2008) as assessed by trait and performance measures should be included here. For example, Mayer and Salovey (1997; see also Mayer *et al.*, 2008) regard emotional intelligence as the integration of four separate abilities: accurate perception; accurate understanding; managing emotion effectively to achieve interpersonal goals; and using emotions to make thinking easier. This model is tested explicitly in their measure of emotional intelligence (Mayer-Salovey-Caruso Emotional Intelligence Test, MSCEIT, Mayer, Salovey, Caruso, & Sitarenios, 2003) which is a 141-item measure assessing performance on eight separate tasks. These tasks are then scored for correctness based on those given by a consensus or an expert.

This may have an impact on deception success and is likely to strongly predict choice of a more effective communication strategy. Some links have been made between emotional intelligence and deception (O'Sullivan, 2005). However, there has so far been no research to explicitly test this. Although a student under the supervision of the first author (Plowman, 2008) failed to find an effect between emotional intelligence and detection ability, for practical reasons he was unable to use a specific ability measure such as the MSCEIT and had to resort to a trait measure. This may have affected the validity of the research and does not preclude relationships between detection ability and ability measures of emotional intelligence. These would apply to both explicit and implicit judgements of deception, but would be stronger for implicit judgements. Additionally, those higher in emotional intelligence as measured by the MSCEIT would be more likely to choose deception as a strategy in appropriate situations and get away with it.

In terms of attractiveness and facial features, research here suggests reliable differences in perceived credibility depending on attractiveness, particularly under conditions of high cognitive load (e.g. Petty, Cacioppo, Strathman, & Priester, 1994) and in terms of the differences between baby-faced and mature-faced individuals (e.g. Masip, Garrido, & Herrero, 2004). One possibility here is that those individuals with such natural "advantages" may not acquire the same level of skill as those without such biological predispositions. This would suggest that they may be better at deceptions where their natural advantages would come into play or when they are younger and more attractive. However, this is unlikely to be a long-term sustainable strategy and they may find their success decreasing later in the lifespan. Alternatively, it may be that attractive individuals are also more popular and hence have more opportunities to develop social networks which give them increased practice in deceptive and honest communication. Research by Berry (1991) asked participants to rate male and female faces varying in both attractiveness and facial babyishness on nine pairs of bipolar adjectives (e.g. strong/weak, cruel/kind, dishonest/honest). Results indicated, while main effects were found for both attractiveness and facial babyishness on sincerity judgements, these were qualified by a significant interaction. People who were highly or moderately attractive were judged as more sincere when they also had more babyish faces. A similar bias known as the "halo effect" (e.g. Nisbett & Wilson, 1977) would also apply to lying as people regarded positively in other domains would be likely to be regarded positively in terms of credibility too.

Later research has suggested this may apply across the lifespan (Zebrowitz, Voinescu, & Collins, 1996). Hence, it appears as though facial structure itself might predict credibility judgements. This is supported by more recent research (e.g. Masip, Garrido, & Herrero, 2004). Higher facial maturity was indeed correlated with lower ratings of "goodness" and higher ratings of deceit. However, as Masip *et al.* point out, these results are based on the ratings of photographs on particular traits rather than detection judgements. In fact, although similar predictions can be made, there is currently no research we are aware of which explicitly compares people with different levels of facial maturity on their actual credibility.

Other biological factors are connected to physiological arousal, the experience of emotion and connections between emotion and facial expressions. If some (high-stake lies) may involve guilt or fear of getting caught, it may follow that those who experience less nervousness in general or who can more accurately monitor their own physiological signals may in fact be better at deceiving. Biological factors that may also have an impact are disorders of emotion and behaviour such as conduct disorder and psychopathy (discussed in more detail in Chapter 5). Pathological deception is part of a cluster of behaviours and personality characteristics that form such disorders (Hare, 2006), hence lying would be expected in these cases. However, this may also influence success at deceiving (Lee, Klaver, & Hart, 2008) and potentially persistence in unsuccessful deception as a result of impairments in empathic functioning (Blair, 2007). Similarly, mood has recently been shown to be related to scepticism and ability to process information.

Forgas and East (2008a) induced positive or negative moods in their participants and then presented them with facial images of six specific emotions. They were asked to indicate how genuine the facial expressions were, whether the emotion expressed was positive or negative and how confident they felt about this. Facial expressions were perceived as more genuine when positive mood was induced and as less genuine when negative mood was induced.

Other research (Forgas & East, 2008b) has explored the impact of mood on scepticism. Participants experienced either a positive or negative mood induction (either watching a comedy film or a film about someone dying of cancer) and then watched interviews of people who were accused of stealing a cinema pass, some of whom were denying truthfully and some denying falsely. Results indicated that those with a negative mood attributed more guilt to deceptive than truthful participants, but those in a positive mood did not show the same ability to discriminate. This suggests inducing a positive mood can affect detection ability and, as is clear from the next chapters, creation of a positive mood is used as a deflection tactic by some deceivers.

Self-efficacy

Bandura's definition of self-efficacy (1986, 1997) is a judgement of one's own abilities to perform a specific task. This differentiates it from self-esteem which refers to judgements of one's own worth. In Bandura's theory, self-efficacy is a belief about how you can match the skills you possess to a specific situation. It is argued that these beliefs are driven by four specific situations: direct experience of mastering particular goals; vicarious experience of watching other people master goals; persuasion/social influence about your ability to achieve specific goals; and physiological/affective information about how well you are mastering particular challenges.

Hendry and Kloep (2002) suggest that realistic appraisals of self-efficacy are important, especially for deception success, as overconfidence can affect both deception and detection ability (e.g. DePaulo, Charlton, Cooper, Lindsay, & Muhlenbruck, 1997). This may be because of low task involvement, which has been shown to increase reliance on non-verbal behaviour

(Reinhard & Sporer, 2008) or because of positive mood. For example, a recent study by Forgas and East (2008b) found that negative moods increased scepticism while positive moods made individuals more gullible when reviewing interviews of people who denied involvement in a mock crime.

As subjective feelings of competence can explain social comparison biases as well as those at the level of individual judgements (Larrick, Burson, & Soll, 2007), the importance of self-efficacy in an interpersonal context such as deception is clear. However, realistic self-efficacy appraisals may not always be possible. A study carried out by Vrij, Semin, and Bull (1996) examined people's perceptions of their lying behaviour and compared this to the behaviour actually displayed during lying. Participants were asked to lie and tell the truth in two interviews: in one they had a set of headphones concealed on their person, in the other they did not, and in both they had to deny possession of them. They were then asked to rate their own behaviour (e.g. gestures, eye contact, blinking, smiling, hand movements, postural shifts, leg and head movements). The videotapes of the interviews were then analysed using the same behaviours. The coding of the actual cues to deception revealed a decrease in certain movements when lying compared to when telling the truth. However, participants' beliefs about their own behaviour were that they had actually increased such movements and had in fact appeared as more nervous. This might be because the individuals felt more nervous when lying or simply because they were paying less attention to their own behaviour and reverted to the stereotypes associated with lying when questioned.

Elaad (2003) provides further evidence suggesting realistic self-efficacy may not always be possible. Sixty police officers were asked to rate themselves on a 9-point Likert scale in terms of their ability to tell lies and then to detect them. Ratings were made relative to other people, so the lowest point on the scale was "much worse than others", the highest was "much better than others", and the midpoint was "as good as others". Participants then made truth/deception judgements and rated their confidence. After they had seen the first tape, participants were asked to estimate how many of the judgements they had made correctly and then either proceeded to the next tape or received one of two sets of feedback. Confirming feedback indicated they had been highly accurate and disconfirming feedback indicated the opposite. All participants then completed a second judgement task.

Results (before feedback) indicated people tend to overestimate their ability to detect lies (with 40 out of the 60 participants rating themselves as above average and only two as below), but actually underestimate their ability to lie successfully (only 18 participants rated themselves as above average, 26 rated as below and 16 as average). When presented with confirming feedback, participants' ratings of their detection abilities increased and the converse was true of disconfirming feedback. Additionally there was one surprising finding – namely feedback also affected perceived ability to tell lies (in the same direction). This is surprising because the feedback itself does not actually refer to this ability. However, it appears that participants are experiencing some form of generalized increase/reduction in confidence as a result of being told they have done well or poorly.

Therefore, because realistic self-efficacy appraisals are not always available, other factors must relate to deception success as well, hence the importance of a range of resources for an adolescent's development. Nonetheless, self-efficacy may explain other aspects of deception, specifically choice of deception as opposed to another communication strategy and may explain the use of deception by young offenders in police interviews, despite clear evidence to the contrary. In fact, for many young offenders in police interviews, self-efficacy has little to do with the choice or success of a strategy. While this is sometimes to do less with the suspect's realistic appraisal of his or her abilities, and more to do with external factors such as the degree of proof the police have (Gudjonsson & Sigurdsson, 1999), there is also a more prominent reason. For suspects in police interviews in the UK, the responsibility for making the decision is removed by the option of having a "no comment" interview. Based on the second author's observations of police interviews, it is clear that the choice to "go no comment" may not actually depend on the case against the suspect or an appraisal of ability, and may have more to do with the presence or absence of a solicitor or the extent to which the young person chooses to co-operate with the police.

Hendry and Kloep (2002) also discuss the importance of previous success in aiding development. However, previous failures and associated feedback are more important for developing deception ability and the ability to choose deception as an appropriate communication strategy than success. This is because failed deceptions can provide useful information about the cues that do not indicate credibility and give us an indicator of what behaviours arouse suspicion in other people (Buller, Comstock, Aune, & Strzyzewski, 1989; Burgoon, Buller, Dillman, & Walther, 1995).

The final element in this category is locus of control. Rotter's original conception of locus of control (LOC; Rotter, 1954, 1971) developed out of social learning theory and was concerned with the extent to which reinforcement was seen as following from a person's own action or from some external factor (such as luck, chance or fate). Those with a high external LOC are more likely to see situations as being due to external circumstances and are more likely to make situational attributions for the engagement in deception.

This is unlikely to have a strong direct role in deception success but may impact on motivation. An interesting finding from our own research (Taylor & Rolfe, 2005) is that when people discuss their own deceptions they refer to situations where they feel the situation was out of their control. This may involve blaming the target for "forcing" the deceiver into a lie and feeling that they cannot retrieve the situation, but instead dig themselves in deeper. This may be exacerbated by an external locus of control and hence may negatively impact on their motivation to succeed at deception. It is also feasible that locus of control will directly impact on the perception that deception can actually be chosen as a communication strategy.

SKILLS

One of the strengths of communication approaches to deception is the focus on skilled behaviour as part of a person's deception repertoire. The skills element of the resource pool is therefore vital to the correct choice of communication strategy and to successful self-presentation. Basic skills in understanding, including attention, memory, language and logic, are vital in the formation of coherent and convincing deceptions and in understanding the types of situations in which deception should occur. Technical and technological skills could be included here too as an understanding of different technologies may increase the scope for choosing appropriate media to deceive more effectively (Carlson *et al.*, 2004; O'Sullivan, 2000).

As deception involves creating a false belief in the mind of a target, an understanding of the existence of other minds is crucial to deception. Although theory of mind is acquired in early childhood (e.g. Wilson, Smith, & Ross, 2003), a more complete understanding is one which develops over time (Hughes & Leekham, 2004; Maas, 2008). Other social skills such as the ability to take another person's perspective, understand when actions are moral or immoral, and levels of general social competence may also be positively related to deception choice and to deception success and this has been demonstrated in research with adolescent samples (e.g. Feldman, Tomasian, & Coates, 1999). Feldman *et al.* asked 11 to 16 year olds to describe their reactions to a pleasant or unpleasant tasting drink. Some were asked to be truthful and some were asked to describe an opposite reaction and these descriptions were taped. A standardized measure of social competence was completed by parents and young people were allocated to high and low social competence groups. Judges then viewed silent videotapes of these descriptions and were asked how much the person really liked the drink being described. While truthful descriptions were more convincing overall, those with high social competence were better at deceiving than the low social competence group. Younger adolescents were detected more often than older ones and younger adolescents who were low in social competence were worse than older adolescents with a similar level of social competence.

Further evidence supporting social skills and self-presentation was provided by Feldman, Forrest, and Happ (2002). They asked three groups of undergraduate students to get to know a new person, one group with a goal of appearing likeable, one with a goal of appearing competent and one not given any other instructions. They were then videotaped in conversation for ten minutes and afterwards asked questions about the conversation (including what was truthful and what was not). Results indicated the two groups with self-presentational goals engaged in more lying than the control group. Both experimental groups told more lies about feelings but the group with a goal to be competent also told more lies about their future plans than both other groups. This suggests self-presentational goal can influence our choice of interactional strategy and indicates the importance of social skill in successful deception.

Finally, normally included within this category would be moral reasoning. Although traditionally linked to deception, this type of skill may in fact have a very specific role in deception rather than being related to deception per se. When we consider deception, we often hear people saying "I know it's wrong but . . ." when they recount details of their lies. Sometimes this will be followed by "but I did it anyway" (perhaps the most honest of the potential responses), sometimes by "but I had no choice" or "but if my dad hadn't stopped me seeing him". In the same way a general attitude towards something may poorly predict a specific behaviour (Fishbein & Ajzen's 1974 principle of specificity), so a classification into a general moral stage will poorly predict engagement in moral behaviour in a specific circumstance. Based on the data collected for the current book, it is clear that people can engage in moral reasoning in a flexible and process-oriented way, they can consider specific goals and this will have some impact on deception choice or on justification for the use of deception.

For example, Box 2.1 presents a series of judgements made in a university focus group by the same individuals over a 45-minute period. Each of these people would be classified into a single stable group based on Kohlberg's Moral Judgement Interview (e.g. Colby & Kohlberg, 1987; Kohlberg, 1984). However, they are in fact reasoning flexibly and across different levels (and it was not the case that different people made these points, these were points made by the group as a whole during the discussion). The group then went on to debate, in a flexible and mature way, the ethics of telling a friend that their partner is cheating on them, if the partner is also a friend. Kohlberg would be likely to argue for a "conventional" level of reasoning (probably Stage 4), with occasional regressions to pre-conventional and occasional overreaching to a post-conventional level. However, a better explanation is that our participants display flexibility and are engaging in a process of negotiating understanding about morality.

Therefore, people's moral motives are equally likely to affect the type of deception chosen, the motivations to lie and the way this is constructed after the fact as to affect whether deception or truth per se is chosen.

SOCIAL RESOURCES

One of the key elements to deception success (including knowing when not to choose deception as a strategy) is the possession of deception skill. A

Box 2.1

Flexibility in moral decision making (university focus group)

Across the duration of this focus group, different moral orientations were identified. These have been classified according to Kohlberg's stages:

1. If I didn't lie then I would never be able to do anything (pre-conventional, self-interested motive).
2. The hardest thing about lying, the thing I can't stand when my parents find out is that they're disappointed in me (conventional – based on interpersonal expectations).
3. It's actually OK to lie about some things but you should never make a promise and then not keep it (post-conventional; universal ethical principle).
4. It was just a silly little lie, and I was actually justified because he shouldn't have asked [to borrow the participant's brand-new digital camera for a drunken night out], but I felt bad because he was a mate (conventional – based on interpersonal expectations).
5. You should keep secrets to yourself (post-conventional; universal ethical principle).

---

vital component of this is the opportunity to receive feedback on the success (or failure) of prior interactions and this will need to occur with a range of people. Opportunities to practise deception and to learn what are the more and less effective strategies are crucial, as with the acquisition of any skilled behaviour (e.g. Anderson, 1982, 1987).

Experience with deceptive communication may lead to changes in the way that knowledge about deception is represented and expertise in deception should be associated with greater flexibility in novel situations (e.g. Chi, 2006). Theories of embedded cognition such as those proposed by Clark (2007) recognize the importance of interaction with the wider world in developing cognitive skills and the role of social interaction in developing reflective thought is predominant in interactionist developmental psychological perspectives (e.g. Vygotsky, 1978). Hence, network size and opportunities for in-depth social interactions (measured by network quality) are important. These provide settings for individuals to hone deception skills and an understanding of when it is and is not appropriate to deceive, although we would predict that this will be more effective when the range of potential targets from both ingroups (peers) and outgroups (e.g. adults) is increased.

Three different aspects make social networks important in adolescence. The first is for social support and social comparison, the second for opportunities to practise skills associated with effective communication and the third for social influence. Given that adolescents increasingly spend more time with peers than with parents during this period (Larson & Csikszentmihalyi, 1978), it is important to consider these relationships.

Early research suggested a lack of stability in adolescents' friendships (e.g. Berndt & Hoyle, 1985) and this was confirmed by recent longitudinal research (Chan & Poulin, 2007) that identified significant short-term instability in the friendship nominations made by early adolescents during a five-month period. This instability increased as network size increased. Additionally, the internet has become a popular means of increasing friendships, with 55% of young people using email, instant messaging or other online communications to establish contact with new people, 25% of people establishing casual online friendships and 14% close online friendships (Wolak, Mitchell, & Finkelhor, 2002). Recent surveys of internet use show 55% of young people have also established online social networking profiles (Lenhart & Madden, 2007) and there is evidence that adolescents use these profiles and associated blogs for self-disclosure and creative self-expression (e.g. Mazur, 2005). Therefore the network, whether physically present or virtual, is important when considering adolescent communication.

Festinger (1954) proposed that we make comparisons to those who are similar but slightly better than us in a particular domain, both for getting information and for self-improvement motives. While later research (e.g. Bogart, Benotsch, & Pavlovic, 2004) has suggested we can make downward social comparisons (with those who are slightly worse than us) to enhance self-esteem, other studies have confirmed these self-improvement motives under certain circumstances (e.g. Burleson, Leach, & Harrington, 2005). When explicitly considering friendships, Mussweiler and Rüter (2003) found university students used their best friends as routine standards of comparison, even when the comparative dimension was one where their friends were extremely dissimilar. This suggests we routinely think of our friends when we are attempting self-evaluations.

Further research (Gabriel, Renaud, & Tippin, 2007) has examined this link between the self-concept and our interpersonal relationships, with the specific perspective that relationship partners and close friends can influence a person's self-concept. Participants were asked to complete a scale to assess how much their sense of self was dependent on their close relationships and were classified into either high or low relational interdependence. They were then primed by either writing a description of a good friend or a celebrity and finally rated their self-confidence. Those primed with the good friend essay generally experienced more self-confidence than controls. However, this was influenced by how much the person defined themselves in terms of their close friendships. Those high in relational interdependence experienced much greater increases in self-confidence after writing about their friends, while a small (non-significant) effect in the other direction was found for those who were low in relational interdependence. Therefore, thinking about a supportive social network can increase self-confidence.

For adolescents, although attachment to peers cannot compensate for attachment to parents in helping to avoid negative mental health effects (e.g. symptoms of depression and anxiety), adolescents' perceptions of their strengths are positively influenced by attachment to both parents and peers (Raja, McGee, & Stanton, 1992). Additionally, a strong sense of community in both neighbourhood and school settings was negatively related to loneliness and worry and positively related to subjective well-being (Pretty, Conroy, Dugay, & Fowler Williams, 1996) and strong dense social networks have been associated with lower reporting of depressive symptoms.

What the above research illustrates is that both social comparison and social support can be gained from good quality social networks. In terms of communication, social comparison could be used to develop assessments about ability and to build self-confidence and self-esteem. Perceptions of supportive relationships may also make it less likely that inappropriate patterns of communication are used.

In terms of interpersonal competence and social skill, a longitudinal study of close relationships and psychosocial adjustment (Laursen, Furman, & Mooney, 2006) indicated that support from close friends was associated with social acceptance, friendship competence and romantic competence. Berndt (2002) found reciprocated high quality friendships were associated with the development of empathy and leadership skills and Kawabata and Crick (2008) found positive social adjustment was associated with high levels of cross-ethnic friendships. Additionally, there is evidence to suggest that those who have been excluded from social groups often behave more aggressively and less prosocially (e.g. Twenge, Baumeister, Tice, & Stucke, 2001). A recent series of studies by DeWall, Baumeister, and Vohs (2008) indicated social exclusion does lead to poorer self-regulation but this can be overcome if there is a possibility of future acceptance. For example, participants were able to self-regulate when given false feedback (a) indicating they could expect negative relationships and loneliness in later life but (b) successful performance on a self-regulatory task was associated with empathy and social competence (which improved future social relationships). As high quality social networks seem to improve social competence, moderate and appropriate levels of lying are positively associated with good quality social networks while exclusion from such networks will be associated with more pathological levels of lying.

The final aspect is social influence. It has been widely documented that peers can influence both adolescent risk taking and positive behaviour. For example, Gardner and Steinberg (2005) asked approximately one hundred people in each of three conditions (13–16 years old, 18–22 years old and 24+ years) to complete two questionnaires assessing risky behaviour and risk preference and to take part in a computer game called "chicken". These were completed either alone or in the presence of two peers. Younger participants indicated greater risk preferences and took more risks in the computer game and the two younger age groups were more susceptible to the effects of peer pressure on risky behaviour. In terms of positive behaviour, Crosnoe, Riegle-Crumb, Field, Frank, and Muller (2008) found a positive effect of friends' academic achievement on maths performance in a group of 13 to 19 year olds. This effect persisted even when the effects of confounding variables were removed. Hence, it appears clear that peer norms and social influence are important in adolescent behaviour and we would expect this would apply to communication patterns. In line with social identity theory and social influence, high levels of deceptive communication within your peer group will "normalize" this as behaviour, in contrast to those groups where deception is not widely used.

Quality interactions with peers, family and other adults may also help to develop a clearer understanding of the nature of trust and the potential relationship outcomes of engaging in deception. This can also be facilitated directly by trust and secure attachments. Evidence by Ennis, Vrij, and Chance (2008) supports a relationship between attachment anxiety and frequency of telling self-oriented and other-oriented lies to both friends and strangers, as well as between attachment avoidance and frequency of telling such lies; hence adult attachment and interpersonal trust may be important. This is because, as previous research on adolescents' deceptions has shown, they perceive lies as being necessary and acceptable to establish autonomy (Arnett-Jensen, Arnett, Feldman, & Cauffman, 2004) and because frequent levels of lying have been associated with lower levels of disclosure, less trust and poorer quality parent–child relationships (Engels, Finkenhauer, & van Kooten, 2006).

Further supporting evidence is based on parental regulation. Adolescents are resistant to parental attempts to regulate behaviour in areas considered personal (e.g. contents of their diaries; Nucci, 1996). Additionally, there may be difficulties in negotiating what issues are personal and what should be under parental regulation. Hasebe, Nucci, and Nucci (2004) constructed a scale to allow assessment of parental authority and areas of adolescent autonomy. This scale allowed two sets of responses: Ideal Control (IC – what would ideally happen) and Perceived Control (PC – what adolescents felt would actually happen). They identified items which fell on to three different scales: Personal Domain Scale (PDC – e.g. what music to listen to); Prudential/Conventional Domain Scale (PCDS – e.g. drinking alcohol); and Overlapping Domain Scale (ODS – e.g. how late to stay out). They then looked at how these perceptions of parental control related to symptoms of psychological problems. Scores on the PC scale were higher than on the IC scale, indicating adolescents wanted less parental control over their behaviour than they were actually experiencing and perceptions of higher perceived parental control in the personal domain were associated with more internalized symptoms of psychopathology.

STRUCTURAL RESOURCES

In this pool is a range of different factors that may directly impact on the individual's ability to deceive successfully in different situations but which may also work indirectly through the detector's perspective. For example, women are more interpersonally sensitive (Hall & Mast, 2008) and better at emotional regulation (Simpson & Stroh, 2004) and this may affect their deception success. Additionally, there may be cross-cultural differences in deception style (Aune & Waters, 1994) or there may be difficulties in correctly decoding cross-race compared to within-race deception cues (Sabourin, 2007). For adolescents, age is a clear structural resource in that there may be developmental differences in early and mid-adolescence in choice of deception compared to other communication strategies. However, the structural resource of age works most clearly when combined with sufficient social skill to recognize stereotype congruent versus incongruent behaviours.

The majority of the research on age differences in deception is based on the understanding of lies and the development of lying ability in early childhood (3–5 years old). One study by Feldman, Jenkins, and Popoola (1979) compared younger and older children and college students in their abilities to mask negative affect associated with an unpleasant tasting drink and found older children and undergraduates were less detectable than younger children. In fact, while younger children were significantly more detectable than the other two groups, there were no significant differences between 12 year olds and adults in terms of detectability. Additionally, Ekman, Roper, and Hager (1980) found children were better able to regulate their facial expressions appropriately as they got older (12 year olds).

However, one reason why the majority of the research on deception and facial control compares younger and older children/adults is that by age 8–12 many of these differences disappear. When Ceschi and Scherer (2003) asked 7 and 10 year olds to suppress facial expressions of amusement, the only differences found were in amount of general facial activity. The actual suppression of smiles and replacement with other expressions were at similar rates. Similarly, Larochette, Chambers, and Craig (2006) found children as young as 8 years old were able to suppress expressions of pain. However, it may depend on other factors such as the degree of knowledge and the behaviour being displayed. McCarthy and Lee (2009) compared children and young people of between 7 and 15 years old in terms of their knowledge about deceptive behaviour and the actual display. Children of 7–9 years of age displayed less knowledge about the impact of eye contact and gaze aversion and tended to avert their gaze more when lying; however, this did not apply to older children. Hence, although there is likely to be a developmental trend in the knowledge about effective communication, display rules and emotion regulation are already in place at the beginning of adolescence and this period is characterized by a refinement of skills rather than a strong age-related improvement.

In fact, as deception is an interactional task, it is possible that structural resources in themselves may not play a strong role in deceptive behaviour. However, when they are considered through other people's perceptions, the role might be stronger. Evidence for how this occurs comes from the social identity perspective. Social identity theory (SIT) was originally proposed by Tajfel (1972) and elaborated by Tajfel and Turner (1979). Tajfel and Turner argued that categorization into ingroups ("us") and outgroups ("them") is a fundamental aspect of social life, but then elaborated on this to include processes of social comparison and self-evaluation. Hence, it was proposed that we gain information about ourselves through our membership of particular groups (our "social identities") and are able to identify the similarities between ourselves and other ingroup members as well as the differences between our own group and other groups. Tajfel and Turner also argued that we display a high degree of favouritism to members of our own groups and we will attempt to maximize the difference between our treatment of our own and other group members. This ingroup favouritism can be partly explained by our desire to be members of high status groups, this being because of the links between our social identities and our self-esteem.

Later research in the social identity tradition made this self-esteem hypothesis more explicit (e.g. Abrams & Hogg, 1988) but also proposed our group memberships reduce uncertainty about the validity of our perceptions and attitudes and help to establish our position in the social world (e.g. Hogg & Mullin, 1999). The uncertainty reduction hypothesis followed on from Turner's self-categorization theory (SCT; e.g. Turner, 1985). Turner argued that we could either see ourselves in terms of our personal or our social identity and if self-categorizing in terms of social identity would display behaviours and attitudes consistent with ingroup norms and values. More specifically, Turner argued that we would attempt to align our behaviour and values with what we perceived as the most prototypical member of our group. This would then give a clear standard of comparison and a clear guide for behaviour. Hence, our social identities may prove invaluable in determining who we are and how we should behave. Despite this, the most important role that social identity can play is through the impact of other people's perceptions. Two related strands of research in the social identity tradition are valuable here: research on identity threats and responses to identity threat, and research on collective action and intergroup conflict.

As Branscombe, Ellemers, Spears, and Doosje (1999) point out, we can experience identity threats to the value of our ingroup and this will be particularly salient to those who are highly identified with the group. One socially creative strategy might be affirmation of the stigmatized identity (e.g. Derks, van Laar, & Ellemers, 2009). For adolescents, if the popular perception of this stage of the lifecourse is as one of storm and stress, rebellion, delinquency and deception, perhaps affirmation of these stigmatized identities is an example of social creativity. This could be particularly applicable to adolescents from groups which suffer further stigma, for example, those from ethnic minorities.

Building upon this argument are social identity approaches to intergroup conflict. Reicher and colleagues (e.g. Reicher, Spears, & Postmes, 1995) proposed a social identity model of deindividuation (SIDE) which argued that the presence of other ingroup members increased identification with the group and hence a greater reliance on social than personal identity. The other proposition of the SIDE model is that the presence of other ingroup members allows expression of ingroup norms usually sanctioned by the outgroup. In an experimental study by Reicher, Levine, and Gordijn (1998), students were given opportunities to endorse or dismiss certain value statements. Some of these statements were approved of by both ingroup (students) and outgroup members (lecturers), some were disapproved of by both groups, and some were endorsed by students but disapproved of by lecturers. High perceived visibility to other ingroup members led to higher endorsement of this last group of statements, hence supporting SIDE.

Later research has extended the principles of SIDE to consider the way ingroup and outgroup relations might develop over time. The elaborated social identity model (ESIM; e.g. Stott & Drury, 2000) proposes a dynamic process where negative ingroup actions and intergroup conflict will arise when the outgroup has a distorted view of the ingroup and can act on it. Research by Drury and Reicher (2000) demonstrated this by analysing participation and conflict during a protest against the building of a link road on the M11 motorway (UK). Some of the protesters had never taken direct action before and believed in their democratic right to protest; they were not causing trouble and the police would be there to protect their rights. When it became clear that the police felt the entire crowd was potentially dangerous and acted on this interpretation, this led to an escalation of conflict and a change in the self-perceptions of the demonstrators.

So it is clear that our social identities can be threatened, that we can respond in socially creative ways and that threats from a more powerful outgroup may lead to an escalation of intergroup conflict. For adolescents, what we have are more powerful groups of people (e.g. parents, teachers, police officers) who may present categorization or value threats to individual young people, perhaps by classifying them as "children", "immature" or "delinquent", or by interpreting harmless behaviour as potentially dangerous. The first author (despite knowing of the dangers of misinterpretation) once found herself experiencing an automatic fear reaction at having to walk through a group of young people to cross a railway bridge and, while this type of reaction is hardly uncommon, overt expressions of fear may be perceived as a value threat. Young people may respond by engaging in social creativity or by exhibiting greater identification with a peer group that provides social support, reduction of subjective uncertainty and self-enhancement/self-esteem.

Support for this analysis in terms of delinquency comes from Emler and Reicher's (1995) work. As part of their analysis, they interviewed hundreds of young people, some of whom had committed delinquent acts and some who had not. Their results supported a model which had three basic elements. First, adolescents are entering the institutional social order on different terms; they are no longer children but are not yet perceived as adults. Second, commission of delinquent acts (or definite refusal to engage in delinquency) is a means of establishing the self as part of this social order, as defining yourself as part of a specific ingroup and identifying salient outgroups. This will lead to a series of behaviours associated with managing reputation within the ingroup. Third, the ingroup provides social support for the individual's position and management of reputation becomes a collective endeavour. Similar results are presented in later chapters and support the role of other people's perceptions in interpersonal deception and in offending behaviour. For example, in Chapter 4 offending behaviour as a means of establishing and maintaining masculinity is discussed while the role of "reputation" and the development or destruction of interpersonal trust is covered in the next chapter.

CHAPTER SUMMARY

In line with the developmental challenge model presented in Chapter 1, this chapter presented some factors that would influence adolescent communication choice and the success or appropriateness of their selection. These factors could be categorized into five different groups: biological factors, self-efficacy, skills, social resources, and structural resources. Facilitation of effective deception was argued to be linked to personality factors such as emotional expressivity and self-confidence, to higher levels of emotional intelligence as measured by the MSCEIT and to increased skills in social competence and the awareness of others' minds. The role of mood in the effective detection of deception and other processing of social information was considered and emotional intelligence was predicted to be linked to effective decoding as well as encoding of communicative intent. Additionally, the size and supportiveness of an adolescent's social network, including the quality of parental relationships and parental monitoring, were linked to the willingness to engage in deception as well as the effectiveness of doing so.

As well as factors relating directly to communication choice and success, elements of the adolescent "resource pool" were considered which related to other aspects of deception. In this chapter, moral development was not considered simply in terms of its links to deception choice, rather it was highlighted as an example of a skill which could be flexibly employed to justify the use of deception in certain situations. In the current chapter, the view was presented that any degree of moral engagement might lead to guilt and that different moral views could be used to reduce the guilt associated with "necessary" deception. This links to the discussions of blame and views of the victims/targets of deception seen in the next three chapters.

Finally in this chapter, a critical appraisal of the role of self-efficacy and feedback in deception success was presented. Hendry and Kloep (2002) suggest that realistic self-efficacy appraisals are essential for development and this view is cautiously endorsed, albeit with some reservations about the scope for such appraisals in the deception domain. Situations are discussed in Chapters 3 to 5 where individuals may feel that they have little choice about lying, where they feel they might not succeed but do it anyway, and where they are not clear about the impression they are making. These add strength to the literature cited on feedback from successful and unsuccessful deceptions in the current chapter.

Therefore, in sum, the current chapter presented empirical research as well as theoretical insights to explain what resources adolescents might draw upon for successful communication. The next three chapters apply these resources to a range of different situations, beginning with inter-personal lies. Each chapter presents both practitioner and developmental perspectives on such lies through the use of case studies as well as additional data and critical reflections on previous research and practice.

3 Deceptive interactions and communications

In Chapter 2, features of adolescent communication were considered. For adolescents to deceive successfully and to choose deception in appropriate situations, they need to possess a range of different features and abilities. Some natural or biological elements may give certain young people an advantage, but even then, as pointed out at the beginning of Chapter 2, the person in question must know (or learn) how to use them successfully.

However, the other important aspect of Hendry and Kloep's (2002) model is the application of appropriate resources to tasks or challenges facing an adolescent. The key word here is "appropriate" and a feature which gives an advantage in one situation may actually be a disadvantage in another. For example, adolescents whose facial features fall into the "baby-faced" category may very well appear credible (Masip *et al.*, 2004) but it is also clear that individuals with these facial characteristics are judged as less intelligent (Berry, 1991). Hence having a baby face may very well help us if we want to convince our parents that we are sleeping over at a friend's house to study for an oral exam instead of going to a party, but may not help us if we are then trying to convince the examiners that we know what we are talking about.

Therefore, it is important to think about how adolescents' deceptions are matched to their goals. A recent review of these goals was published by Massey, Gebhardt, and Garnefski (2008) and covered research between 1991 and 2007 on a range of different adolescent goals. The most common general goals related to education and occupation as well as success in social relationships. However, the content of these became more realistic in later (compared to earlier) adolescence. Additionally, while females tend to report fewer goals than males, they tend to identify more educational goals and report greater commitment to goal attainment. The role of the wider systems can be seen here, with parents who encourage autonomy in their children having adolescents with greater "leadership and independence" goal endorsements. In contrast, young people whose parents discourage autonomy tend to endorse greater financial and extrinsic goals.

Although the literature above suggests that adolescents have a range of general life goals, for interpersonal deceptions there are two main tasks facing an adolescent: these being to establish autonomy and to protect the self and others from the consequences of the lie or the event/action being lied about. The importance of autonomy to goal endorsement has already been suggested and the above review (Massey *et al.*, 2008) also indicated a relationship between problem behaviours and the endorsement of (i.e. wish to have) freedom–autonomy goals.

A third, less important challenge facing adolescents in deception terms is effectively enhancing the self. Self- and other-protection and self-enhancement are not new motives and adolescents' searches for identity may lead to a requirement for self-protection, if not self-enhancement. Although DePaulo *et al.*'s diary studies (e.g. DePaulo *et al.*, 1996) did not make a clear distinction between the reasons for self-oriented and other-oriented lies, both of these categories included protection and enhancement of either the self or another person. It is not, however, clear from this research how self-protection and autonomy are differentiated, as lying to benefit the self psychologically could include the establishment of autonomy. And it is the creation of opportunities to be independent and to make one's own decisions which is the primary motivation for interpersonal lies in adolescence. Adolescents' lies in these situations are not always negative and are often necessary. However, the majority of previous literature does not recognize these positive aspects.

A review of the literature makes it clear that the large proportion of research on "deception" in adolescence refers to delinquency or conduct disorder. This may be because the manual most widely consulted for classifying different disorders, the American Psychiatric Association's (1994) *Diagnostic and Statistical Manual of Mental Disorders* (*DSM-IV-TR*), uses frequent lying to obtain goods or favours as one of the diagnostic items of conduct disorder. While the *DSM-IV* guidelines make it very clear that diagnoses of conduct disorder would only be given when this frequent or persistent lying was accompanied by other behaviours violating societal or age-appropriate behaviours, this imbalance of research implies that all adolescent lying may be considered pathological.

Even some of the more recent research on interpersonal deception (e.g. Engels, Finkenhauer, & van Kooten, 2006) that attempts to separate out frequent and occasional lying to parents still starts from an implicit pathologizing of adolescents' lies. This is problematic and contrasts with other research considering moderate levels of lying performance (Feldman, Tomasian, & Coates, 1999) to be indicative of high social competence, and with their own earlier research (Finkenhauer, Engels, & Meeus, 2002) which indicates a positive relationship between secrecy and emotional autonomy. In the current chapter, it is clear that there is a distinction between moderate and pathological levels of lying and that moderate lying is indeed both an indicator of social skill and necessary for adolescent autonomy. This will be demonstrated through a review of existing literature, an analysis of some data obtained from focus groups and interviews (see also

Taylor & Gozna, 2010) and specific case studies. Most of these cases are taken from the main data corpus; however one is adapted from a weblog posted by a concerned parent. For each of these case studies, perspectives from developmental psychology and from "practitioners" will be discussed. In the case of the non-offending young people covered in the current chapter, this will be from the perspective of a parent or a teacher faced with the deceptions listed. Given that such lying may be considered in the academic literature as "problematic" (i.e. associated with parental over/disengagement, lack of trust and school or peer problems), it is important to consider some of the challenges faced by parents and teachers in this situation.

Some of the earliest research focusing on adolescent deception was carried out by Knox, Zusman, McGinty, and Geschleidler (2001). This questionnaire study asked people to complete 26 different items about deception of parents in high school. As well as basic demographic information, Knox *et al.* asked which parent was lied to the most as well as what topics were lied about. Results indicated that 65% of their undergraduate sample had lied at least once during high school about where they were, 49% had sometimes lied about their sexual behaviour, 41% about who they were with, and 42% about their alcohol use. They also discovered that adolescents did not consider themselves dishonest (85% said they were basically honest), that females were more likely to lie about sexual behaviour, that all young people were more likely to lie to the opposite-sex parent and that deception was more likely in two-parent households. More recently, a study of the character of American young people (Josephson Institute, 2008) indicated that while 96% of them felt it was important that people trusted them and 84% considered that it was not worth lying or cheating, when it came to specific behaviour there were some differences. When asked how many times in the past year they had lied about something significant to a parent, only 18% said that they had never done this. Similarly, 64% had lied once or more than once to a teacher about something significant, 54% had cheated at least once during a test at school, and 82% had copied another student's homework. Rates for internet cheating were lower, however, with only 36% of students claiming to have copied an internet document for a classroom assignment. We should also treat these results with a little caution as a substantial proportion of the group also admitting to lying at least once on this survey. And what neither this study nor the one by Knox *et al.* (2001) did was to consider why these lies might have occurred. Knox *et al.* do provide some suggestions, mainly based around social control, but this does not get to the complexity of liars' motivations. The current study explored this in more detail.

The main analysis in this chapter is based on a sample of non-offending young people who were recruited through local schools and universities. This sample comprised 16 university students aged 18–21 (13 females and 3 males) and 35 young people from local schools aged 11–17 (18 females and

17 males). Interviews and focus groups were conducted by the first author and were transcribed by the same author before being subject to thematic analysis as outlined by Braun and Clarke (2006; see also Smith, 2008). This method involves six stages and the analysis was treated as a "recursive process" as recommended by these authors.[1] Although this was primarily inductive (with themes being derived from the data), it should be noted that the superordinate themes were generated by the researchers when developing the interview schedule and were confirmed by data analysis. All sub-themes were, however, generated entirely from the data and relationships between superordinate themes were also generated through examination of the interviews.

Following initial reading and re-reading of transcripts to ensure familiarity with the material, initial codes were generated and checked with reference to the transcripts. These were then refined and a final list of themes was derived. The four "superordinate" themes were based on the questions asked, motivations, targets of lie, strategies/success, and acceptability. However, each contained subthemes and these will be discussed in turn.

MOTIVATIONS FOR LYING

Three main motivations for lying emerged from our data. The first was a straightforward "self-protection" motive. This comprised not only lies to protect participants from getting into trouble for wrongdoing but also lies which allowed participants some material advantage. Some of our participants freely admitted to "risk taking" either now or earlier on during adolescence, and stated that they lied to parents to avoid punishment (e.g. "being grounded") or even parental reactions (e.g. parents expressing disappointment in the young person's behaviour). Within this group, few lies were admitted to that directly provided some physical advantage to the deceiver. However, some were identified which provided psychological advantages (e.g. exaggerating a story to make yourself seem more exciting than you actually are, or to be accepted into a group).

One other area of self-protection/advantage was identified. However, this was more problematic to classify as it showed some overlap with the next category – lies told to establish autonomy. Interestingly, one of the strongest examples of this came not from a younger participant but from a 20-year-old university student who lied to his mother about completing university coursework to avoid the hassle of being told to do it. Box 3.1 presents this case study as well as the challenges faced by parents/teachers and a developmental approach.

These results fit in with those by Arnett-Jensen *et al.* (2004) who compared groups of high school and college students on responses to questions about the acceptability of lying and on frequency of lying to parents about

Box 3.1

Case study 1: Chris, 21 years old

Chris is a 21-year-old student at a university in the UK. Although the institution in question has a large proportion of students from its local area, Chris has moved away from home to live in rented accommodation, first on campus and later in a house in the vicinity of the university. In the course of an interview, Chris described a range of lies, mainly to his mother but also to his friends. His lies to his mother were mainly designed to stop her "nagging him" about having completed university coursework and he regarded these lies as quite minor, necessary to have a quiet life and almost an expected part of the interaction with his mother. He felt that she regarded his responses to questions such as "Have you done your essay?" as almost rote or necessary, just as he saw the questions as one way of indicating that she cared.

Later in the interview, he revealed that his relationship with his mother had been damaged the year before as a result of him being "caught out" in a more serious lie. At the time, his mother had been concerned that he was "going to turn out like his older brother" who had persistently lied about where he was, what he was doing and the degree of trouble he was in. She had not been angry with him when she found out; instead she had expressed disappointment and he considered that to have been "worse". For this reason, he revealed that he would feel uncomfortable with telling her more serious lies and in fact had a relationship with her which was based on disclosure. This meant he felt particularly uncomfortable that he had been "forced" to lie to her about one particular romantic relationship. In this case, the girl that he had been seeing was actually in another long-term relationship and wanted to keep her involvement with him a secret. He described the way that this caused conflict for him, as he would have been happy with disclosing their involvement but did not want to "cause any trouble" for her. He described the process as incredibly isolating, as he was not able to tell anyone about the high or the low points and ultimately it was this secrecy which led to the end of the relationship.

In terms of his relationships with his friends, he mentioned that he lied in order to maintain a sense of privacy. He described his friends (by this he was referring to casual "mates" rather than close intimate friendships) as wanting to know all about him and what was going on. Therefore lying in this case seemed easier than having to overtly withhold information or to disclose facts which would "give them ammunition to wind him up".

Issues and challenges for parents/teachers

In such instances, the need to deceive is born out of a requirement to reduce stress or anxiety from a completely unrelated aspect of the individual's life. Hence in this case, the deception is told in order to avoid being pressured and to gain a level of autonomy which is appropriate for the stage of life – as in a university student. However, the mother's need to continue to treat Chris as a child or as someone in need of nagging highlights not only her concern about him becoming like her other son, but a difficulty in letting go of her son and allowing him to make his own way as an adult. The relevance here for the targets of the deception

Box 3.1 cont.

is that the purpose of a lie can be indirect to the reason why it has been told. In this case, avoidance of admitting to not completing coursework allows Chris to have some freedom and feel reduced pressures. Hence the need for teachers to consider wider perspectives when they feel that a student is not being honest with them. In cases of non-submission of coursework, it requires some further investigation in order to potentially support the student but also the consideration that there are malign reasons underpinning the behaviour.

The developmental challenge perspective

Chris's interactions with his mother are based on a high degree of familiarity in their communication. Prior experience with similar situations, in this case successful as well as unsuccessful meeting of the "challenge" of lying, has given Chris a more realistic appraisal of his available resources. However, Chris also appears to experience a high sense of guilt, as evidenced by his reaction to having to lie about his relationship with his girlfriend and his description of "needing" to lie to establish privacy with his friends. This would, combined with the memory of the previous "serious" lying situation, increase the resources required to successfully meet the challenge of carrying off the lie. This could explain Chris's reluctance to make more than "rote" responses, as he could feel that he would not be able to (or perhaps not want to) attempt more "elaborate" lies. The degree to which Chris chooses deception in the situations with his friends might highlight the importance of different social networks. Perhaps Chris does not perceive this as a highly supportive situation and this is why he chooses deception in the circumstance.

specific issues. Participants indicated how often they had lied to parents about using alcohol and drugs, money issues, attending parties, time spent with friends, dating and sexual behaviour. They rated a vignette where a 17 year old lied to his or her parents about spending the night at a friend's house instead of being with a partner. This was rated in terms of the acceptability of this act when faced with 19 different motives and then rated the acceptability of three different transgressions (betraying the confidence of a friend, cheating in school/university and being physically violent towards a peer). Additionally, participants completed a scale measuring degree of self-restraint and two scales assessing family environment (family cohesion and family control).

Results indicated that high school students lied more often to parents than did college students, this being significantly more for lies about friends, parties, dating and alcohol/drugs. However, it is likely that this is because high school students will be living in the family home and this will provide a greater need and opportunity to deceive. In terms of the vignette, lying was regarded as most acceptable when it was to give the person time to spend with a partner who was experiencing stress and needed support or because the liar had the right to make his or her own decisions. However, as Arnett-Jensen *et al.* (2004) point out, acceptability judgements were only made on one vignette and hence more data are needed on the motives and judgements of different types of lies. Our interviews and focus groups with young people examine this issue and provide a deeper exploration of the reasons behind the lies.

Arnett-Jensen *et al.* (2004) regard the differences in numbers of lies as indicative of a qualitative difference between adolescents and emerging adults (and hence support for a stage). However, while we believe that their results are valid, we do not think that this suggests a qualitatively distinct stage. Instead we suggest that this fits into the developmental challenge model. Arnett-Jensen *et al.* admit that they did not compare college students who lived at home and those who lived on campus and we would argue that differences in lies about parties, drinking, friends and dating may in fact be indicative of situational differences between Arnett-Jensen *et al.*'s adolescent and college samples in terms of this specific aspect. In our interviews, young people from the same age group told different types of lies depending on the degree of financial and practical dependence they had on their parents. This would suggest a strategic and flexible response to the different challenges presented by varying family circumstances.

What the earlier example also illustrates is the importance of topic avoidance as predicting deception (included as a subtheme for motivations, being directly predicted by self-protection and autonomy). This is consistent with other research on topic avoidance in parent–adolescent communications (e.g. Mazur & Hubbard, 2004) as well as responses to legitimate versus illegitimate authority. Mazur and Hubbard (2004) asked 119 late adolescents (18–22 years of age) to report about their relationships with a parent (73% reported on communications with the mother, 21% on communications with the father, and 6% with other parental figures). Adolescents were asked to recall the most recent time that they had not wanted to discuss a topic which the parent had raised and they had been forced to discuss, however briefly. They were then asked to indicate what type of topic it had been and to recall in detail what was said by both themselves and their parents. Results indicated that adolescents only engaged in a full and truthful discussion about the topic in 17.6% of the occasions, and that the most frequent responses to such topics were deception (44.5%), aggression (19%), and terminating the conversation (17.6%). Indirect rejection of the topic, including postponing the conversation and "meta-communication" (e.g. making an issue of parental nagging or shouting), was used in approximately 16% of instances, as was an assertive reinforcement of the adolescent's position. This indicates the importance of deception in helping to maintain boundaries in interpersonal relationships. Further support for this boundary maintenance explanation can be found in research on disclosure and secrecy/privacy (DePaulo, Wetzel, Sternglanz, & Wilson, 2003) which demonstrates how deception is sometimes necessary to protect privacy (although privacy can be used as an excuse rather than a justification for deception in some cases).

The final motivation for lying identified by our participants was "other-protection". While "other-oriented" lies were also found in research by DePaulo *et al.* (1996), our research suggests a slightly different view of these lies. In DePaulo *et al.*'s research, lies were very clearly classified as being told to protect or benefit the self (e.g. telling a story to make yourself seem "cooler" than you really are), or to benefit other people (e.g. telling someone they did a really nice presentation because you don't want them to feel bad). Some of the lies told were indeed other oriented/other protective. For example, one of our university students did not want to tell her parents just how homesick she was feeling, as she knew that this would distress them. However, while some of the lies told by young people clearly fell into this latter category, there were some which were told with the apparent intention of protecting parents or friends but which might, in terms of content alone, appear self-protective.

One possible explanation for this is that our participants were simply justifying the lies and used an "other-oriented" motive to explain them and this is likely for some lies. However, for others the participants genuinely believed they were protecting the other person. This particularly applied to parents. Some young people had an extremely protective attitude towards their parents and believed that they would not be able to "handle" hearing about the risk-taking behaviour. For example, one student told us about her friend at another university who had forgotten to pay her course fees. This was a serious error for which she could have been excluded. However, she did not tell her parents because she did not want them to be worried about the situation and she felt she could sort it out on her own. Similarly, Box 3.2 highlights a clear case of "other-protection" motives.

Box 3.2

Case study 2: Amanda, 21 years old

Amanda is an international student at a university in the UK. She had moved to the UK two years previously and had left her parents in her home country. Amanda is a highly academic student whose motivation for leaving home was to further her education and improve her English. However, she had been extremely homesick during her first term and had lied to her parents about the degree to which this was affecting her. In the end, Amanda felt the pressure of constantly pretending that everything was fine and was relieved one day when her father hinted that he knew she was not being honest. At this point she disclosed the entire situation and she and her family worked together to find a solution. She had found it easier to lie because she was only communicating with them by telephone and made it clear that she would have felt too guilty if she had done this face to face.

Despite this deception, Amanda displayed a general reluctance to tell lies for other than "altruistic" motives, although this may have been due to discomfort at disclosing more self-oriented lies in this interview. She also described a situation where she had been lied to, this time by a friend of her ex-boyfriend who contacted her online pretending to be someone else. She described the feelings of anger, hurt and confusion when the truth was revealed and indicated that she did not want to be the cause of similar emotions in another person.

Issues and challenges for parents/teachers

The problem for parents and teachers when young people tell lies in order to protect either themselves or others is that the motivation for this is largely positive and altruistic. Hence the response should be to understand why the deceit occurred and how the situation can be rectified as a result of the exposure of the deceit. In this case, Amanda is grappling with the need to lie to protect her parents but also has a good insight into how it feels to be the target of a lie, and as such is unlikely to engage in serious deception.

The developmental challenge perspective

Amanda's description of her deception to her parents is a key example of the "other-protection" motive. Amanda disclosed that she had a strong positive relationship with her parents. However, her decision to move to the UK to study had been largely as a result of her parents feeling she would "do better" here. In her country of origin, the UK (according to Amanda) was seen as somewhere that people went to improve their prospects and as Amanda is white and spoke reasonably good English she did not envisage problems fitting in. Therefore, her response could be seen as being based on wider cultural expectations of life in the UK, combined with a desire to maintain her close relationship with her parents. However, in line with a dynamic systems perspective, we can see that the initial deception changed her perception of her relationship with her parents, exacerbating the effects of her geographical distance and increasing her distress and sense of isolation. At the resolution of the situation, the prior experience with her parents provided a conversational opening. It seems likely that, knowing that she was unhappy but knowing what her likely reaction would be to a direct challenge, the indirect "hinting" was a useful way to re-establish contact. This also allowed her parents to communicate their potential reaction and provided a secure basis for disclosure.

For Amanda, being a victim of a lie might be a painful experience for several reasons. One reason could be of the closeness of her relationship to her former boyfriend. Also she could be upset because of the betrayal of trust and partly because the situation was so unexpected and unpredictable. However, it is also likely that Amanda's prior attitude to deception and the appropriateness of lying in different situations affected her response here – possibly through her ability to empathize with and take the perspectives of other people. Therefore existing attitudes and this experience have interacted to "harden" her attitude towards all but altruistic lies.

One aspect of "other-protection" that emerges from our interviews is its link directly to secrecy/disclosure. A number of these scenarios were based on keeping secrets for another person. In this case, our participants generally felt it was important to maintain confidentiality and keep the information secret but they did have boundaries. There was some consensus however that certain individual differences including age and previous experience influenced this choice. All participants questioned indicated that they would keep "silly secrets" (e.g. who their friend was attracted to) and there was general consensus about secrets involving harm to the friend in question (e.g. from bullying or taking drugs). However, two of our 12-year-old participants indicated that they would find it difficult to disclose a friend's being bullied if they had been asked not to. Also older participants said they were less likely to disclose if, for example, a female friend suspected she was pregnant. Our university students were also more willing to keep more serious secrets if necessary. This might be because older participants felt that they and their friends could deal with any difficulties without needing help from parents or authority figures. Box 3.3 presents a case study which highlights these boundaries.

Box 3.3

Case study 3: Jack, 12 years old

Jack is a 12-year-old boy at a school in a rural community in the UK. This area is somewhat economically deprived but contains greater pockets of affluence than some of the other communities (e.g. Case study 4 – Carla's community is more economically deprived than Jack's). Again, Jack was interviewed as part of a peer group; in this case the other boys in the group were not just peers but also close friends and "partners in mischief". Jack described a range of different lies which he told to parents, teachers and other adults, but again he did not often lie to friends and classmates. The exception to this was that he would lie about being interested in a particular girl with the goal here to avoid being "wound up" by his friends.

For Jack, the most frequent types of lies told were to avoid getting into trouble at home or at school. This included lying to teachers about why he had not done his homework and about who was responsible for bad behaviour in the classroom. In fact Jack and his friends cheerfully acknowledged that they would often blame Robert when caught messing about. But when Robert was asked how he felt about this, his response was that he didn't mind because he was in detention most weeks anyway and always told his mum that he was playing football instead of in detention. For Jack and his friends, Robert's willingness to take the blame was a feature of their friendship and a means for Robert to establish his reputation. However, in other circumstances, Jack, Robert and the rest of the boys would feel aggrieved when blamed for things they had not done. They considered this to be highly unfair and would either protest vigorously about the injustice or would change their view of the person accusing them.

Which response was adopted would depend on the role of the person making the accusation; all of the boys were more likely to protest to parents and siblings and more likely to simply change their view of teachers.

Although Jack was willing to lie to get himself out of trouble, he had very clear boundaries about his deceptions. For example, when Jack and the boys were asked about the school's bullying policy and what they would do if a friend was being bullied but asked them not to tell, two of Jack's friends said they would tell a teacher but would not be happy about doing so. In contrast, Jack was very clear that he should tell a teacher and would not feel guilty about betraying his friend's trust; in this case the severity of the situation overrode the requirement to keep a secret. Additionally, the single occasion that Jack had been involved with the police represented an important boundary for him. Jack and some of his other friends had been playing in a local scrapyard and had been throwing gas canisters through the windows of an old bus. The police had been called and when they arrived, all of the lads ran away. Jack described himself as not having "run fast enough" so was caught by one of the policemen who took him home and explained what had happened to Jack's mother. Jack described himself sitting on the sofa, listening to the police officer's account of the situation and then being asked by his mother if this was a true account. He said that he could not have lied to her at that point because it was a "serious situation" as the police were involved.

Issues and challenges for parents/teachers

This example outlines the boundaries that are created in the minds of these young people where they identify what is acceptable in terms of deceit and what is not. There is an acknowledgement that certain individuals or certain topics can be lied about but that there are situations in which the seriousness will prevent further deception occurring. In this situation, Jack and Robert appear to be used to being in trouble and can handle the relative routine of being accused. However, it is important that parents and teachers realize that for some young people the accusation occurring as a default response to a situation can lead to the decision to become more embroiled in trouble. Hence the more young people are considered guilty of a minor indiscretion (regardless of reality) the more this can become a chosen way of life. It is therefore the opposite of the boy who cried wolf in that parents and teachers should be wary of making accusations toward typical troublemakers unless they have evidence to back this up.

The developmental challenge perspective

Of interest here are the distinctions that Jack makes between different types of lies and the indications that he would not lie about certain things. This may be as a result of parental socialization, as Jack's relationship with his mother seems very strong. There may also be a role for his school experience, having been "social-ized" into a new school with a clear anti-bullying policy and having a strong peer network also seem to be important in predicting Jack's behaviour. Certain types of lies (e.g. "messing about" in class) were considered to be acceptable, again perhaps influenced by cultural expectations within the school environment but also within his wider peer group of friends and extended family at different schools. Finally, Jack's definition of a "serious situation" as one involving the police

Box 3.3 cont.

may say something about his wider attitude towards them, the power that they hold to punish him and their role in his particular community. The officer's response, as described by Jack, seemed a pragmatic one and one which might be associated with his own local knowledge; knowing who Jack was and that he was not a "bad lad". It seemed clear from talking to Jack that, despite this involvement with a police officer, Jack regarded his actions as "risk" rather than "offending". This may illustrate the difficulty associated with labelling a young man of Jack's age as an offender for a single antisocial action; his reaction here was to desist from being so "stupid". It is possible that a different punishment would have produced a different reaction.

Interestingly, "other-protection" motives did not just apply to deception but also to truthtelling. One individual recounted how she had been the one to tell her younger sister the truth about her mother's death – because this girl had heard so many different versions of the event from other people she asked her big sister to be honest. To this day, the truthteller is not sure whether she has done the right thing but as she says herself: "so I told her the truth and I didn't know if she was too young to deal with the truth but then she will know in future that she's always been told the truth . . . and that she can trust me in the future" (P01, 19).

This links to research by Bavelas, Black, Chovil, and Mullett (1990) on equivocal communication. Equivocation is something which occurs in very specific circumstances when we are faced with an "avoid–avoid" conflict. Their situational theory of equivocation predicts that when we are in a situation where we either have to lie or tell an unpleasant truth, we will actually equivocate. They tested this in two phases: first judges were asked to scale messages generated by the research team along different dimensions of clarity. Then, once established independently as clear or equivocal, the messages were given as choices to undergraduate students in response to a particular dilemma. For example, participants were told they had received a gift from a good friend in another town which they did not like. They then had to write a thank-you note, choosing one of four alternatives:

1 "The gift is perfect: I really love it."
2 "I don't like the gift and I am going to exchange or return it."
3 "I like you but I don't like the gift."
4 "I appreciate your thoughtfulness" (all taken from Bavelas *et al.*, 1990, p. 68).

In the original study, 79% of Bavelas *et al.*'s participants chose option four, even though this was also independently rated as the most "equivocal". It was rated by judges as being clear in terms of what was being said and in terms of being the speaker's own opinion. However, judges did not feel that this was directly addressed to the target and certainly did not feel that it was a direct answer to the question. Nevertheless, this is not a lie. Evidence from our participants indicates that these types of communicative conflicts are being dealt with as a part of everyday interaction and that sometimes they will pick the whole truth, sometimes an outright lie, sometimes a partial lie, and sometimes they will equivocate. This supports our contention that we should remove the simple truth/lie dichotomy both from research and as a way of understanding everyday social interaction.

Target of the lie

Here young people in our research revealed the clear majority of their lies were told to parents, some to friends and some to relational partners. Interestingly, there was a developmental trend in our interviews. Although all participants lied most frequently to parents, younger participants reported they would tell more lies to friends and would be less likely to tell lies to parents. There were also some lies to teachers, to people who were acquaintances but not friends, and occasionally lies were told to other authority figures. Again, younger participants were more likely to lie to teachers, even more so than older participants who were still in school.

There was a link between target of the lie and the motivation for lying; with autonomy goals applying to lies told to parents (or other older relatives) and other protective lies being told to parents and friends/partners. The goal of the lie might also explain the trend towards lies being told more to parents as adolescents become older and a decrease in lies told to teachers. Younger participants may very well expect greater parental controls and may therefore regard it as more legitimate. Hence, they may be less likely to lie about where they were going and who with. This fits in with the research cited in the previous chapter by Hasebe, Nucci, and Nucci (2004) which identified differences in perceptions about parental regulation of behaviour and by similar research by Smetana (1995) which identified conflicts over the definition of specific behaviours as personal or subject to parental regulation.

In these data, the target of the lie also links to the type of strategies used. However, the one thing that seemed to predict the likelihood of lying is the quality of the trust between the liar and the target. This is not to say that liars will not lie to those they trust. However, they will feel less comfortable about doing so, may take greater steps to justify this and will do it less often. In fact, this notion of trust was often cited by participants as explaining why they were less likely to lie to friends. However, if someone betrays that trust then they deserve to be lied to: "If they're a friend which you can't really trust, you say, 'I can't trust you no more and I don't want to be your friend'" (P02, 12).

Returning to the study by Smetana *et al.* (2006), in terms of prediction of adolescent disclosure and adolescent secrecy, multiple regression models were calculated to assess the rates of disclosure of personal, school, and peer information and the rates of hiding in these three categories. Adolescents who perceived a high degree of obligation were more likely to disclose information and less likely to keep secrets in all categories (supporting the notion of internalized moral awareness and guilt as discussed in Chapter 2), while disclosure across all types of situation was positively predicted by higher adolescent trust. Our analysis (as detailed above) is highly supportive of this.

Similarly, research by Kashy and DePaulo (1996) looked at data from two diary studies (one with a college student sample, one with a community sample) and examined frequency of telling self-oriented and other-oriented lies to different people. Instead of just looking at the relationship per se, Kashy and DePaulo took self-reports of relational closeness and used this as a primary predictor. Overall, participants told fewer lies to people they felt closer to and a greater proportion of the lies told were other oriented. This is also supported by research from Ennis, Vrij, and Chance (2008) discussed in Chapter 2 which indicated securely attached individuals told fewer lies. Overall, research on targets of lies from both our own and previous research would suggest trust is an important mediating factor in decisions to lie.

STRATEGIES AND SUCCESS

Four subthemes emerged here:

1   Deflection.
2   Manipulate expectations.
3   Use truth.
4   Behaviour, nerves and cognitive load.

Deflection

The first theme, deflection, was identified by our participants as being very important for success as successful deflection minimized, shortened or avoided the lie. The difficulties associated with lying (e.g. Ekman, 2001) can be guilt, fear of getting caught or cognitive load and hence any action which minimizes these will also maximize the liar's chances of getting away with the deception. For our participants, this minimization was achieved through deflecting attention. As deflection did not necessarily involve telling a lie, we have linked it to our topic avoidance theme. For example, a young person might choose this point to disclose they have been slipping behind at school rather than answering questions about where they were last night. Of course this will only work if: (a) the person can switch the conversation easily without making their parents suspicious; (b) achieving at school is important enough to the parents for them to be interested in this news; (c) if the lower achievement is not then linked by the parents to the young person's social life and used as a way to develop the conversation! Some of our participants (although not all) used tears or other evidence of strong emotion as a deflection tactic. This had the effect of making targets feel guilty and less likely to focus on the topic at hand: "I can make the other person apologise for accusing me" (P03, 19). While some participants found it too difficult because they were unable to summon tears at will, Box 3.4 highlights a case study where other forms of deflection were highlighted as being used.

Box 3.4

Case study 4: Carla, 17 years old

Carla is a 17-year-old girl who is in the sixth form of a school in an economically deprived area in the UK. She has a high level of academic achievement, and plays a key role in the school community with responsibility for mentoring peers. Although pupils from this area are more likely to be going to university than, say, ten years ago, the fact that she is planning to do this marks her out as different from many of her classmates. Carla was interviewed as part of a focus group with members of her class and discussed a range of interpersonal situations in which she was prepared to lie. Carla described how she would lie to her parents about where she had been and whether she had been drinking with her friends. Although underage, the majority of Carla's peers would also drink alcohol and this would be considered a normative behaviour for teenagers of this age. According to Carla, the most frequent reason for her to lie to her parents would be to establish some privacy and she described how sometimes she felt "forced" to lie as a result of their questioning. She would respond to this by sometimes "turning on the tears" and saying that "something had happened" which she was not ready to talk about just yet. Her parents would then be uncomfortable about questioning her further and would leave her until she was ready to talk. This would give her time to formulate a more convincing lie about what had actually happened which would then deflect her parents' attention. More elaborate lies to parents were aided by the involvement of a good friend. Here the selection of an appropriate collaborator was necessary, Carla highlighted that she would select a friend whom her parents knew, liked and trusted and would reciprocate if necessary by lying to her friend's parents. Despite this, Carla would not lie about anything which she considered "dangerous" or overly risky and made clear distinctions between risky and non-risky activity.

For Carla, the majority of lies that she told would be to her parents. She did, however, lie to teachers occasionally about completion of homework and this was made easier if the entire class would "collude" in a lie to a replacement teacher about whether homework had been due in. However, this required collaboration from the entire class and some planning. Lies to friends were occasionally told, but Carla and her classmates all felt this was less acceptable as trust was highly

Box 3.4 cont.

important in such situations. Nonetheless, when lies were necessary, new technology was really helpful as Carla would ensure she was texting on her mobile phone at the same time as delivering a lie so that any hesitation could be attributed to her being distracted by the message she was composing.

Issues and challenges for parents/teachers

The methods used by Carla to deceive others illustrate a sophisticated understanding of how she can deflect or manipulate a situation in order to provide herself with more time whilst making her accusers feel uncomfortable in asking further probing questions. Her ability to perspective take in interactions means that she is adept at responding to challenges faced by deception and can handle the situations using the resources she has to hand. In such instances it is difficult for teachers or parents to respond to these reactions negatively, although it is always beneficial to monitor whether the emotional outburst or the avoidance is long lasting (as in something really might have happened that is negative) or shortlived which can indicate a higher likelihood of deceit.

The developmental challenge perspective

A dynamic systems perspective here would first pick up on the relationship between Carla and her parents. The first question would be whether Carla really had any choice about lying in these circumstances. Is Carla trying to be "difficult" or manipulative or is she simply searching for a level of privacy which most adults would take for granted? In terms of resources, there is a clear role for the structural resource of age as mediated by other people's perceptions. In this case, it may be that Carla's age does not give the same "right" to privacy in the eyes of adults around her. Therefore her response, to use their concern as a means of getting this privacy, may be seen as a reaction to that. As a 17 year old, Carla may feel that she is able to distinguish between risk and safety; however, the reaction of adults around her may reflect a view of her as more helpless than she feels she is. Carla's choice of deflection strategies suggests a high level of interpersonal skill, including an awareness of other people's expectations and her own limitations in being able to carry off a lie successfully. It would be interesting to see Carla's actual lying performance and how she applies these principles in practice.

One important aspect of deflection is to be able to get away with distracting attention without making it immediately obvious that this is what you are planning to do. Participants in our study emphasized the importance of appearing casual and used self-distraction techniques to avoid any nerves or to give a reason for hesitation in answering: "and you say 'that's when I was texting someone, that's when I've said it'" (P04, 17).

This fits with research by Strömwall, Hartwig, and Granhag (2006) that, although based on a mock crime scenario and hence not indicative of everyday lying, identified plausibility and simplicity as two verbal strategies identified by liars as ways of being convincing. Taylor, Nicholls, and Fisher (under review) compared high and low self-monitors' (Gangestad & Snyder, 2000) strategies for telling successful truths or lies. The first study asked participants to give written answers. The second study used a semi-structured interview methodology and both studies asked participants to generate successful truths and lies in serious and trivial situations. Participants in this study indicated they were likely to be given away in trivial situations if they made too much of an effort to lie. Over-elaborate stories with a great deal of planning were likely to appear rehearsed and participants felt these would raise questions about why they were making so much effort over such a trivial matter. Although planning was regarded as important for serious lies, the notion of over-planning was also seen in our research, particularly when involving friends: "The thing is, someone messes up then . . . it all gets mixed up if you're questioned" (P05, 15).

The importance of deflection as a strategy for success is supportive of previous research on deception strategies. Taylor and Rolfe (2005, under review) interviewed 27 participants and asked them to generate lies in four different situations: serious/difficult, serious/easy, trivial/difficult and trivial/easy. They were asked to generate all lies for one of three different targets: stranger, acquaintance and intimate. They were then asked for details about the lie and what sort of behaviours a liar would be expected to display. Lies were generated in a range of different situations, including real lies with the participant as liar, target and observer and hypothetical deceptions. However, despite these variations, the overarching theme from this research was "distraction and deflection".

In the Taylor and Rolfe study, participants dealing with intimates and sometimes acquaintances would use their previous knowledge of the target to make this more convincing (e.g. pick a topic which was always designed to make the person angry or to capture their attention). Although this deflection is deceptive (providing information the sender knows to be incorrect), it has more in common with excuses and justifications than lies. This illustrates both the complexity of deception and the futility of treating lies as separate from other forms of strategic communication. Although the use of excuses has negative connotations in everyday life (Schlenker, Pontari, & Christopher, 2001), they are widely employed.

Support for this position comes from a paper by Tyler and Feldman (2007). They conducted a series of four experiments that manipulated the conditions under which excuses were delivered and considered the consequences of these. Results showed, while valid excuses resulted in more positive character appraisals, invalid ones resulted in appraisals that were more negative than in a "no excuse" control condition. This research would therefore suggest you should avoid making an excuse rather than use one which lacks believability or suggests disrespect for others. As we saw in the previous chapter, matching action and situation requires a great deal of social skill and excuses and minimizations are still used in very serious situations, despite these being ineffective.

Manipulate expectations

This can operate in two different ways. First, for people we know, we can work to establish a "reputation" that creates a set of expectations in the minds of our targets. This can sometimes work in our favour but may occasionally work against us. For example, a group of 11 and 12 year olds described a recent detention situation where one had taken the blame for two other members (see Box 3.2 for more detail). Although he had been involved as well and was not alone in the act, he was the only one to receive school detention for this offence. All group members attributed this to his "reputation" (the boy in question was in his first year at the school and had already been in both break-time and after-school detention on a number of occasions). Interestingly, neither the boy himself nor his two friends felt his taking the blame was a problem. This may of course have been because of the consequences (detention after school rather than arrest and charge), or it may simply be that he "knew the system" now and was less affected by the impact of this particular punishment. This ties in with research which will be presented in later chapters on persistent young offenders.

Another interesting aspect that emerged from discussing negative reputations concerned the degree to which, once established, these were permanent. One 15 year old recounted an occasion where she had been caught out lying to her parents and claimed she had reduced the number of instances where she lied to her parents and expressed concern they would not see her as honest: "I'm straight up with her now . . . I've lied in the past, serious lies to my parents but now I can be more open to her . . . I wouldn't be able to do it any more. . . . My mother found out about what I lied about in the past . . . don't want to go through it again" (P06, 15). In terms of the developmental challenge model, this significant negative experience has altered perceptions of the resources available to meet a challenge with deception. The 15 year old's experiences have led her to think she is less likely to succeed in deception with these targets as well as reducing her motivation to lie (by making "betrayal of trust" salient).

If some young people have managed to acquire a negative reputation, there are also those who have managed to establish "credit" with a specific target which could be used for a really necessary situation. This was a strategy discussed by some of our university students as being extremely useful. This relates to research by Tarrant and Campbell (2007) which demonstrated that violation of group norms was more likely to be tolerated if this was done by someone who had previously established themselves as supportive of the group. This also ties in with the research conducted by Emler and Reicher (1995) who argued behaviour within a specific situation does not just have an immediate impact, but will also have indirect consequences which are more far-reaching. They also argued that, when people go into a specific situation their previous reputation has an impact on the way this progresses. Their research did suggest some general reputations that developed and which were agreed upon by both delinquent and non-delinquent young people, suggesting reputations are developed and delinquent youth know what reputations they are likely to have.

Next, expectations can be manipulated in a specific situation if there is a prior relationship with the target. For example, younger participants were very clear on which teachers they could try a homework excuse with and which not. Additionally, choice of friend to establish an alibi or validate a story was sometimes governed by their parents' perceptions of this person, although this did have to be managed quite carefully: "My friend kind of spilled it. He goes 'Was camping good?'" (P07, 14). "If, like, your mother is really fond of one of your friends and she believes everything they say and you get them to lie for you, she'll be like 'Oh well, they wouldn't lie so you must be telling the truth'" (P08, 15).

Knowledge was acquired through direct experience or observation but did not have to relate specifically to the deception situation: "Yeah, you improve the next time then!" (P09, 15).

"Manipulating expectations" was also found in Taylor and Rolfe's research, although here participants referred less to general reputations and more to expectations in specific situations. Participants in Taylor and Rolfe's research would mention going out with people the target knew (and preferably liked) to enhance the credibility of the account. Similarly, one participant said he would deliberately over-elaborate the background when lying to his mother (who had limited patience). In the end, she would lose patience and either stop listening or tell him she had heard enough and he was able to minimize or avoid the lie. Taylor and Rolfe also found expectations of situationally appropriate behaviour in lies to acquaintances and strangers. For example, if you were phoning the receptionist at work to call in sick, you would make yourself sound ill. Similarly, if you were being questioned by the police about the death of a close relative, participants felt you would display some distress. This pattern did not emerge in the current data. However, this might be because lies to unknown people were mentioned relatively rarely and further research should explore this in more detail.

Use truth

One specific strategy mentioned by participants was of using the truth (or a partial truth) to successfully avoid a specific topic of conversation. We have already discussed this when it comes to deflection. However, it is important to be aware there are other ways of using the truth. Participants felt they should stick as closely to the truth as possible as this would make the lie easier to carry off but also because this could then be used as a mechanism for creating guilt if they were not believed.

Again this supports Taylor and Rolfe, where participants would use the creation of guilt in particular to intimate targets. For example, there were two participants who had been unfaithful to their girlfriends. When questioned, both emphasized the positive feelings they still had for their girlfriends and avoided specific questions about where they had been, who had been there and what had happened. One participant who had been away from home at the time even used examples of how often he had called home to make his girlfriend feel guilty for doubting him. In the current analysis this strategy worked most effectively when the person using it was aware of what the target would expect.

The three strategies outlined above have a number of features in common. First, there is no simple dichotomy between truth and deception and so treating these as separate phenomena is unrealistic. This links back to equivocation as discussed earlier in the chapter. Surface examination of some of the messages used in the equivocation experiments would suggest these are lies and should be treated as such. However, Bavelas and colleagues conducted a number of rating studies which indicated equivocal messages were rated as true rather than false. Therefore truth and lies may not be entirely separate from one another.

"Deceptive miscommunication theory" (DeMiT; Anolli, Balconi, & Ciceri, 2003a) also dismisses the notion of deception and truth being treated as separate communication strategies. Deceptive miscommunication is not simply an alternative to truthful communication but is part of a family of potential miscommunications (including politeness, pretence and mistakes). Therefore the wider context in which deception occurs determines the structure of the communication. Anolli *et al.* argue that the same processes of planning and execution apply to deceptive miscommunication as to all other types of communication and all include the same variety of verbal and non-verbal behaviour. Anolli *et al.* are able to use the DeMiT perspective to address differences in linguistic style across different types of deception. They identify three main linguistic styles (vague, unverifiable language, avoidance of giving information and depersonalization) and argue that this range of styles means communicators are able to choose a strategy which fits their communicative goals.

The second common feature is flexibility. This does not link with traditional research on believed cues to deception (see e.g. Akehurst, Köhnken, Vrij, & Bull, 1996; Global Deception Research Team, 2006) which emphasizes the importance of ingrained stereotypical beliefs. Akehurst and colleagues compared the beliefs held by police officers and students about their own and other people's behaviour. They asked about 64 different behaviours, ranging from verbal cues such as clichés, use of short, simple sentences and response latency to non-verbal cues such as facial twitching, unfriendly facial expressions, shaking and shrugging. Results indicated that both police officers and students held inappropriate beliefs about the cues to deception, believing lies were associated with nervous behaviours.

Similarly, the Global Deception Research Team (2006) conducted two studies (Study 1 in 58 countries and Study 2 in 63). The first study asked participants a single open-ended question "How can you tell when people are lying?" while the second used the most popular content categories from Study 1 to create a structured questionnaire. Participants again showed beliefs that suggested liars would behave nervously, with the most popular response being gaze aversion. In terms of the differences between their findings and ours, we would argue that traditional research is designed to elicit such stereotypes.[2] By providing no opportunity to elicit a specific lying situation, participants draw on generalized representations of deception and hence retrieve stereotyped beliefs. Some support for this comes from our own research (Taylor & Hick, 2007) where differences were found in beliefs between self-generated trivial and serious situations. Similarly in the current research semi-structured interviews were used that allowed participants to think about specific lying situations and to identify strategies rather than generalized perceptions.

Behaviour, nerves and cognitive load

When questioned directly, participants did believe that nervous behaviour would be associated with deception. This is supportive of research such as that by the Global Deception Research Team (2006). However, they qualified this belief in two important ways. First, they supplied reasons why nervous behaviours would be expected (e.g. the target of the lie made it difficult, the degree of planning made them feel the lie was import-ant and highly skilled liars would feel less nervous). Second, they expected these cues to be shown by other people more than by themselves. Those asked generally rated their lying abilities as better than other people their age.

When it came to cognitive load, participants acknowledged more diffi-culties when lying and some participants described elaborately planned lies which would include other parties as confederates. Interestingly, these lies tended to be directed towards teachers and parents and included careful selection of targets and confederates (e.g. select people that your parents know but not too well, in case they feel they know your friend's parents well enough to check with them). The degree of planning engaged in often resulted in participants regarding these lies as creative enterprises and being quite upset if they were denied the opportunity to air these "works of genius" (e.g. when faced with a substitute teacher who didn't ask for home-work to be handed in). However, participants also recognized difficulties with too much planning and often felt that a lie could look over-rehearsed and as if they were trying too hard. Sometimes this was best avoided by using an "automatic" lie (without any planning), at other times the planning actually consisted of not making the lie sound as though they had made too much of an effort. This fits with research by Taylor, Nicholls, and Fisher (submitted) who found that low self-monitors were more likely to "overdo" minor lies and minor truths by putting in too much information and hence appearing less credible.

ACCEPTABILITY

The final theme identified was lie acceptability. Two elements emerged here: lies were considered as more acceptable when they were told to preserve secrecy or to control disclosure; and participants would use strategies of blaming the targets of their lies to reduce the degree of guilt and to increase acceptability. When compared to the forensic lies discussed in Chapters 4 and 5, and in particular the avoidance of responsibility in some of the case studies presented, there is a much wider range of methods used to establish acceptability, including co-perpetrator blaming as well as victim blaming.

Victim blaming could be explained as an attempt to minimize empathic distress (Hoffman, 2000) and has been seen in other research on the acceptability of deception (Taylor & Rolfe, 2009). Taylor and Rolfe found that lies to intimate targets were often accompanied by this type of blame, with targets being regarded as gullible, overly possessive, controlling or suspicious and hence "deserving" of the lie. These kinds of judgements are also evident in our interviews, as were judgements about others who are observed to be liars: "to start sort of a ripple effect, and my mum's gonna start nagging. . . . I guess I sort of see it, it's best for both of us" (P11, 20). "when you see people in high places are lying, you think to yourself 'Oh I don't see why I can't lie'" (P12, 15).

What is clear from this analysis of young people's interviews is that everyday deceptions are a complex process, involving clear choices and boundaries, awareness of the other person's reactions and strategic self-presentation. Lies are told most often to protect the young person's autonomy and privacy and to avoid difficult topics of communication. However, these are not necessarily negative and are often told in the context of good family communications. Adolescents are also aware of the nature of trust and are less likely to manipulate others who have displayed genuine trust in them. Although some developmental trends can be identified, we see no evidence for specific stages in the development of deceptive communication ability and instead have evidence to support this as a flexible process, influenced by a wide range of factors.

There is, however, one limitation in the current analysis – our young people were by definition not delinquent or "at risk". While the schools and university from which these participants were recruited are all in South Wales (an area with pockets of very high unemployment and associated social problems), participants were regular attendees at their academic institutions and in some cases held positions of responsibility within them (e.g. prefect). These results may very well not apply to adolescents who are either delinquent or "at risk" of becoming so. Similarly, they may not apply to those with conduct or personality disorders. However, the transition to risk may also be seen as a developmental process. The final case study in this chapter (Box 3.5) presents a mother's concerns about her teenage son's behaviour and is adapted from a weblog. This illustrates the way that "normal" adolescents may move into risky behaviour and provides a link between this chapter and the cases discussed in Chapters 4 and 5.

Box 3.5

Jamie, 15 years old

When Jamie was 15 he began a relationship with a girl which quickly became extremely intense. He began to see her to the exclusion of his friends and to spend his limited earnings on taking her out and buying her clothes and gifts. Jamie's mother tried to discourage him but he did not pay any attention to her. Jamie's new girlfriend (Leah) engaged in persistent lying and manipulation of those around her and encouraged Jamie to lie to his family and existing friends. The situation became such that nothing Jamie said could be believed by anyone. He lost contact with his previous peer group and developed a friendship with another 16-year-old boy who was an alcoholic (Clive). Clive lived at home with his mother who was unemployed but did not have contact with his father. Jamie and Clive started to get into "trouble" – this included violence and harassment of other people in the area, of his mother and of Jamie's younger brother. Jamie also began taking drugs and drinking heavily. His mother reacted by using punishment and pleading with her son to come home, to not see these friends and to stop drinking. This was then followed by attempts to separate Jamie from his friends. This just made Jamie even more angry and he began to threaten the family on a more regular basis and to "take out" his frustration on inanimate objects in the house. Finally, his mother felt she had no option but to call the police and have them intervene with a curfew and a behavioural order. This, according to Jamie's mother, was one of the main factors in getting Jamie to realize what he was doing and to persuade him to seek help. The other contributing factor identified by his mother was that Leah had left him and set up home with Clive. Jamie stopped contact with Clive and Leah and began to attend counselling regularly. While the situation was not completely resolved, significant progress had been made in rebuilding the relationship between Jamie and his family and he had begun working again to pay off his debts.

Issues and challenges for parents/teachers

This example highlights how quickly a situation can spiral out of control and from the perspective of a parent lead to feelings of helplessness in terms of being able to intervene with their child. On the one hand the parent needs to allow their child to make mistakes, but when such mistakes are identified as getting more risky and illegal they become self-destructive to the adolescent. Many parents reading this example would hope their child would never become involved in such situations, although this is not always preventable and hence there is a need to foster a relationship of open communication and trust throughout childhood and into

Box 3.5 cont.

adolescence. Respect for privacy is obviously important, but the knowledge that a child will always inform a parent when things become difficult or dangerous is perhaps the most positive way of managing such situations. This is also sadly highlighted in circumstances where teenagers take their own lives because the pressure of exams and the future is so intolerable. Many parents report little or no knowledge of the anguish their child was experiencing prior to their death. Such pain can remain secret from parents and although they are left with huge levels of guilt and a feeling that it could have been prevented, in many instances, the child chose not to disclose their inner trauma more widely. Ultimately, the more openness and trust that can be fostered by teachers and parents during times of difficulty or risk with adolescents, the better such situations can be managed.

The developmental challenge perspective

While it would be difficult for any parent to see a way through this situation and the common reaction for most people would be to blame Jamie for his actions, the dynamic systems perspective provides a clear insight into the gradually escalating process. Jamie was initially extremely defensive about his mother's reaction to his girlfriend, seeing Leah as his "ideal woman" and his mother as attempting to undermine this. His mother's perspective was that she was protecting her son from getting hurt too quickly. However, Jamie saw this as an attempt to take control away from him. Jamie could be seen as lacking the resources to balance a new relationship with his existing friendships and removed from his social support network he received less validation for his hardworking prosocial lifestyle. The normal sources of social comparison were not available to him; in fact at the time the only peer group member that Jamie was able to compare himself to was Leah. The system in which Leah had developed her "pathological lying" is not outlined. However, it seems likely that exploring her circumstances would reveal a pattern leading to this development. Jamie's feeling of being stifled by his mother may have prompted him to use deception as a way of establishing himself as an autonomous adult. However, for his mother the deception served to underline her view that Jamie could not be trusted to take care of himself.

When Jamie met Clive he was already separated from his existing peer group and may have seen Clive as a way into a more adult, less restricted lifestyle. After all, Clive also lived at home with his mother but was not being "nagged" all the time to spend less time with (and less money on) his girlfriend. Jamie may have lacked the resources to see his mother's perspective. However, his mother's actions also make it clear that she perceived her resources as inadequate to meet the challenge. This situation of "decay" continued for a significant period of time until the new challenge of Jamie threatening his younger sibling made his mother reappraise her own resource pool. This forced her to realize that there were wider societal resources available (in this case the police) which could at least be tried and she brought these to bear on Jamie (the organism within the system). Independently of this, in another part of Jamie's system, his girlfriend had begun to display overt signs of the behaviour he had been warned about. This may have made him more willing to accept the help offered at the same time as the sanction.

CHAPTER SUMMARY

The current chapter outlines a comprehensive analysis of different lies, motivations for lying and strategies adopted by non-offending adolescents, those who were actively engaged with the UK education system and whose home circumstances were generally supportive. Lies were told to protect the young people themselves and those close to them and were also told to establish autonomy and privacy from parents. The target of the lie was often blamed for "forcing" the liar to adopt this strategy, either through gullibility, over-regulation or some other negative behaviour. This could be seen as an attempt to justify a negative action.

Despite lying to a range of different targets, all the young people interviewed showed very clear boundaries, either in terms of content, consequence or relationship, and indicated that there were some things they would not lie about. Deflecting attention, as in previous research, was identified as a key strategy for success, with more skilled adolescents being able to manipulate others' expectations of them. The use of truthful information to enhance the credibility of a lie clearly illustrates that young people do not see truth and deception as entirely separate and therefore perhaps academics and practitioners should not either.

In terms of the developmental approach, evidence was presented in this chapter for lying as skilled behaviour designed to establish goals of particular relevance to adolescents. Five case studies were used to develop this point, highlighting both issues for practitioners (in this case parents and teachers) and the way that a dynamic systems approach might interpret such behaviour. This strategy will be continued in Chapters 4 and 5, outlining practitioner challenges and developmental insights for lies in offender populations.

NOTES

1 Instead of following the six stages linearly, Braun and Clarke (2006) recommend that researchers move backwards and forwards between stages as required by the data and the purpose of analysis.
2 A positive move was the Global Deception Research Team's (2006) description of their research as "two worldwide studies of stereotypes about liars" (p. 60).

4 Strategies and tactics in interpersonal interactions

This chapter will consider a range of interactions with young people involved or alleged to have been involved in criminal activity. The purpose of this chapter is to present and develop a discussion about how to approach and understand young people in pre- and post-conviction environments. Our approach is not to establish that all young people involved in criminality are routinely engaging in deception, but to enable a heightened level of insight to allow practitioners to distinguish between those individuals who are lying from those who are not. By reviewing the resources and challenges of the young people in question, it will also be possible to understand the skilled nature of this behaviour, even among a group of young people who might be unsuccessful liars having been caught and convicted as a result of evidence gained during a police investigation. Therefore, identifying skilled as well as less skilled deceptions produced by unsuccessful liars can act as a cautionary note to practitioners about the varying levels of challenge presented by such young people. It will be possible to demonstrate how young people feel that deception is appropriate, even in situations where most of us would consider truth to be a better strategy, and to show that this may create challenges for practitioners in this and other settings. This is because it is important for practitioners to understand the young person's perspective and motivation to enable more effective interactions.

In order to explore some of the challenges further, we will focus on the first accounts of young people in police interviews, assessments for court, and research interviews with prolific young offenders. All the individuals included in this discussion present differently and as such we emphasize a holistic approach to the assessment of credibility. As will be discussed in Chapter 5, the challenge of working with young offenders can be enormous when accounting for myriad factors of vulnerability, offending, personality and adolescence. To understand the nature of deception in adolescence and have awareness of the tools at our disposal to assess credibility and respond appropriately, it is necessary to take a step backwards from the minutiae of the verbal and non-verbal behaviours exhibited (as was discussed in Chapter 1) and instead consider a broader perspective.

Although relevant across a range of domains for practitioners working with young people, our rationale for understanding and improving credibility assessment is illustrated only too clearly when rates of recidivism are considered: that is, the reoffending rates following prior convictions for offences. The ability to identify deceit and levels of risk is of paramount importance to those practitioners working in the criminal justice system. In terms of offence prevalence and prolific offending, 59% of male and 44% of female young people in prison had been in custody before (HMIP, 2007) and 79% of males and 57% of females aged 15 to 17 years released from custody reoffended within two years (Ministry of Justice, 2008). Furthermore, the Ministry of Justice (2008) state that overall the reoffending rate for those who were reconvicted in the 2006 cohort was 38.7% which amounted to a total of 48,938 offences including 407 considered "serious" which included murder, manslaughter and sexual offences. Statistics for March 2009 (Howard League for Penal Reform, 2009) report current numbers of children in secure custody at 2602 (secure children's home 183; secure training centre 225; prison 2194). Although this might appear to be a relatively low statistic within the wider population of young people, the figures are increasing and do not account for offences that occur when there is no criminal justice intervention and represent a general issue in relation to the reduction of recidivism. This is especially the case when speaking with prolific offenders who will disclose involvement in offences where they had no police inter-action. In particular the prevalence of prolific young offenders within community and secure settings and reoffending rates illustrate a requirement to understand and heighten the skills of practitioners who routinely interact and work with this client group. Further, given that offending and deception are considered by the young people themselves to be an effective use of resources to meet the challenges of day-to-day living, more effective and honest interaction can lead to a better understanding of the wider systems in which young offenders are embedded. This will itself assist with more effective interventions to reduce reoffending.

There is a range of situations in which we can become the target of deception by adolescents, the majority of which are unproblematic incidents associated with a need for young people to push boundaries, break rules and rebel against societal norms, preserve their privacy and protect others. Although such interactions provide us with insight into how adolescents view the world and manage their subsequent interactions with adults, it is our experiences with young offenders in applied forensic settings that provide the opportunity to observe deception in criminal settings.

In general, delinquent acts tend to occur frequently within groups who explore social interactions within their own comfort zone. With increased experience in criminal activity, the need for the additional support provided by the presence of peers (co-defendants) during offending is reduced and instead starts to become a hindrance to success. The journey through adolescence for some brings with it heightened experience in offending, and the comfort blanket that peers can provide which aids confidence and increases bravado can become surplus to requirement. Furthermore, the type and range of offences committed can alter to those which necessitate an individualized rather than group approach. This is also illustrated in "gang" membership where some young people will eventually strike out alone and gain criminal independence and individual status. In developmental terms, the challenge of offending has become less difficult and therefore requires fewer resources, such as those of social group support. Additionally, the young people themselves have developed a more realistic appraisal of their own self-efficacy which allows them to offend successfully without receiving the validation from, and social comparison with, other group members.

Variations in offending during adolescence can further impact on the assessment of credibility, that is, the extent to which young people become immersed in a criminal lifestyle. Three categories appear to emerge from assessing the literature on offending during adolescence:

- one-off involvement in crime
- adolescence-limited offending
- life-course persistent offending.

For example, a group of young people may break into an unoccupied property whilst under the influences of alcohol and be arrested and cautioned by the police. Such actions for some individuals may be a "one-off" prank, for others generally low level offending will be contained in adolescence or as the result of a particular event or trigger. For others, such behaviour will be part of an ingrained criminal lifestyle which might initially include vandalism, stealing cars, drink-driving, joy-riding, setting fires and burglary – with little or no thought of the consequences. The skills gained during adolescence for persistent offenders can influence their views and perspectives in adulthood and in such instances crime also becomes a life skill to accompany deception. Ultimately though, any decision to lie about illegal activities will be the result of a complex set of considerations by the young person and their evaluation of the likely success. In other words, any decision to lie in these circumstances will depend on the young person's appraisal of the challenge and the resources available to meet that challenge (Hendry & Kloep, 2002).

When considering deception in forensic settings, it is important to differentiate between the way events are presented by the young person in pre-conviction, court, and post-conviction settings and how this depends on the stage of the investigation and likelihood of conviction. This is because the motivation and reason behind interactions with practitioners will likely alter over time. Observations of young people in police interviews require consideration of impression management, previous experience of offending, personality and orientation to authority amongst other factors (e.g. Gozna, 2008). Hence, to isolate behaviours and identify particular responses to questions as indicative of deception is potentially precarious. As well as being contrary to the systems approach, this course of action raises difficulties for practitioners. It can ultimately result in the wrong interpretation of behaviours, bias or an incorrect focus in further questioning. Similarly, evaluating behaviours in pre-court assessments and post-conviction settings can have potential drawbacks and the emphasis is to tailor the focus of any interaction with a young suspect or offender, keeping practitioner objectives at the forefront of the interaction.

To explore further the ways in which young offenders engage with practitioners in their encounters in pre- and post-conviction settings, we consider three types of interaction:

- the first accounts of young suspects provided in police custody
- pre-court assessments of dangerousness and fitness to plead
- the beliefs of prolific young offenders in youth justice settings.

SUSPECT INTERACTIONS IN POLICE INTERVIEW

Evaluating the personality and mindset of a young person who is suspected of committing an offence can be achieved by exploring their initial account provided in police interview. This is one opportunity in addition to that presented at time of arrest where a suspect can provide their own perspective of what occurred during the offence. This takes place once the individual has been formally cautioned and is being audio or video recorded in interview. The benefit for police interviewers is that the initial account is uncontaminated, that is, it is solely the narrative of the young person and their choice to express themselves (albeit in some cases following advice from a legal representative). The account has not been altered through focused questioning and targeted discussion about certain aspects of the offences and legal "points to prove" for the prosecution. This provides a valuable account of how the young person perceived events and the way in which they are likely to further view the situation during the police interview. The manner in which information is presented by young suspects through the implementation of particular strategies can hugely assist in a general assessment of credibility, but also incorporates an opportunity for practitioners to further plan their interactions to increase the effectiveness of interviewing.

The police interview is an excellent opportunity to understand the intricacies of deception as it is presented within an interpersonal interaction. The ways in which young people present their accounts of events following arrest can hugely assist practitioners in identifying truthful and deceptive narratives. As discussed in Chapter 1, there is a general lack of holistic research focusing on ways in which people deceive in forensic settings, and to date the literature has largely relied on generalizations from laboratory studies with non-offending populations.

The opportunity to observe police interviews live and record the initial accounts of suspects has allowed some interesting insights to be made that are crucially relevant to the consideration of deception in such settings. In our research (Gozna, Teicher, & Boon, 2009) a total of 69 interviews were observed which involved young suspects aged between 13 and 21 years (average age 18 years) and included 8 female suspects. Prior to discussing the initial accounts of these suspects, it is important to describe the sample we observed and to consider the wider implications for the detection of deception. All our suspects were arrested for high volume crime offences although a subsection of the cohort had prior convictions for major crime offences. The suspects were all interviewed by a specialist team of police officers who are assigned to a prisoner interview and intelligence team. Of the 69 arrested, 19 (27.5%) had not previously been involved with the police and had not been interviewed before. This left a sample of 50 suspects who between them had been convicted for a total of 263 offences (range 0–20, average 4 offences) although had been associated with a total of 542 offences (range 0–59, average 8 offences). This overall figure of suspected crime was not fully illustrated in the previous histories of these young people but this emphasizes that for some there was substantial experience in being interviewed by the police and spending time in police custody. This has important implications for interpreting deceptive interactions, particularly when considering the alleged offences committed by the suspects. In the sample of interviews observed, 29 (39.1%) young people had been arrested for offences against the person; 8 (11.6%) for offences against property; 23 (33.3%) for theft; 4 (5.8%) for drug offences; 3 (4.3%) for public order offences; 2 (2.9%) for possession of an offensive weapon; and 2 (2.9%) for driving offences. Of the offences observed, 12 were domestic incidents involving the suspect and a partner or member of their family. All of these offences present different challenges for the young people involved and all had different resources available. However, despite this variation and the importance of taking a flexible approach, Gozna *et al.* (2009) were able to identify some commonalities in their initial account.

The presence of co-defendants in offences committed by young people is important to consider when discussing the detection of deception. Criminal behaviour during adolescence has a heightened likelihood of involving multiple offenders due to the nature of social interaction and the need for a reliance on peers to support successful offending. Our research identified a reduction in the number of co-defendants when individuals reached the age where there was the potential to be sent to an adult prison (rather than a young offenders institution). The reliance on peers can be beneficial and a resource of young offenders who are learning the ropes but once experience has been gained, some will no longer have a need to commit offences in groups. Offending in groups increases the likelihood of being caught (heightened chance that one person will be arrested) and convicted (more likely that one person will "grass" during the police interview or be caught on CCTV). Therefore, during police interviews with young people there is the potential for more than one suspect for any offence. Although this could be perceived as an advantage to police officers, the criminal code of loyalty amongst peers (Gray & Gozna, 2010) can result in lower disclosure rates during interviews or the projection of blame onto others which can cloud the interpretation of accounts given. The option of involving peers in offending also depends on the offences being committed and hence certain offences will by their nature only involve the suspect and aggrieved/victim. In the interviews we observed 34 (49.3%) suspects had committed the offence alone; 14 (20.3%) with one other co-defendant; and 21 (30.4%) with 2–5 others. Although the length of interview is a consideration of deception detection in high volume crime, the initial account allows the first assessment to occur, although it is crucial that changes in the suspects' objectives and responses to pertinent questions are monitored throughout. Of the interviews observed in our research, the length ranged from 6 to 54 minutes although the average length was 27 minutes. Although these appear relatively short when compared with major crime interviews, the wealth of material that can be gathered is immense.

The presence or absence of a legal advisor during interviews is a further factor to consider when identifying the strategies and tactics that young suspects might employ. This includes those strategies that might be recommended by legal advisors and could impact on the impression presented to police interviewers. The young suspects we observed exhibited a limited tendency to opt for the provision of legal advice once they had been arrested where 18 (26.1%) had a solicitor present during the interview and 3 (4.3%) obtained telephone advice pre-interview. The presence of an appropriate adult within the interview is more a part of the procedure to protect vulnerable young persons and ensure they understand the police caution and any subsequent questions. Therefore, in the sample of young people observed in interview 16 (23.2%) had an appropriate adult present. The presence of legal advisors and appropriate adults may act as an additional resource for the young people involved; perhaps by presenting additional strategies or relieving the sense of "isolation" that might be associated with a police–suspect interaction. However, in the case of a "known" appropriate adult (e.g. a parent, guardian or familiar social worker), this can present an additional challenge for the young person due to additional impression management requirements or the difficulty in admitting what you have done to the police and a close relative (as was highlighted in Chapter 3). Of the 69 young suspects observed, there were initial accounts provided by 48, the remaining being the result of the manner of the questioning (no initial account provided) and "no comment" interviews.

Strategies and tactics

Following the observations of the initial accounts, it was possible to identify a range of strategies and tactics used by suspects in order to present a particular impression to interviewing officers. Before we discuss specific cases of suspects in interview, the strategies and tactics are explained in Table 4.1.

Table 4.1 Strategies and tactics used by young suspects in police interview

No comment	Suspect responds to all police questioning using "no comment".
Minimize – language	Minimization of the offence through the way in which the information is presented to interviewing officers – reduction of severity of violent behaviour (pushing, scuffle, hitting, punching).
Minimize – culpability	Minimization of personal criminality by emphasizing that the suspect is non-violent, could not have committed the offence (through some inability).
Projection of blame	Projection of blame onto aggrieved or onto co-defendants in order to avoid direct culpability for the offence.
Projection of honesty	Emphasis of honesty through statements that overtly state that the suspect is telling the truth in response to questions: "Honestly", "To be honest with you".
Malicious allegation	The suspect emphasizes that the allegation is malicious and has no substance to it.
Protection of others	The suspect avoids responding or providing specific information that refers to their co-defendants or names and places which could be used as evidence.
Loss of memory	Lack of memory for offence – the suspect emphasizes that they have a total lack of memory for their actions during the offence.
Partial memory	Suspect has a partial lack of memory for the offence illustrated by patchy recollection of some aspects of their actions.
Remorse	The suspect expresses remorse for their actions.
Mental state of aggrieved/victim	A negative mental state regarding the aggrieved is emphasized in that they are considered to be psychologically disturbed (e.g. paranoid, depressed, anxious) or is under the influence of alcohol and/or drugs which negatively impacts on their behaviour (including aggrieved lack of memory).
Skimming	Skimming over the information with a lack of detail – listing events with little depth of description of the actions.
Vague	Vague detail presented to interviewing officers about whereabouts, actions, behaviours but without overt loss of memory.
Deflection	Deflecting the topic by coverage or irrelevant information – speaking about topics that are wholly unnecessary to the main focus of the interview.
Defensiveness	Defensiveness in responses to questioning by the police – responding to questions with questions, exhibiting verbally aggressive language.
Coercion	Emphasis of lack of intent and coercion in the commission of the offence – influence of a third party in the commission of the offence: "I didn't want to do it but . . ."
Provocation	Emphasis that the offence was committed following provocation by the aggrieved therefore they had no choice but to respond as they did.
Victim	Suspect is the victim of an abusive, dysfunctional or violent relationship regardless of gender – this is emphasized to the interviewing officers.

continues overleaf

Table 4.1 (Continued)

Alternative version	Offering an alternative version of events which links to the alleged actions but avoids the admission of the offence itself.
Omission	Omission of relevant/crucial evidential information regarding culpability until directly asked or challenged.
Distancing	Distancing through account provided and to align oneself with the law-abiding community – not a violent person, use of references to aggrieved as a "gentleman", appearing as though a credible member of the community.
Admit culpability	The suspect admits they are in the wrong and were culpable for their behaviour: "I can change when I am drunk."
Responsibility	The suspect takes responsibility for their behaviour in the offence – awareness that the offence was the fault of the suspect (internal locus of control).
Excuses	The suspect presents a range of excuses for their behaviour during the offence – alcoholic, having a bad time, needing to let off steam.
Helpful	Suspect is helpful in the information they provide with additional elements mentioned that are not directly related to the questions posed. Illustrated an attempt to tell the police everything in one session in order to present an honest impression of the events.
Compliant	The suspect is compliant in their responses to interviewing officers and tries to respond to questions in the best manner they can – irrespective of whether they truly believe what they are saying is accurate.
Admission	Admission of involvement in offence.
Denial	Denial of involvement in offence.
Partial	Partial denial or partial admission of actions during the offence.

Initial accounts

In this section a number of the accounts provided in interview are presented to form discussion of the tactics and strategies used by young people who are suspects of crime. The aim of this is to highlight the subtleties of the language used in the accounts and to provide practitioners with some important factors to consider when interviewing young people. As illustrated in Table 4.1, there were diverse objectives for the suspects in interview and many of these appeared to ensure a good impression was provided to those interviewing and presenting the case to the Crown Prosecution Service. The provision of an initial account by suspects in interview should be seen as an opportunity to identify their perspective with regard to the offence. Therefore, there is potential here to gain an insight into how the young person is intending to present their version of events and whether there are particular issues being emphasized that will impact on the way police interviewers tailor their questioning. It is important to acknowledge that an understanding of suspect strategies presented during the first account can also identify the lack of involvement a young person might have in an offence.

However, these different strategies and tactics have a tendency to co-occur within the accounts of young people and so on a higher level it is possible to unravel the focus of the interview. The various perspectives taken by suspects during the initial accounts are explained in detail below and can also be applied to other interactions with young people when practitioners or parents are information gathering.

Damage limitation

The emphasis for the young person here is to limit the perceived damage that has occurred as a result of the alleged offence or indiscretion. The mental state of aggrieved/victim is emphasized, and suspects tended either to deny the offence, partially deny, or minimize (through the use of language and/or legal criminality). Further tactics included claiming they had been coerced to commit the offence, deflecting the discussion towards irrelevant issues or stating a loss of memory. Other options included highlighting that the arrest was a result of a malicious allegation, or that they were unable to provide information due to protecting peers who might have been involved in the crime. Hence the overall presentation was to project honesty and innocence through the impression given to the police.

Admitting

Although generally perceived as a rare event in police custody in terms of the admission of involvement in an offence, there were some instances where suspects admitted culpability for the offence, admitted their actions and accepted responsibility for their behaviour. This was more prevalent with young suspects who had been arrested for the first time and had little experience of police interviews and what their potential resources were should they choose to utilize them (e.g. give a "no comment" interview). This emphasizes that such young people are less entrenched in an antisocial disposition and do not opt to present a dishonest impression to the police. However, it is possible that depending on the outcome of their admission they might choose to deny involvement if they were to be arrested in the future.

Storytelling

One aspect that tends to be ignored in the interpretation of deceptive accounts is the ability to be engaging and develop a storytelling aspect to the information disclosed to police. In certain interviews, young suspects created very vivid stories to explain what had occurred. This was a particularly interesting aspect of their account and included quotes from third parties and also of their own verbal interactions. The main consideration with the storytelling capability in young suspects for practitioners is that they can become drawn into the story and less focused on the content of the information. This can become an effective way for suspects to deflect the interviewer towards elements of the offence that are irrelevant to any prosecution. It also has the ability for the suspect to build rapport and take control of the interview. This should therefore be a factor that practitioners consider when interacting with young people who can present in an inter-personally alluring manner and links to the personality characteristics which will be discussed in Chapter 5. Additionally such strategies can be linked back to Chapter 3 where we saw that non-offending young people used distraction, deflection and strategic truthtelling in a similar manner and with reference to the "reputations" that non-offending young people have created for themselves. For example, one of our 17 year olds indicated she could distract the target of her deceptions so successfully that she could get them to apologize for accusing her. It was clear from the interviews conducted for Chapter 3 that young people would choose the situations they lied about and often would spend some time establishing themselves as honest before including a lie. While it may be the case that those suspected of offences have different reputations and are less selective in their use of deception, it is still important to remember that the content of such stories can be as successful as those used in Chapter 3.

Avoiding

The theme of avoidance was a further tactic utilized by young suspects during interview and incorporated accounts where information pertinent to the offence was skimmed over, there were omissions of information and a general avoidance of disclosing evidence that would result in a prosecution. Although similar to the topic avoidance theme discussed in Chapter 3, the choice of avoidance here would be less effective as a strategy, given that the purpose of the interview was to discuss the offence itself and omissions would be more likely to be noticed. Additionally, non-offending young people in Chapter 3 were more likely to use topic avoidance with those they knew well and who might be more easily deflected on to different topics of conversation.

Blameshifting

The focus of this suspect strategy was to project blame towards a third party involved in the commission of the offence. Hence, there was an emphasis that they had been provoked to act in a certain way and therefore provided excuses to explain their criminal behaviour. Again, this is similar to the "victim blaming" seen in Chapter 3.

Distancing

Suspects attempted to provide as much distance as they could between their actions and the offence that has occurred. However, it was not possible to ascertain the true veracity of their accounts. The main emphasis within the initial explanation was that they had no involvement in the offence, they provided an alternative version of what had occurred and were generally vague about their own actions. In some instances, the suspects were credible in their accounts and in other cases the overall impression left by the young person was one that required further clarification and questioning.

The following case examples of young suspects are presented in order to illustrate the variations in the presentation of the initial account and the background information available to police interviewing officers. To maintain anonymity, the identity of the individuals involved and all names and places have been altered.

Case examples

Box 4.1

Geoffrey

Background

The suspect was seen at night walking along the street. When stopped and searched, a large knife was found on his person. The suspect explained to police officers that he was on his way to his sister's house to feed her dog. The arresting officers noted prior to the search that the suspect became agitated. The suspect has a history of mental health problems and has been diagnosed with paranoid schizophrenia. In interview the suspect explained that his sister was on holiday and he was looking after her house and dog. He was replacing the carpet in her house using the knife, and in the process it became blunt. He took the knife to a friend's house to get it sharpened, and was on his way back to return the knife when he was stopped by police. The suspect points out that he was very co-operative and immediately admitted that he had a knife in the front pocket of the hoodie he was wearing. Throughout the interview the suspect repeats several times that he had a reasonable excuse to carry the knife, but is unable to provide an address stating "but I can take you to where he lives" or a telephone number – "he doesn't have a mobile" for his friend who sharpened the knife for him.

Initial account

It was earlier on about . . . 12 o'clock. I left my sister's house, and um, went over to my mate's Chris's house, don't know exactly where he lives, don't know his second name. I know, I know where he lives, but I don't know the road name of where he lives, or what number it is. And um . . . I went to his house 'cause I knew he had . . . sharpening stone, because after been using the c-, knife to cut carpet and, like, cut up sandpapers, it was getting blunt anyway and, I, I've, I don't want that. My sister has to go and use it and find out that she couldn't cut through even . . . a piece of bread with it, because it was . . . completely blunt. So I took it round to his house so he could sharpen it up. Stayed there till about . . . quarter past four, twenty past four, played on the Wii with him . . . And watched some DVDs, and going on

Box 4.1 cont.

MSN and talking on the internet with him. And then, start walking home . . . [inaudible] I was less than, pretty much about two minutes away from my sister's house when the police decided to stop me, called me over "Oi", and drove past me. I walked over there, started speaking to them . . . And they're like . . . asked me what am I doing here, I was like "Well, I just came from there." And they said "Got any sharp objects?", and I said "Yes I have a knife in my front pocket, because I just came from my mate's house and am going to my sister's house just up there." He got out, took the knife out . . . and that's it, I got arrested.

The suspect

Geoffrey was a 19-year-old male who had previously been arrested eight times and convicted six times. His previous convictions included four offences relating to police/court/prison including three for assaulting police officers, two for theft, one for drugs and one miscellaneous. The suspect was arrested for possession of a bladed weapon (knife). The evidence against him was moderately strong consisting of the knife found on his person. The suspect was charged with the offence.

The interview account by Geoffrey (Box 4.1) illustrates the problem with discerning the intent of a suspect when an alternative version of events is disclosed that is considered credible. Ultimately though, the suspect has previous convictions and the lack of detail provided to prove his intentions leads to problems in determining why he had possession of a knife. In the case of individuals who are diagnosed with mental health problems, the account from the suspect becomes all the more challenging to evaluate in terms of wider risks posed to others. From the developmental perspective, two specific considerations are seen here. The first is the suspect's previous behaviour and reputation which means that any attempt at a legitimate explanation as to why he was carrying a knife is likely to be challenged. While in some offenders, the reputation (previous interviews or convictions) might also be associated with a greater ability to use feedback and greater experience – both leading to greater success – for Geoffrey, the presence of mental health problems impairs his ability to learn successfully from the feedback and to present a more credible account. Geoffrey is a vulnerable individual and this example highlights the complexities surrounding understanding the accounts of young people who present with a range of difficulties.

Box 4.2

Mitchell

Background

The suspect has been previously diagnosed with ADHD and is on medication. He has been living with his grandmother for the past six years. It is alleged that the suspect and his grandmother had an argument over the use of the computer. The grandmother was concerned with the amount of time that the suspect was spending on the computer. When his grandmother pulled out the power cord, the suspect apparently "lost it" and started hitting her with a pillow. After hitting her several times, it is alleged that the suspect followed her into the kitchen, picked up a knife and threatened her with it. The grandmother then called the police and the suspect was arrested. In interview the suspect admits everything, and describes how the argument started. He describes how, after hitting her several times at the back of the head and side of the face, he followed her to the kitchen and threatened her with the knife, but put it back immediately when told to do so. The suspect also says that whilst hitting her he had a "blackout", and only remembered the specific details of his actions after reading his grandmother's statement.

Initial account

Um, I was on the computer, like, the PC . . . laptop. And, um, my nan said I can sh-, ca-, she called me . . . at eight o'clock saying that, um, I can have a bit longer on the computer. And then, she phoned me at, um, quarter to twelve saying "I'm coming up to bed now." And I said "Hey," and she come up and . . . I said "I'm not gonna get off the computer." And then she pulled out . . . the internet lea-, um, the charger lead, and um . . . like, I went to go and grab it and, and scr-, scraped my hand at her and . . . like, she started saying "You're not gonna have it tomorrow." And, I just like, I don't know, just hit her . . . for some reason. And then um . . . [2 sec pause] like, and then she like, like sat down on her bed, like after I hit her, and I picked up a cushion, and I started hitting her with it . . . around the head. And then like, she went to go to the door, going upstairs, I hit her with the cushion again. And then, she went downstairs . . . and I followed her . . . to, downstairs, to the kitchen, and then . . . um, I kicked her in the arm . . . and, like, oh yeah, and one was in, when I was like, when she went on to her bed, I kicked her in the arm as well. [2 sec pause.] And wh-, as we went downstairs, I kicked her . . . again. [2 sec pause.] And, I started saying, I started shouting, calling her names. And then . . . [2 sec pause] like, I don't, don't know, but then, next think I know the police turned up at the door.

The suspect

Mitchell was a 13-year-old male with no previous convictions. He was arrested for battery. The evidence was moderately strong and consisted of a statement from the aggrieved and photographs of injuries. The suspect was cautioned for a first offence.

The suspect Mitchell in Box 4.2 was particularly open in interview, although the level of violence he used during the assault on his grandmother illustrates his propensity for reactive behaviour and to an extent associated characteristics of Attention Deficit Hyperactivity Disorder (ADHD). Mitchell admits a level of responsibility for his actions during his initial account, but does attempt to evade responsibility in the way he recounts the events. The irascibility exhibited in addition to impulsive reactions to this perceived slight illustrate a difficulty in responding to authority and provide evidence of the type of issues that might result in the need for him to engage in deception. Deflection and evasion of responsibility were seen in Chapter 3, but success here was associated with a high level of social skill. That Mitchell is unsuccessful here is perhaps evidence of having had fewer opportunities effectively to develop such social skills and therefore being less aware of other people's perspectives and expectations. As we saw in Chapter 3, blaming someone else can work. However, this is facilitated if the target of the blame is a credible one (e.g. a highly restrictive parent or suspicious partner). In Mitchell's case, trying to deflect blame on to someone who has established a reputation as being caring and supportive in the face of extremely challenging behaviour is unlikely to have been successful.

Box 4.3

Kevin

Background

The aggrieved was the suspect's girlfriend, and the two live together in a flat. Police were called by the aggrieved's sister, who had a telephone conversation with the aggrieved and heard her and the suspect arguing. When police arrived, the aggrieved stated that the suspect threw a plate at her, threatened her with a knife, and eventually sat on her and pulled out some of her hair (a lump of hair was found in the flat). However, she does not want to provide a statement. In interview the suspect states that they had a verbal argument, and that he believes she might say that he has pushed her because she wanted him out. He explains that he was out drinking with friends, and returned home to have dinner with the aggrieved. An argument started during dinner, as the aggrieved was apparently unhappy about the suspect going out with his friends. The suspect explains that both were shouting at each other, and that she wanted him out – but he had nowhere else to go. The suspect denied any physical violence between them and stated that he loves her to bits. When asked whether he threw a plate at her, he responds, "No, don't remember that at all." The suspect also denies pulling her hair or threatening her with a knife stating, "I'm shocked that she's saying that." When asked about the lump of hair found in the flat, the suspect suggests the aggrieved might have pulled it out herself, and reiterates that she is the love of his life. When told by the interviewing officer that the aggrieved stated that she wanted to end the relationship, the suspect started to cry.

Initial account

Um . . . We had a big argument, big row. Um . . . I had been away all weekend, out with my mates. I don't think she liked that very much. Um . . . started getting ab-, like, abusive but of-, with our words to each other. Um . . . I think she ended up ringing the police. I think she really, she just wanted me out. I think she might have s-said that I pushed her or whatever she said, as a way of getting the police to remove me. And she just wanted me to be locked up for the night. That's my, that's the only . . . that's the only thing I could think of why she would say that.

The suspect

Kevin was an 18-year-old male who had previously been arrested 25 times and convicted for 14 offences including two offences against the person, eight for property, two for theft, five for Section 5, three related to police/court/prison, three for drugs, and two miscellaneous. The evidence for the offence was weak because there was no formal statement from the aggrieved and she did not inform the police. The outcome of the case was no further action taken against the suspect.

One of the greatest challenges in ascertaining credibility in the initial account occurs with domestic incidents when one party is arrested. It is very common for the projection of blame to move from the suspect to the aggrieved in response to any statement made about the alleged offence. In the case of Kevin (Box 4.3), it is unclear whether he was responsible for the offence for which he was arrested and on evaluating the evidence the lack of a statement from the aggrieved provides little support for the potential prosecution. In cases of domestic assault, it is common for the actions to be regretted following the incident and statements from suspects to include remorse (including pseudo remorse), expressions of love for the aggrieved or victim and statements that reduce the likelihood that the suspect could exhibit violence toward others, e.g., "I'm not a violent person." This may contrast with non-offenders' motives for using similar impression management strategies – which may be as a means of reducing empathic guilt (Hoffman, 2000). It is therefore difficult for interviewing officers to ascertain the correct course of events due to the higher levels of impression management from all parties and a need to increase personal credibility through the projection of blame.

Box 4.4

Nathan

Background

The police were called to the suspect's flat after neighbours heard him arguing with his partner. When officers entered the flat they found a bag of cannabis (mostly stalks/leftovers, plus a small quantity of cannabis resin) in his room, and

Box 4.4 cont.

arrested him on suspicion of possession of class C drugs. The suspect reacted by jumping up and headbutting one of the officers. In interview the suspect admits that the cannabis stalks are his and leftovers, but denies possession of the cannabis resin found in the same bag. Asked to describe it, the suspect states that "it looks like shit weed to be honest," but refuses to say to whom it belongs ("I'm not gonna go saying that, am I?"). When the officers ask him about his drug habit and whether he arranged for someone to bring the cannabis to him, the suspect says that he smokes it all the time, and although he did not ask for anybody to deliver drugs he recalls seeing a friend of his in the flat a few hours before police arrived, suggesting that he might have left the resin behind. Asked why he assaulted the officer, the suspect responds that he does not know why he did it, but says that the officers were not very nice to him. After the interview the suspect states that he wants to make a complaint about the arresting officers' use of force, "They gave me a good beating."

Initial account

Um . . . To tell you the truth, I don't know nothing about that. I wouldn't have had it lying around if I know police were there, you know what I mean. Like, obviously, that ain't cannabis, that's like stalks, and that's like from what we've, what I've smoked, like, in the past and I've just saved up the stalks and that, innit.

The suspect

Nathan was a 21-year-old male who had been arrested 58 times and convicted for 16 of those offences. His previous offences included 13 against the person, one sexual, nine property, nine theft, five public disorder, 16 police/court/prison, two drugs, and three miscellaneous. He was arrested for assaulting a police officer and possession of a class C drug. The evidence was strong in relation to "points to prove" and consisted of physical evidence of cannabis found at the property, and statements from attending police officers who witnessed the suspect headbutting one of the police officers. The suspect was charged with the offences.

The limited account provided by Nathan (Box 4.4) appeared to be largely the result of extensive experience of being interviewed in police custody and an unwillingness to accept responsibility for his actions. It is apparent that he has a good knowledge of the law in relation to the alleged offence and has therefore minimized the severity by denying possession of a proportion of the drugs found in his flat. However, this clearly was not an effective strategy and although Nathan has a level of experience but is not effective highlights that his implied expertise in such situations does not lead to development and improvement. This suggests that wider factors are necessary for successful interaction and further interviews with someone like Nathan might explore some of these factors, including his ability to produce realistic appraisals of his own self-efficacy.

Box 4.5

Aden

Background

It is alleged that there was an altercation between two males and another group, and when the two males retreated to their flat, the suspect's group followed them and exchanged words. The aggrieved was living in the flat and was the girlfriend of one of the men. She alleges that the suspect made threats to kill over the intercom, and one of the males accuses the suspect of kicking his car mirror. In interview the suspect states that he went out to a shop with a friend. On their way back they came across a scuffle, and the suspect realized that it was his brother Steve fighting with two males. When the suspect arrived, the fighting stopped, and the two males ran back to their flat. The suspect, his brother and cousin followed them and exchanged words. However, the suspect denies making threats to the male's partner and kicking the car mirror.

Initial account

Well, basically I was in . . . my home address in ********. I was in there with . . . my cousin, my mate Jack . . . a few other people that I can't remember . . . and um, my brother Steve and his girlfriend was there I think. And I've gone down the shop with my cousins, my mate Jack . . . basically was i-, who was in the house, but not Steve and his girlfriend. So everyone left our house but Steve and his girlfriend. We've walked down the shop, straight past, obviously, Dave's and Chelsea's house, walked straight down past there. And, I've been in the shop, and then, basically, I've walked my stuff out of the shop, and I've come around to the corner of, um, by the co-op to walk back up towards my house. And as I'm walking up the road, I've heard my mate say, "Ah, they're scrapping, they're scrapping." And I've looked up, and at first I didn't realize who it was, so I've carried on walking. Then I looked up again and seen it was my younger brother being attacked by two people. So I am straight up there. By the time I ran up there, it's stopped. It was Steve and Jamie fighting. Steve wasn't fighting, Steve was being beaten up by Jamie, someone who is near enough twice his age. And as soon as me and my cousins ran up the road, it all got, it stopped. They all went into . . . Carl, no, Dave, and Jamie, and two others, I don't know who it was, ran into Chelsea's house. Um, there was a few words exchanged on the landing, picking on children and all that, pick on someone your own size. And then Dave come out with a gun. We've, we're trying to cross to the bottom of . . . well if his landing is up here, you run to the bottom at this side. And the other three had, no two of them had knives. I don't know who the oth-, it was that Jamie had a knife, Dave had a gun, and there was a person in a red, I think it was a f-, England football t-shirt that had a knife as well. Um . . . Yeah, so basically after that, they all went in, we stayed in the middle of the community area, 'cause everyone was coming up to ask what had gone on. Um, but as they was fighting, Steve and this matey, Steve ran off, and um, I didn't notice this at this at this point, 'cause I was worried about who'd hit my brother, and I wanted, so after that everyone went and dispersed. I went up to my mum's house, see Steve on the phone to my dad; big lump on his

Box 4.5 cont.

head. As soon as I saw that, I ran back outside, ran over to Dave, they was all gone. And I said to him, "You wait until I see you mate, you wait until I see you." That, of, no, I didn't see Chelsea the whole time, she didn't even come out. The only time I spoke to Chelsea was, when my dad w-, ev-, basically everyone, there was a little scrape, they went in, we stayed over here, my dad came down . . . Um, we spoke to Steve, soon as Steve told my dad it was a 30-year-old man, we went over to Dave's. We rung the buzzer, because they wouldn't come. So we rung the buzzer, and that was the only time I physically spoke to Chelsea. I couldn't make out what she was saying, she was ranting and raving. And it's all over, the whole situation was to do with Steve and Chelsea. I think something went on there, while Dave was in jail. And this what I think the whole lot of this is to do with. Something went on, I don't know what exactly, but I could probably guess. But I don't know. And . . . Dave pulled me over . . . a couple of days ago. And he said to me, "Keep your brother away from me." And I said to him, "At the end of the day Darren, you won't lay a finger on my brother. You've 30-odd years old, you won't touch him." Then I thought that was the end of it, until I walked up the road last night and seen my little bruv attacked by two grown men.

The suspect

The suspect was a 21-year-old male who had no previous convictions and had not been arrested before. He was arrested for criminal damage and threats to kill. The evidence was weak consisting of a statement from the aggrieved. After the suspect is released, detention officers discover that he has thrown food against his cell walls. Following the suspect's initial release on bail, no further action was taken.

The initial account provided by Aden (Box 4.5) shows the complexities of the strategies and tactics employed to present the events within the offence. The suspect uses a range of methods to attempt to explain the offence and present an honest and open impression to police interviewers. The level of detail within the account is high, although this does not necessarily result in increased credibility. As in Chapter 3, when talking about interpersonal lies, sometimes the provision of such detail can be inappropriate to the situation or cannot adequately overcome the presence of additional evidence. In cases such as this, regardless of the account provided by the suspect, the accompanying evidence tends to be mostly influential. However, if interviewing officers are convinced that the account provided is truthful, the way they present this to the Crown Prosecution Service can exhibit this belief and act in favour of the suspect. Hence, it is in the suspects' best interests that they appear compliant and detailed in interview to project an impression of unstated honesty. In a similar manner in interpersonal settings (see Chapter 3) an adolescent who presents an impression of compliance and detail can sometimes minimize the punishment or sanction received, even when the evidence against them is strong. In line with the resources discussed in

Chapter 2, adults often have a view of how young people should behave and the kinds of characteristics they should exhibit. It may be that the compliant and detailed account fits effectively into that worldview and hence is regarded as more credible.

Box 4.6

Stacey

Background

The suspect was arrested after fighting with the new partner (aggrieved) of her ex-boyfriend (witness) in the street. During the fight the aggrieved went to the ground and broke her arm. However, it is unclear whether it was an accident or deliberate action by the suspect. The suspect sustained some cuts to her knees. In her initial account the suspect describes the events leading up to the incident. She states that she was at a friend's place having a few drinks (and later hints that her drink might have been spiked, possibly by a man her friends tried to set her up with) but when she wanted to go home nobody would call her a taxi. As she did not have any money on her, she called her ex-boyfriend who lived close by and asked him to lend her some money. They agreed to meet, but when the suspect arrived at the arranged place she saw that he had brought his new girlfriend with him. An argument started between the suspect and her ex-boyfriend, and at some point the aggrieved got involved too. The suspect alleges that the aggrieved pinned her to a lorry, she pushed her away, and the next thing she remembers is getting thrown to the floor and cutting her knees. When asked more questions about her relationship with her ex-boyfriend and the call she made, the suspect explains that they have been together for nine years, but that she split up with him two months ago. The suspect mentions that she recently received a caution for assaulting him, and that was why he was annoyed with her. Hence, when she called him initially he told her to "fuck off," but when she rang back he agreed to meet her (she had also spoken with the aggrieved who initially negotiated between the two). The suspect also elaborates a bit more about the actual incident, stating that when she pushed the aggrieved away from her the aggrieved fell to the floor. The suspect then walked off, but was stopped by the police who had been called by her ex-boyfriend. When confronted with the allegations by the aggrieved (who describes the suspect as aggressive and "in their face" right from the first moment), the suspect denies being the aggressor and instigating the physical attack, but admits using abusive language once the confrontation escalated. The aggrieved also alleges that the suspect was grabbing and twisting her arm, causing her a sharp pain and throwing her on the ground. However, the suspect insists that she only pushed the aggrieved once she was pinned against the lorry. Both the statements of the aggrieved and witness fail to account for the injuries the suspect sustained.

Initial account

Um . . . I was staying at a friend's, um, Sharon, she invited her partner, Mark around, and his brother Simon. And Sharon wants me to . . . have a relationship with Simon, but I'm not interested. Um, things got a bit heated last night. I only had

Box 4.6 cont.

a few to drink; and I've felt the way I did that night. I felt quite dizzy, and I didn't feel . . . right. Um, so I asked to go home, and no one would order me a taxi. So I left her flat . . . [2 sec pause]. Um, and the only person I could call was my ex-partner Dan. Cause I had no money on me at all. So I called him . . . um . . . he said he would meet and give me the money . . . for the taxi. Um, as we were meeting at the bottom of ******* street, when I arrived there he was with . . . he said she was a friend, but I think she is a girlfriend or something. Um, then he started having a go at me about getting arrested for assault. And I said that I won't hear about that, I just needed to borrow a tenner to get home. His um, the girl that was with him then started . . . again, in my face saying, "You hate him, don't you, you hate him, you wanna hit him," and I said "No." Um, and then things just got out of hand. She pinned me up against a lorry that was there. Um, I pushed her, and then all I remember is being thrown to the floor, cut my knee, she had me by the hair. I heard Dan say, "Get off her hair" [2 sec pause]. Um, then I, she let go, I stood back up. And as I went, my mate Sharon stood in front. That's all I remember.

The suspect

Stacey was an 18-year-old female with no previous convictions. She was arrested for GBH and the evidence was weak because the aggrieved and witness statements were not independent and although the aggrieved had a broken arm it was not clear whether it was broken accidentally or intentionally. The suspect was bailed pending court.

It is important to mention here that in general the accounts provided by female suspects involved an additional factor for police interviewers to consider which related to a self-orienting disposition. Therefore, initial accounts had a tendency to include a victim stance and a generally different demeanour towards interviewing officers. When interviewing young females it is important for practitioners to consider the gender differences in presentation of accounts and also ensure that there is an awareness of the characteristics discussed in the the next chapter focusing on borderline and histrionic personality. The account in Box 4.6 was given by Stacey who was a young female suspect accused of the offence of grievous bodily harm (GBH) following an altercation with her ex-partner's new girlfriend. As mentioned above, domestic altercations are more challenging to investigate due to myriad complex issues within the relationships and the problem of identifying who is providing a credible account. Hence the reliance on evidence of injuries and wider statements allows for a broader assessment to take place. Therefore, for the young people in these situations their own personal resources may not be sufficient to ensure deception success. However, a realistic appraisal of the wider evidence may very well influence the decision to lie, even in a situation where the protagonist has little control over the outcome.

PRE-COURT/SENTENCE ASSESSMENT

A particularly challenging aspect of credibility assessment for practitioners occurs when interviewing or assessing young offenders prior to a court hearing or prior to sentencing. This is usually in response to specific instructions from defence/prosecution counsel or the court and can involve the administration of various psychometric and clinical tests to assess, for example, propensity for suggestibility, compliance, and anger. The reason for our inclusion of pre-court and pre-sentence assessments in this chapter is because the outcome can potentially influence the evidence presented or decision making for sentencing and can become a further opportunity for deceptive impression management by young people. The implications of inaccurate or misleading assessments are broad and can influence the court and in certain cases a jury. Hence it is crucial that practitioner assessments are accurate and reflect the true nature and circumstances of an individual and that the manipulation of information is minimized.

One difficulty that practitioners can have when interacting with young people, especially those in early adolescence or who are diagnosed with particular learning disabilities, is the accurate assessment of vulnerability and how this impacts on the interpretation of motive, intent and the offence. In some instances, the culpability and maturity of a young offender appears to be at odds with their age and stage of life. Hence it is vital to have knowledge of the baseline presentation of an individual in addition to a full insight into the alleged offence/s they have committed. Pre-court assessments that occur in the home of a young person can assist in establishing credibility due to the likely presence of other family members and the option to gain additional information. Furthermore, the home environment can highlight peripheral issues that might affect the level of candour and ultimately influence the perceptions of events in an accurate way. In prison or other secure settings, the difficulties in assessing alter slightly and practitioners need to be sensitive to the use of various "masks" that can be employed in order to present a certain image to peers or to cope with the adverse environment. In particular, young offender institutions can be incredibly challenging environments and result in the need for a young person to present a front of invincibility. This level of change in presentation can result in initial or enduring misperceptions of the true personality of a young person and inhibit any true vulnerabilities being identified.

Ultimately the identification of the mindset and personality of a young person and whether they have the capacity to commit particular offences needs to be undertaken with care to ensure that truthful and deceptive accounts of events can be ascertained. Pre-court assessments facilitate recommendations for how a hearing is conducted or potential sentencing, to identify whether there are certain vulnerabilities that pertain to the commission of the offence or the process of the court case. The following case examples are taken from a range of real-life assessments with young offenders in prison and community settings. The purpose of presenting these cases is to outline the various challenges in assessing credibility and this is therefore less about the particulars of individual assessments *per se* and more to outline the different presentations and factors that can influence young people where the interview objectives are different again from those in pre- and post-conviction settings.

Usually when we consider "truth" within the criminal justice system it is ultimately the outcome of the perception that the court gains from the evidence presented to them and subsequent decision making by jury members or the judge presiding over the case. This may be influenced by a common view of "good" versus "bad" adolescent behaviour and the degree to which the information gleaned as part of an assessment fits into this. In some cases the assessment of a young offender will have no bearing on their case and will not be admitted as evidence – ultimately the findings influence the outcome of use in terms of benefit or otherwise to the client. However, assessments of young people prior to court require impartiality regardless of initial judgements that practitioners might have regarding the case. Taking this approach may mitigate the impact of the (natural) adult worldview held by practitioners when faced with challenging clients.

Sophie

Sophie was arrested for assault (initially recorded as GBH) on a female peer at school following an argument where she observed her best friend kissing her boyfriend. She has prior convictions for violence-related offences and public order although has to date not received a custodial sentence. Sophie is 13 years old and has an educational level paralleling that of an 8-year-old child and has limited involvement in formal education due to behavioural management problems. This suggests a problematic relationship with wider "systems" of family and school and her disengagement with the system means that she has limited opportunity to replace the behaviour with more prosocial and effective behavioural strategies. She lives with her older brother (17 years) who has previous convictions and is unemployed (an individual who not only acts as a role model but is an example of Hendry & Kloep's 2002 concept of discontented stagnation), and her grandmother who has been her guardian since the age of 3 years. Sophie admitted to the offence allegations and was being assessed in order to provide recommendations for sentencing and identify the nature and level of risk she poses within the community. In interview Sophie presented as childlike, quiet and shy and was reticent to respond to questions about the offence. Her grandmother supported wider evidence from third parties that she can be volatile and violent, reacting to minimal slights whether directed at her or her peers. Throughout the assessment Sophie maintained a static demeanour and was uncomfortable speaking about topics that did not paint her in a positive light. However, when topics were discussed which relate to the offence, she obscured her face with her hand and only exposed non-verbal communication through her eye expressions. Throughout the assessments and interview, Sophie presented as vulnerable and incapable of exhibiting the offence behaviour. This suggests that she has achieved some success in the past at using other people's stereotypes of feminine and childlike behaviour and has some awareness of what would be expected by an adult in this situation. That she is unsuccessful in this case may be more to do with her reputation and the presence of other evidence against her.

Ultimately the baseline assessment of her behaviour conflicts with her offence actions – the question resulting from this being whether she is masking her true persona. The ultimate conclusions and recommendations resulting from such an assessment can only be fully considered when taken with collateral information which accounts for the discrepancies in her presentation. In this case, any assessment of credibility can be challenging to undertake. Although we should acknowledge that it is common for individuals accused of offences to wish to present in an innocent and honest manner regardless of their true actions, this should be seen as but one opportunity to learn about an individual. Assessments for appropriate sentencing options require wider considerations relating to concerns of vulnerability and the interventions that would best assist the reduction of reoffending and refocus the life course in a more positive way. Given Sophie's history, it is likely that this will require a reappraisal of the wider systems and her interactions with them (particularly the micro- and exo-systems). The impression given to the practitioner is potentially biased and manipulated by a number of sources resulting in conclusions that require solid justification.

Stuart

Stuart was arrested and charged with GBH with intent following an altercation where he allegedly intervened in a fight in which his friend was being assaulted. Stuart was observed by bystanders repeatedly kicking and punching the protagonist which induced a comatose state. The assessment, conducted at his family home where he resides with his parents and two younger siblings, was to evaluate Stuart's mental state with regard to the offence and additional factors of suggestibility and compliance and implications for questioning in court. During the police interview Stuart gave "no comment" responses to questions and intended to plead not guilty in court depending on the evidence that materialized. Hence although he acknowledged his guilt privately, his intention was that the court should prove this was the case. Stuart has a medical history which includes a diagnosis of autism, ADHD, and reported high levels of defiance to authority. In the home environment his parents reported that Stuart could be extremely irascible and prone to frequent angry outbursts including assaults. He has assaulted his parents on numerous occasions and when reported received a police caution. Stuart reported regular use of cannabis and consumption of alcohol in his home and with peers which is provided by his parents.

The assessment was conducted privately with Stuart in order to create an environment that enabled free disclosure of information and a reduction of internal family scrutiny. Stuart was superficially compliant during the administration of psychometric tests and collection of general demographic and lifestyle information. However, he exhibited frustration and suppressed fury when discussing his alleged offence. Given that Stuart has clearly experienced standardized testing as part of the process of being diagnosed with ADHD and autism, he may have developed a strategy of compliance as a means of coping with such situations; and explicit training of such skills is often used with autistic children (e.g. Barry & Burlew, 2004). However, when faced with the more "difficult" task of discussing the offence, Stuart's coping strategies prove ineffective and he is less able to manage his impressions successfully. He admitted responsibility in relation to the offence during the assessment although stated that he had no intention to admit this publicly unless additional evidence showed unequivocally that he committed the act. This was in relation to his likely sentence length and optimizing his circumstances. Ultimately, it was Stuart's conscious intention to work the court situation to his advantage by exploiting his diagnoses and developing an overt perception of a vulnerable young man in the hope that the jury would find him not guilty. In terms of the assessment for court, the purpose was to gain an accurate and full assessment of mental state, particularly given the open disclosure of deception to the investigation team and court. Young people have to weigh up the likely outcome of a court case and the implications of different courses of action. Therefore crafting a particular presentation and altering this with the addition of new information or disclosure of evidence means they retain some level of control over how they are perceived within various interpersonal interactions.

Liam

Liam was remanded to prison following allegations from his girlfriend resulting in a charge of false imprisonment and domestic assault. The purpose of the assessment was to evaluate his levels of risk and dangerousness and provide recommendations for sentence planning and treatment options. Liam presented as a quiet softly spoken 17 year old and appeared to be open in his account of the events leading to his arrest. He was reticent to engage with a female practitioner and exhibited noticeably defensive body language when interviewed. Direct questions about certain topics relating to the offence failed to result in open disclosure. However, indirect discussion which enabled Liam to adopt a victim stance allowed wider information to be gained. The assessment was therefore inhibited by the gender of the interviewer due to the young person's general perspective towards women.

The offence had involved the assault of his pregnant girlfriend whom he had later locked in a room in the house where they resided. Liam's two prior relationships had been acrimonious and he had two children whom he did not see or have access to. He exhibited a pattern within his relationships of increasing control over partners and excessive and pathological jealousy. This illustrates the value of taking details about the relationship history as part of an assessment and suggests that a wider life history (including family dynamics) could be beneficial. Similarly, it is worth noting that the acrimony and failure of the two previous relationships (despite the presence of children) would have reinforced Liam's "decision" to adopt an overly controlling attitude in his current relationship. It seems likely that Liam had not learned more appropriate strategies for dealing with difficulty and conflict in his relationships and could have interpreted relationship failure as indicating that he had been "right" not to trust his partner and should in fact be more controlling in the future.

The assessment was challenging in relation to identifying pertinent information and gaining the confidence of the young person in order to fully assess risk and sentencing options due to the perspective towards females and an inability to hold an individualized view of women. Given that this attitude itself and the approach taken to previous partners and other children would in fact be useful in illuminating the offence, such an outcome creates a level of uncertainty in credibility assessment and illustrates the importance of having an awareness of the dyadic interaction in addition to the objective of the assessment.

Jack

Jack was arrested for the sexual assault of an elderly woman in sheltered accommodation. Initially Jack denied the offence although he admitted to burglary and maintained he returned to the property the following day to plead with the victim not to contact the police. It was on this second day that the alleged offence occurred. Although Jack denied anything sexual had occurred between himself and the victim, he further stated that he had little recollection of events due to his consumption of alcohol that same evening. Following further interviewing, Jack admitted that he had returned to the property with the intention of rape although digitally penetrated the victim because he had not been able to achieve an erection.

The purpose of the assessment was to ascertain risk and make recommendations for tailored sentence planning. Jack was interviewed and assessed while on remand at a young offenders institution. He was calm and relaxed in presentation, eloquent and appeared confident in the presence of authority. Throughout the assessment Jack behaved appropriately and was deliberate in his speech when answering questions. Overall he presented as a well-adjusted young man, although when speaking about his offence he showed a complete lack of insight into the severity of his behaviour and little genuine emotional response or ability to perspective take. As Jack had a high level of awareness about appropriate behaviour when not referring to the offence, this suggests that he was at some level aware of how his behaviour would be perceived by others. Even though he may not himself have regarded the behaviour as serious, possibly as a result of his reluctance (or inability) to perspective take or experience empathy, Jack's reticence and initial denial show an intellectual understanding of how others would view the offence.

When presented with evidence of his involvement, Jack further attempted to deny what he may have thought that others would consider the most heinous aspect of the action (his experiencing sexual pleasure) by claiming that he did not experience an erection. He was reticent to discuss further issues surrounding his sexual interests and relationships, although this would have provided useful information which would have further illuminated the offence behaviour. Ultimately, the changes in disclosure in police interview appeared to be a result of the availability of wider evidence and the realization of this. The risk assessment here is therefore based more on the requirement for intervention and assessing credibility in order to ascertain appropriate recommendations than whether the offence occurred. In such an interaction, there will be additional risk factors to consider due to the inability to ascertain a level of depth of understanding about the young person being assessed. In the same way that non-offending young people in Chapter 3 found using the truth strategically and demonstrating socially appropriate compliance to be effective ways of "getting away with" some part of the lie, Jack's behaviour can act as a highly effective obstruction to the kind of information gathering necessary for intervention.

OFFENCE-SUPPORTIVE BELIEFS OF YOUNG OFFENDERS

Holistic approaches to understanding and interpreting the offence-supporting beliefs of prolific young offenders have hitherto been largely neglected in attempts to understand continued involvement in crime. This is despite their importance in understanding both this continued involvement and the assumption or denial of responsibility for their offending. However, there have been attempts at identifying specific risk and protective factors. For example, Ge, Donnellan, and Wenk (2001) identified the influence of involvement in crime as one prevalent factor, while others have focused on the influence of family background (Farrington, 2005; Sullivan, 2006). Ge *et al.* (2001) employed self-report measures, caseworker interviews and official records to examine the development of persistent young offenders.

Family environment significantly impacted on arrest patterns and suggested that "unstable" family backgrounds influence early onset offending and its prevalence before 17 years when compared with individuals from "stable" backgrounds. This was further supported by Hart, O' Toole, Price-Sharps, and Schaffer (2007) who emphasized the requirement for a stable and supportive family environment. Although dysfunctional backgrounds tend to be linked with a greater likelihood of offending, the exact factors contributing to such behaviour are both complex and varied owing to the multifaceted nature of the chaotic existence of many young offenders. Further individual causal factors in offending have been found to relate to the use (usually to excess) of alcohol and drugs (Ge *et al.*, 2001; Hart *et al.*, 2007). In particular it is alcohol that ultimately reduces inhibitions on a general level predisposing involvement in situations where criminal behaviour is likely.

The experience of a chaotic lifestyle requires young people to have the resources to effectively deal with conflict and challenging situations. Further, as discussed in Chapter 2, the resources required to meet such challenges will be different for young people from different backgrounds. Wong, Pituch, and Rochlen (2006) identified that males holding negative views towards exhibiting emotions were more likely to restrict the display of them. This outlines the potential for such emotions to remain unresolved or avoided or displaced in ways that are ultimately potentially negative or illegal. Jackupeak, Tull, and Roemer (2005) suggest that men can fear vulnerable states because they are at odds with traditional gender roles showing that fear of exhibiting emotion was a significant predictor of overt expressions of anger which could ultimately result in displaced aggression through violence. Hart *et al.* (2007) provided evidence that emotional regulation can be a significant factor in offending and found that an inability to deal with shame resulted in violent offending in young people. This was considered to be a result of the projection of the negative feelings on to others (known or unknown) which in turn resulted in violent actions. Such projection of violence has been associated with enhanced masculinity and the need to be seen as a dominant male who is always in control (Mullins, 2006).

One factor that appears to influence the beliefs and perspectives which young offenders have towards offending is the concept of masculinity. For young people who spend a lot of time on the streets, the need for a masculine identity is key and often requires accompanying violence to either support or maintain a particular reputation (Mullins, 2006). Abrams, Anderson-Nathe, and Aguilar (2008) used an ethnographic framework to explore the construct of masculinity within a US prison setting, drawing on observations and interviews with young incarcerated males. Results suggested that young males were consistently exposed to an unhealthy view of masculinity (e.g. prison guards were observed to encourage unhealthy competition between males) and this was linked with additional inappropriate role models for normative levels of masculine ideals. Messerschmidt (2000, cited in Mullins 2006) suggested that young males use violence in response to a threat to their masculinity which through conflict enables males to reassume control following any threat. Lopez and Emmer (2002) investigated the influences on young offenders – specifically focusing on the reasons why young people commit violent acts. One reason identified was the need to portray themselves as a protector, specifically of women. This fits with the "protective" aspect of lying found in non-offending adolescents in Chapter 3. However, in this case the protection further reinforced traditional gender roles. In order to maintain dominance, the woman was required to maintain a passive stance and rely on a significant male to fulfil their needs (Mullins, 2006). Challenges to this perception may provoke aggression or violence from males experiencing such a threat. Research on domestic violence has identified the processes that violent males will use to justify violence towards their partners (Henning, Jones, & Holdford, 2005) with strategies such as minimization, denial and the externalization of blame (towards the partner). As we saw in Chapter 3, minimization, denial and victim blaming can occur in interpersonal lies and, in that case, were used to reduce the experience of empathic distress of the liars (Hoffman, 2000). Here, however, we see a much more ingrained set of beliefs which are used to justify systematic violence rather than occasional deceit.

To explore further the beliefs of young offenders in relation to criminal activity and wider lifestyle factors, a series of interviews were conducted (Gray & Gozna, 2010; Gozna, Gray, & Boon, under review). The purpose of the interviews was to identify how young offenders view their world and how this can impact on their capacity to interact in situations where they may choose to deceive. In particular we were interested in the beliefs that perpetuate their actions and the implications of this on deception detection. The young offenders who participated in the interviews were all considered to be "prolific" in that they had extensive involvement in offending and were serving a range of community orders (e.g. referral orders, supervision orders, curfew orders, or intensive supervision and surveillance programme, ISSP). In order to further discuss the views of the participants, we have changed their actual identities to protect their anonymity. Therefore the seven young offenders are referred to as Paul, Jordan, Chris, Ryan, Stuart, Matt and Ashley and were all aged between 16 and 18 years. The previous convictions of the young offenders included public order offences, driving (while intoxicated/without a licence), burglary, actual bodily harm (ABH) and grievous bodily harm (GBH). The participants had been previously sentenced to a range of community orders and four had experience of young offender institutions. The average number of offences committed was ten (range 6–14) and all had similar backgrounds with regards to family, education level, employment status and history. Furthermore, all had experience of parental separation, had numerous siblings and step-siblings, and general family discord. Six participants had left school

Table 4.2 Thematic analysis of interviews with young offenders

Master theme	Subordinate theme
Reputation	• Group reputation • Self-serving reputation • Threats of reputation
Role of women	• Women as subordinate • Relationships with women
Victimization	• Projection of blame • Targeted by the police • Police conspiracy
Peripheral influences	• Chaotic lifestyle/families • Alcohol and drug use • Regulation of emotion

prematurely (usually within secondary school although one participant had been excluded from primary school) and none were employed at the time of the interviews. One participant was enrolled in part-time education. Hence the young males potentially had similar resource pools although might still choose to pick different resources in order to meet their diverse needs.

Our interviews focused initially on a discussion about the first time the young person had ever had involvement with the police and this enabled the disclosure of further information about general offending behaviour and associated beliefs. Generally the interviews covered topics including offence history, attitudes to offending, views towards authority, and wider issues of family, girlfriends, interests and aspirations for the future.

The interviews were analysed in order to draw out similarities and differences within the group of young offenders and four principal themes emerged (see Table 4.2) and we have incorporated relevant quotes from the discussions to illustrate these themes.

Reputation

The three subthemes illustrating the key features of reputation highlighted an overwhelming need for the young people to live in accordance with a specific persona defined by a certain reputation. In Chapter 3, the establishment of reputation was seen as a choice and a strategic move, in some cases designed to prepare for situations when the young person knew they would need to lie. One young person (12 years old) had established a reputation as the "class troublemaker" and spent most of his time in detention. However, he still showed little evidence of being "governed by" his reputation and indeed still felt that he would have a great deal of choice if he decided to establish an alternative identity. This may illustrate an important difference between our non-offending sample and the young people in the current analysis, all of whom appeared to be more tied into their reputations. In terms of our developmental approach, the non-offending young people in Chapter 3 had more "degrees of freedom" than the offenders; in other words their life courses were less restricted. In each case this reputation had far-reaching consequences – governing not only how they lived, but also where they could/would go, who their victims were likely to be, and the likelihood of personal victimization.

Group reputation

The discussions concerned rivalry within and across peer groups or "groups/ gangs" from other geographical neighbourhoods and it was demonstrated by the young people that such rivalry could emerge in response to a single fight between two young people:

> Yeah, no it's not really . . . dunno, it's just stupid, say if one of their people had a fight with one of our people then everyone would just turn on them just . . . big ruck innit.
>
> (Ryan)

Established rivalries and a mutual understanding of another group's turf appeared to restrict young people from entering other areas as a result of likely victimization:

> If any of the X lot get seen round here they are getting killed and if any of the Y lot get seen in X they are getting jumped.
>
> (Matt)

This not only demonstrates the rivalry between groups of young people but also a need for each group to elevate their own reputation above that of the rival group. The issues of "turf" and "reputation" were shown to be core to an extension of masculine identity for individuals and also within the group to which they identified. Therefore, any level of external threat to their identity results in predicted repercussions, that is, illegal, aggressive acts which will ultimately lead to further need to protect oneself within any interactions with practitioners such as the police.

The need to establish and maintain group reputation appeared to present an overt threat to rival peer groups, but also served as protection for any particular individual. This dovetails well with the extant literature articulating the reasons young people become members of "groups/gangs" including the need for reputation and protection (Decker & Curry, 2000).

Self-serving reputation

The young people further highlighted the importance of own reputation in the area with which they associated. In particular, an external reputation of being someone not "to cross" ultimately established them in the role of the "the alpha male". Such a reputation required the young person to behave in a manner that supported the beliefs about them. Hence, these accompanying behaviours can perpetuate offending through the requirement to project an impression of strength and power within the group of young people. This can include the reputation that females derive from associating with a particular group or gang. Therefore, there is a reciprocal relationship between the reputation of the gang as a whole and those of the individuals within it:

> Well some people do but most people don't, like some people think I'm, well most people think I'm the local um . . . well some man the other day said I'm the leader of all the gangs round my area.
>
> (Paul)

This young offender explained it was a negative thing that they were viewed this way as it often led to unwanted attention from those wishing to challenge his perceived status, whether it was peers or the police. However, for some reputation appears to serve as protection for both them and their family:

> Urm, I dunno cos like . . . I'm not trying [to boast], I'm quite well known so nobody really like challenges my family and that, and I've got loads of mates in X.
>
> (Chris)

This young offender's emphasis on wider family members being protected from unwanted attention is particularly important when considering the phenomenon of psychological "compartmentalization". This occurs where an individual holds close family or certain assets in rarified reverence that is not extended to the population at large. One view of the root of this compartmentalization is that such people and objects (e.g. cars) are perceived by offenders to be an extension of self and the identity they portray to the world. As such they are included in a "protection zone" as though they are the self (Boon & Gozna, 2008). This narcissistic presentation is important to interpret in the context of what an individual chooses to disclose or how they explain their decision making and offending behaviour. The need for a self-serving reputation has been reported previously (Mullins, 2006) and emphasizes the importance of masculine identity. The aspiration towards a hegemonic lifestyle, the dominant form of masculinity (Evans & Wallace, 2008), allows social approval in the form of a higher male status that subsequently ensures the protection of self and wider family and peers.

Threats to reputation

It was highlighted in the discussions that the maintenance of a reputation ultimately takes on a life of its own and can result in displays of violence. Hence any perception (real or imagined) of disrespect towards individuals or a group is challenged with violence to exert and regain control over the situation:

> I walked past him and he wouldn't get out of my way and he was sitting on the floor . . . so I told him to get out of my way and he started getting laary to me and then like I said to him, "I'll have a fight wiv you now" and then we got up and started fighting . . . and then, I just bottled him . . . stabbed him in the head with the bottle.
>
> (Jordan)

This description provided by one of the young offenders emphasizes how easily such altercations occur with others who are deemed to challenge status or reputation. In particular this incident highlights how the benign actions of another male are misconstrued as disrespectful and ergo a direct threat to reputation – particularly in regard to the expectations of his and others' peer groups.

The following quote also shows the ways in which altercations can occur from an initially benign interaction:

> Well, well I've had a fight with one person, that was the last thing I done . . . some boy basically, I went down to this place and we were all sitting there and I said to the matey, can I use your phone an he said I ain't letting you touch my phone or summink like that, then he swung at me and I said, "If you do that again I'm goin' to hit ya" and then he swung at me again so I hit him, ended up beating him up. And then he got me arrested.
>
> (Ryan)

This further illustrates the need these young offenders have to challenge others and the ways that situations can develop into something serious. It also shows the way that blame is placed on the ultimate victim for calling the police and suggests that these offenders perceive violence or fighting as a normal method of self-policing and resolving situations.

When discussing a serious assault another young person spoke of involvement with his older brother and an ongoing feud:

> Yeah I hit some guy in the floor with a bike helmet and fractured his, somethin on his head or summink, not fractured like damaged or cracked the bone or summink, f**k knows. I knew him, cos he chased me before and f**kin, he's massive and he's me brother's age. . . . and

f**kin smacked him one, knocked him out and I just hit him with the bike helmet and one of me mates video recorded it and the police ended up getting it.

(Stuart)

The lack of remorse and entitlement exhibited by the young person on recalling this serious assault is rationalized in a post-conviction discussion. However, the young person was regularly involved with the police through a heightened level of interest from his prolific offending. Therefore he would regularly give a "no comment" police interview to reduce the likelihood of the charge for an offence being pursued.

The concept of disrespect and related links to reputation have been identified (Mullins, 2006) as attempts to legitimize the use of violence whilst reinstating reputation. According to Evans and Wallace (2008), men associate "being male" with external aspects such as physical size, willingness to fight and power and dominance. Therefore, existing within a criminal society with its own system of policing requires any overt signs of masculine weakness to be hidden through compensation by other means. However, this can result in those who do exhibit overt signs of hypermasculinity becoming targets of inappropriate interest from other males within their community who feel threatened and have a need to challenge this self-appointed male superiority. Such actions can validate the beliefs held where reacting to challenges from other males is an appropriate response and hence the rationalization assists in avoiding blame and minimizing responsibility.

Role of women

A further subtheme linked to perceptions of reputation and masculinity related to beliefs about traditional gender roles and the experience of relationships with women. This supports the role masculinity plays in offending and it was apparent that the young people had experienced conflicts in the relationships they had with women, whether female family members or girlfriends. These conflicts appeared to occur particularly in interactions where a young person's projected masculine superiority was challenged and the traditional female role was not maintained. Therefore, any response from females at odds with the expectations of female behaviour would evoke a negative reaction and conflicted with the role of male protector.

Women as subordinate

The community and general environment in which the young people lived provided support for the general female dependency on males and as such there is a greater expectation of protection and support of action if threats are perceived towards "their women". Hence females were more likely perceived as "owned" by the young persons and as such they were directly responsible for them, whether all females within a family unit, direct girlfriends or girlfriends of other group members. Therefore women were perceived as unable to defend themselves:

> Three weeks or two weeks ago I saw some man shouting at a woman and I had a full on fight with him cos he was shouting, I said don't shout at her like that. I hate . . . men shouting at women and f**king rapists and shit especially if I saw some boy hit a girl, I'd smack him up.
>
> (Stuart)

This young person illustrated that he felt obliged to respond and rescue any woman whom he perceived to be threatened either verbally or physically by another male and further required no knowledge of the cause of any altercation. The maintenance of a masculine ideal and the need to react and protect appears in certain circumstances to occur impulsively without due consideration of the consequences.

The view of women as defenceless was expressed in another interview:

> Never hit a woman . . . won't even think about scaring em, it's just bang out of order really. A man can look after himself . . . not saying women can't but obviously men can put up a better fight.
>
> (Jordan)

This highlights that violence is perceived as justified when the other person targeted meets a particular criterion, in this case, being male and maintaining the view that women are less capable of self-defence. Although the participants held beliefs that violence towards women in general was wrong, and some had previously reacted to protect an unknown female or family member, there was little awareness of why such beliefs were held:

> Um dunno . . . it was just that one night, because I was on the train so. . . . some matey just hit the bird with the coat so I just jumped up and chased him for some reason.
>
> (Paul)

The response to situations where women are being threatened by other males appears to be largely reactive and uncontrolled in terms of the accompanying cognitive process. This has implications for interviewing young offenders about such altercations, particularly when their belief is that the behaviour was entirely justifiable.

Relationships with women

The requirement to ascribe to a purely heterosexual perspective was apparent in the behaviour and beliefs of the participants. In one instance, a belief of a loss of control within a relationship led to views becoming malign and resulted in physical assaults when challenged. This was illustrated by one young person who had been hugely affected by a previous relationship:

> I was like proper in love with her and wanted her all to myself. When she'd go out I'd get pissed off and she would play with my mind and I'd get in more trouble. I dunno. . . . she just, like playing with my head like . . . she'd do it like slyly kind of thing.
>
> (Chris)

His attempt to restore control was expressed through anger and violence and the relationship ultimately ended. The same young person further proudly described juggling three girlfriends and boasted his ability to avoid getting caught out by developing a range of excuses. This illustrated a propensity to engage in deception without remorse due to his objectives of pursuing multiple females and a belief of superiority in that he could so easily get away with his behaviour.

The lifestyle of the young people followed a route of least resistance in relation to income and living expenses. This was achieved by their involvement in financially lucrative offending, claiming multiple welfare benefits or both. The entitlement beliefs held concerning the provision of material goods as a result of minimal effort appeared to heighten their perception of being a "breadwinner", enabling a life free of wider responsibility. On recalling a prior relationship, one offender stated:

> I liked that girl loads and what I was giving her should have been good enough, but it wasn't.
>
> (Ashley)

Therefore a lack of appreciation from women, particularly when fulfilling a traditional gender role was considered a snub despite the knowledge that their lifestyle was supported by crime.

Another young person discussed his history of exhibiting violence towards males as an attempt to attack and destroy those who were perceived as successful. He saw this in terms of masculine ideals which included sexual virility. Military personnel in particular were the focus of targeted aggression due to a belief that they were more successful in their sexual liaisons with the local women. Worse they were seen as "outsiders", again highlighting the importance of territory and with contingent implications for "claims" over women in his area. In order to interpersonally and internally justify a preference for military personnel and, by definition, a rejection of local males, references to such females were denigrating using terms that implied they were loose and "sluts". The outcome of the perceived defiance from any local girls who associated with the military personnel was to create a negative reputation that they were "sloppy seconds" creating an atmosphere to ostracize them. Hence, views of women were polarized – at once considered virtuous and to be protected yet demeaned verbally or physically if their behaviour results in a perceived or real slight on masculinity. The underlying influence of such beliefs was identified as triggering much of the aggression and violence discussed by the participants, directly or indirectly.

Victimization

There were various ways in which participants presented as a victim, whether of circumstance, the police or their lifestyle. The rationalizations provided for engaging in crime were many and varied. However, there were some particularly pertinent core factors that are discussed here which relate to how the young people justified their actions to themselves and others. This impacts on how offending behaviour is communicated and ways in which they react to questioning and the potential reasons behind their engagement in deception. Overall the impression is of a low level of personal responsibility taken for actions and this means that there is little acknowledgement of wrongdoing but in parallel there is avoidance of being caught by the police in order to maintain a particular lifestyle.

Projection of blame

When speaking about offending, the young people were consistent in stating that they had no responsibility and attempted to shift blame on to a variety of external explanations. For example, one offender stated that in many cases, the victim could be blamed:

> Everyone's like yeah this kid's been stabbed, I get stabbed yeah, it'd be on the news ah this 18-year-old boy has been stabbed, but I could have gone and robbed some boy for all his shit, d'ya know what I mean? . . . People don't know nothing!
>
> (Ashley)

In particular, he emphasized the lack of understanding of the culture of crime where some actions were a consequence more of necessity than choice. Another stated:

> If I moved . . . if I didn't hang around with the people I did and if I didn't grow up in a violent place.
>
> (Paul)

Other explanations for offending included being used as a scapegoat for older males living in the area and such excuses illustrated an unwillingness to accept any involvement in culpability and hence externalizing blame on to something or someone. As mentioned before and in Chapter 3, externalization of blame also occurs in interpersonal settings but to a lesser extent and only in very specific circumstances.

Negative police interactions

A particular problem perceived by young people was heightened interest by the police in their activities as a result of reputations of being prolific young offenders. This illustrated a deep antisocial orientation towards authority, particularly from those who were regularly involved with the criminal justice system, had extensive previous convictions and a reputation for committing crimes. Although the criminal histories of many of the young people we spoke with were not vast, they admitted being involved in many more offences than they had been caught for. This mirrors the findings of the first accounts of young offenders in police custody.

Reported targeting by the police often resulted in participants stating that they were regularly stopped unfairly and questioned for any crime that occurred in their area. Each young person stated that they had a reputation with the police:

> Yeah . . . they think I'm like the cen [centre], anything that happens in my area, I get stopped and they'll be like ah something has happened in this area matching your description, when it ain't even matching my description.
>
> (Jordan)

However, the young offenders were ultimately unwilling or unable to see why the police targeted them and appeared angry and frustrated as a result and this heightened resentment towards authority:

> No . . . and um . . . like then, then I kept on getting blamed for stealing motorbikes even though it weren't me and like um, that annoyed me.
> (Paul)

The reported strained relationship between the police and young offenders allows a greater distancing from the responsibility of criminal acts. It also deflected the focus of the discussion from the actual offences which one participant disclosed he was still committing but not being caught for. It was apparent that there was a further requirement to portray the police not only as an authority and "them and us" perception, but also to derive kudos from police incompetence in investigating offences. The offending lifestyle was normalized such that the participants were known to the police on first name terms, although any perception of wrongdoing by the police was considered a breakdown in the pseudo level of trust expected:

> Like yesterday one of the police officers that said that I was only going to be on, like I got told I was on an ABC [particular community order] and he told my mum I was goin' on an ASBO [anti-social behaviour order] when I go to court an I think that's a bit harsh cos I reckon he should have told me that not my mum kind of thing. Cos he's meant to be making a kind of relationship with me to talk to me an that . . . but he's telling other people . . . instead of me.
>
> (Ashley)

Although this young offender emphasized a breakdown of trust in his relationship with the police, further discussions illustrated his deep levels of disrespect and the extent of antisocial beliefs towards authority in general. The assumption of increased targeting by the police was further outlined by another of the young offenders:

> Yeah cos all the police know me and are going to be on me, say if I do anything wrong . . . they are going to be straight on me.
>
> (Chris)

Rather than act as a preventative intervention for the young offenders, knowledge that the police are monitoring their behaviour appears to result in heightened offending. However, the police interest in their actions resulted in an element of pride with the accompanying reputation which further enhanced exhibited masculinity. There was an additional factor of game playing identified in the run-ins that the young offenders had with the police:

> I see these lights just flashing behind me and I'm like oh no, just keep revving it and then they [police] tried knocking me off and then um, I got to my area and went through this alleyway and they tried to chase me, they had the baton out and everything and I had to like swerve out the way and then like all my mates were there and I got away.
>
> (Paul)

The enthusiasm and vitality exhibited when such stories were recounted showed the "buzz" that resulted with the increased interest from police.

The police interview in particular was identified as a further opportunity where participants felt they could be set up in some way for offences they had not committed:

Ah . . . I dunno they try and trick ya, trust me I know they do. I've said to them before "Don't try and trick me." They ask you questions and then they try and talk you around them questions, d'ya know what I mean?

(Stuart)

This belief was common among the young offenders and appeared to manifest in many of their interviews with the police:

Cos if it ain't me then they've got no proof that it's me have they . . . Then if I say "no comment" they can't try and twist my words or nothing . . . cos I ain't said nothing.

(Jordan)

The continued emphasis on victimization from third parties was prevalent throughout the interviews and illustrated further anti-authority and an antisocial perspective exhibited by the participants.

Peripheral influences

The subthemes presented here relate to those factors that were found to influence the young offenders and either to create or support the environment and associated criminal activity. These would be features of the exo- and macro-systems as well as micro-systemic factors. These included chaos within the family, the influence of alcohol/drugs, and the expression of complex and challenging emotions experienced during adolescence.

Chaotic lifestyle/families

All participants had experienced chaotic family environments which included parental separations, the presence of step-siblings, negative relationships within the home, and generally challenging and sometimes hostile environments. One participant spoke about his family situation:

Well it's like, I didn't really like my dad to be honest anyway, he used to do my head in, he always used to cause arguments with me . . . and like ever since he cheated on my mum and hit my mum, I ain't like seen him as my dad like properly.

(Paul)

The chaotic environment was characterized by arguments, infidelity, and the exposure to violence between parents/step-parents:

> They know how to push my buttons straightaway. I don't know how
> they do it but they do it . . . it just makes me flip so I just go out and
> then come back in a bit.
>
> (Matt)

This young offender reported that due to constant arguing at home he only
resided at the property to sleep and as a result spent significantly more time
with pro-criminal peers in order to physically and psychologically escape.
This heightened his involvement in offending due to the amount of time
spent on the streets and involvement with negative influences.

Emotional responses

The hair trigger reactions and impulsivity of the young offenders appeared
in part due to an inability to regulate emotions when experiencing
challenging life events:

> Err dunno, I just take fings out on other fings or people . . . like, cos
> like I don't sit down and cry or anyfink I just, like hit summink . . . to
> take my anger out . . . I've said to my mum I wanna get a boxing bag . . .
> so I can just go in my garage . . . I wanna start boxing as well.
>
> (Paul)

This encapsulates the essence of how difficult emotions can seep out via
expressions of anger and aggression that are focused towards the source of
the problem or indirectly towards unrelated people or objects. Much of the
anger and frustration occurred as part of a cycle where young offenders
perceived a marginalization by society and the police and claimed to be
unable to work legitimately. Further problems within the home also
exacerbated this. Hence, emotional volatility was in response to attacks on
their failure to achieve meaningful and functional lives and the accompanying macho reputation (e.g. Jackupeak *et al.*, 2005).

Alcohol facilitating offending

The absence of responsibility for actions was further illustrated through the
consumption of excessive alcohol and illicit drugs. Alcohol was reported to
lower inhibitions and increase the irascibility towards others, potentially
increasing the likelihood of committing an offence:

> Uh, I dunno, say if I've been drinking and I go into X, I'm bound to
> get nicked [arrested], it's is like 100% that I will definitely get nicked.
>
> (Chris)

It was unclear whether intoxication increased the likelihood of straying into geographical areas which are "off limits" or if it made the young offenders more provocative in their interactions with rival groups. However, there was a general awareness of the impact that alcohol and drugs could have on exhibited violence:

> [Alcohol] makes me more aggressive . . . vicious . . . that's why if I drink, I drink in here [home] or at me mate's. If I'm on the street, I'll just be drinking and then someone will say something that will make me, make a problem.
>
> (Matt)

Another young offender recognized that different types of alcohol were more likely to have a negative effect on his behaviour:

> Well it depends what I drink . . . if I, if I drink like spirits that makes me really angry, if I drink beer I'm alright I spose . . . it's just vodka and that that makes me [violent].
>
> (Ryan)

The influence of alcohol is further used as a method of minimizing responsibility and externalizing blame:

> Nah . . . I fink if I weren't drinking I wouldn't have done it, I would've just left it there. If I hadn't been drinking I probably wouldn't have got caught if I did do it but . . . cos I would be looking out for fing like that.
>
> (Paul)

This implies that the presence or absence of alcohol impacts on the failure or success of an offence in terms of avoiding police detection. The reduction of inhibitions and subsequent criminal actions emphasize the lack of behavioural controls that are exacerbated "in drink" and drugs. However, whilst there was some awareness of this, the ability to avoid or abstain from such substances was poor to the point of being negligible throughout the sample.

Our extensive discussions with young offenders enabled us to take a holistic perspective to understand more of the relevant beliefs and experiences that support their criminal lifestyle – illustrating the incredibly complex and multifaceted nature of interactions. Notably, the emphasis for the detection of deception should include consideration of reputation (criminal and adolescent), heightened masculinity and the expression of emotion. In particular, it is likely to be as a direct result of developing masculine identity that young males will become more interpersonally obstructive in police interview and respond in a manner that makes deception more likely to occur.

CHAPTER SUMMARY

This chapter has presented and discussed research findings and practitioner-based experience in relation to interactions with young people who have become involved for a range of reasons with the criminal justice system. In our understanding and evaluation of the ways in which young people can present in such situations, it is necessary to consider the interpersonal strategies used and the content of speech, what is emphasized and what is avoided. Deception by omission, that is the avoidance of a particular subject, can be as informative as when a young person chooses to present in that way. Hence the importance of focusing on all aspects of interpersonal presentation with wider consideration of motivation and risk can assist in the interpretation and assessment of credibility.

5 Challenges of conduct and personality

The picture of adolescence and deception becomes all the more cloudy when the psychopathology of young people is contemplated. In Chapter 4 we considered the ways in which young people present their accounts within the environment of the criminal justice system. In this chapter, we move on to focus on mental health aspects, specifically those "disorders" that are relevant to the general assessment of adolescents including those who become involved in criminal activity and the associated deceptive communication and challenging interactions that may occur. It is important to emphasize at the start that this chapter refers to a specific group of young people and a clear differentiation should be made between those with disorders and those with other challenging behaviours. In fact, care should be taken to separate those without disorders but who display challenging behaviour from those with the disorders covered in the current chapter. It is anticipated that the information presented here will assist practitioners in making these distinctions.

To further the understanding of deceptive communication in adolescence, it is crucial to examine the characteristics of conduct and personality disorders that can impact on parental and practitioner interactions. Although the diagnosis of personality disorder is not officially recognized (APA, 1994) until "adulthood" has commenced, we believe that certain characteristics develop and will manifest during adolescence. These are helpful to understand when interacting with young people, and in particular those who commit criminal acts or are at risk of doing so. Our interpretation of the term "young offender" within the concept of adolescence requires us to widen our focus to consider young people aged between 10 and 21 years which incorporates adolescence as a variable life stage and the ages of criminal responsibility as defined by law. Our focus is to account for variations in individual development and in particular vulnerability. These are relevant to our view of deception as a skill that has the potential to be enhanced by specific personality characteristics whether prosocially or antisocially interpreted. For those working directly with adolescents, a heightened awareness and knowledge of the beliefs, attitudes and behaviours of adolescents exhibiting challenging behaviour and those engaging in various levels of criminality will assist in the interpretation of deceptive communications should they occur. In terms of Hendry and Kloep's (2002) developmental approach, the presence of such personality characteristics may themselves create new challenges or drains on resources. However, these are likely to be further exacerbated by the responses made by individuals around those with conduct and personality disorders. These responses can often indicate to young people what elements of their behaviour are most likely to be successful in what circumstances and can provide reinforcement in the form of attention for negative behaviour.

Further, as we can all attest to from personal experience, being faced with challenging and difficult behaviour from a particular individual can often make it difficult to provide a constructive response. Our inability to respond effectively can itself further escalate a problematic interaction (as seen in dynamic models of interpersonal and intergroup interaction discussed in Chapter 2). While the presence of such a disorder can make interaction challenging for all concerned, including the young people themselves, we do not subscribe to a deterministic view and hence we believe that the young people concerned still possess a choice and responsibility for their actions. However, because these disorders present a specific set of resource constraints, they deserve special attention. Further, highlighting the features of such disorders and their associated behaviours will signal to practitioners the likely outcome of their own communication choices and allow for easier identification of circumstances where their own behaviour may contribute to a problematic interaction.

The characteristics relevant to potentially challenging interpersonal interactions and in particular deception include conduct disorder, personality disorder (particularly Cluster B: antisocial, borderline, histrionic and narcissistic) and Psychopathy. Although it is crucial not to pathologize the behaviour of young people and to ensure that negative labelling is avoided, it is however helpful to consider the ways in which some of the mental health considerations might result in a need to deceive, as highlighted in the developmental challenge model in Chapter 1. Hence, the aim is to create a holistic assessment of credibility and more specifically the identification of likely deception and any resulting implications.

Although such considerations will not be relevant to all interactions (and indeed all young people) in adolescence, fluctuations in the presentation of challenging interpersonal characteristics can be identified throughout a range of settings including home, school, mental health and forensic. The characteristics we will discuss can be seen in varying degrees and formal diagnosis need not have occurred for practitioners to benefit from an understanding of this behaviour. However, it is important to be aware of the presence of particular characteristics and how they co-occur to create more complex presentations in interviews and wider interactions.

The discussion of relevant disorders in this chapter is not meant to assist in formal diagnosis but to enable the identification of a range of behavioural presentations that practitioners working with adolescents might find helpful when considering the detection of deceit and general credibility. It is hoped that this knowledge will assist parents and practitioners in their understanding of such characteristics and, more crucially, how to respond to them effectively during both deceptive and truthful communicative interactions.

CONDUCT DISORDER

The diagnostic criterion for conduct disorder (CD) – as described in the *DSM-IV-TR* both supports the validity of a systems approach to behaviour and highlights the difficulties faced by practitioners. The characteristics of CD are relevant to the way in which young people behave and interact when engaging in deception, whether as part of their normal interactions or criminal activity. The breadth and depth of potential deceptive behaviour and actions of CD adolescents are particularly challenging when coupled with a requirement to assess or develop interventions, be it social services, probation, police, court or post-conviction settings.

CD can be divided into two types: child onset, where behavioural characteristics can be observed before the age of ten, and adolescent onset, where characteristics are seen later in childhood, occurring after the age of ten. CD can be mild, moderate or severe, depending on the number of criteria and the frequency of occurrence of each. The diagnostic criterion for conduct disorder (APA, 1994) involves consideration of four high-level factors that, when taken together, aptly describe an individual who exhibits behaviour rejecting of social norms. These high-level factors are especially helpful to acknowledge during the detection of deception because they allow practitioners to visualize and develop their formulation of the young person through the implementation of a holistic perspective. However, the importance of such knowledge is to inform the tailoring of interactions rather than being prescriptive. Again as with any feature of a dynamic system, such characteristics cannot always be considered in isolation of other disorders. However, here it is the relevance to credibility assessment that is of interest rather than a general description or diagnosis of behaviours.

1   *Aggression towards people and animals.* CD characteristics include the display of aggressive behaviour accompanied by frequent involvement in bullying, threatening and intimidating others. This includes the initiation of physical fights and the willingness to use of a range of weapons (e.g. bats, bricks, bottles, knives and guns) which increase the likelihood of provocative violence whether intentionally deployed or with weapons procured from the scene as required. Individuals further engage in physical cruelty towards people and animals, stealing items overtly from victims (e.g. mugging, purse snatching, extortion, armed robbery) and using force and coercion in sexual activity with others.

2   *Destruction of property*. Fire-setting and the more general destruction of property is a further characteristic of CD. In terms of arson, the nature and prevalence is important to consider, particularly in relation to intent and whether the use of fire is an additional aspect of violence towards others or could be interpreted as pathological. Criminal damage to property further requires reflection in terms of the nature and likely intent of an offence and whether a young person is portraying the true picture of what occurred – hence motive is crucial to understand.

3   *Deceitfulness or theft*. The history of deceit in CD is both interpersonal and criminal and therefore individuals are likely to have a history of property offending (e.g. breaking into residential homes, offices and cars) and will frequently engage in lying and deception to obtain goods or to avoid a range of obligations. Ultimately theirs is a "needs must" approach which can include overt or covert theft of items of a non-trivial nature (e.g. shoplifting/forgery). This emphasizes a flexible approach to criminal activity where the skills (resources) necessary to commit the offence are used to achieve necessary goals (meet developmental challenges). This particular theme is hugely relevant to deception detection, although it is still unclear how successful adolescents exhibiting different levels of CD characteristics are at lying.

4   *Serious violations of rules*. The boundaries of individuals displaying characteristics of CD are flexible and in no true way conform to social or moral expectations. Hence individuals will often flout parental/ guardianship rules regardless of prohibitions. This tends to commence prior to age 13 years and a cursory look into the home background of the young person will reveal a history of running away from home overnight at least twice while living in parental or parental surrogate home (or once without returning for a lengthy period). It is therefore also likely that parallel behaviours such as truanting from school will be recorded.

To consider a diagnosis of CD, an individual is required to exhibit evidence of these behaviours to a significant extent that impairment occurs in different settings across social, academic and occupational functioning. It is likely that there will be incidents where young people have a history of behaviour which might not be overtly recognized as indicative of CD and is ultimately normalized within the particular community in which they live. This illustrates support for Bronfenbrenner's (1979) approach and further highlights how it is that some young people will not have come to the attention of official recording mechanisms and will be unknown in terms of their personality and behavioural history. Although adolescents diagnosed with CD can be immensely challenging to live and work with, there will be cases where their behaviour exists within a micro-system (or even an exo- or macro-system) characterized by a wider chaotic existence. It is important to note that in some instances, CD forms a precursor for antisocial personality disorder for which the onset is officially considered to be from 15 years onward.

As seen from the above *DSM-IV-TR* (APA, 1994) criteria, persistent lying features largely in CD. Hence, practitioner expectations would be for children and adolescents exhibiting such characteristics to engage in deception more frequently than those without such a diagnosis. Although such deception might be more frequent, as mentioned previously, the success of deceit is less well understood for those diagnosed with CD.

The destructiveness of CD behaviour is externally and internally displaced via aggression and violence within and outside the home and self-destructive behaviour illustrated by excessive risk taking, criminality and loss of control. Hence, when considering the most effective ways to interact and work with young people who exhibit such challenging behaviours, practitioners are required to evaluate much more widely than the assessment of credibility and deception. In addition, there is a need to think broadly about wider systemic factors including the personality, lifestyle, background, environment, peers, family, schooling and criminality of the individual.

The characteristics of CD are prevalent within populations of young people who become involved in criminal activity and in particular prolific young offenders. Perhaps most notable is the nature of the diagnosis that readily describes the behaviour, beliefs and lifestyles of adolescents who engage in such behaviour. Practitioners therefore require an understanding of the young person's general focus and view of the world in order to subsequently evaluate the interpersonal interaction and credibility of accounts and related deception. This is particularly important in such circumstances as the worldview of a young person with CD is unlikely to share any features with the established adult view of appropriate adolescent behaviour. In fact, the actions of a young person with CD fit so well with the "storm and stress" stereotype of adolescence that practitioners need to be careful to avoid even implicit acceptance of this view (e.g. Gross & Hardin, 2007). Awareness of CD symptoms may help to avoid this challenge.

The picture of the young person becomes more complex as one considers further the factors relating to personality and mindset and how these can influence behaviour. Our discussion now turns to that of personality disorder which, in general, work with young offenders has largely neglected. We have chosen to include it in this chapter because it outlines the foundations for understanding the chameleon offender (presented later) and further assists our pursuit of a holistic understanding of deception and its detection.

PERSONALITY DISORDER

The core personality characteristics of adolescents continue to develop throughout their journey from childhood into adulthood. With regard to more complex and challenging manifestations of personality, knowledge of four personality disorders identified in *DSM-IV-TR* (APA, 1994) can greatly assist in tailoring interactions and in heightening flexibility in the communication with, and ultimately the assessment of, young people. Therefore the disorders described in this section are presented as especially relevant to practitioners working in a range of settings (including forensic and mental health) with adolescents whether in community or residential establishments.

Antisocial Personality Disorder

Antisocial Personality Disorder (APD) describes individuals whose disposition toward life, society and others is antisocial. This can develop throughout childhood and adolescence and is potentially reinforced by a range of factors, not least offending. To fully explore the impact of an antisocial perspective, it is important to discuss the characteristics of APD, how this influences the assessment of credibility and how such individuals choose to engage in deceptive activities and interpersonal communication. A cursory look at the characteristics in relation to APD highlights parallels with conduct disorder, although these characteristics are further entrenched and developed as a way of life.

An overall lack of conformity to social norms is indicative of the anti-social personality and particularly relates to illegal activities. Therefore, the presence of extensive involvement in criminal behaviour and prior convictions is particularly pertinent. The use of deceit within an antisocial lifestyle is evidenced through repeated lying, the use of aliases and conning of others for either profit or pleasure. Deceit in this regard is enacted to serve a particular purpose for the individual, although this will not neces-sarily be developed enough to be continually successful over time. Such inconsistency in deceptive success is perhaps because a number of different resources are required, most importantly the ability to adopt different perspectives and understand how others make sense of the world around them (discussed earlier in Chapter 2). Over time and with experience, this ability can be honed and incredibly well executed especially when there is a motivational underpinning to the actions. Therefore the manipulation of others is entirely deliberate and such individuals openly brag and boast about cons, scams and conquests to impress those around them. Ultimately there is a purpose to the actions and conscious intent of their manipu-lations, which if denied in some regard through meeting their match can quickly result in a change in demeanour from seemingly compliant albeit focused in motivation to intimidating, hostile and critical responses.

Interestingly, while the deceit itself may be well executed, suggesting an understanding of how the target is likely to behave, the perception that this will impress others may be less successful and may depend on the moral code and interpersonal politeness of the selected audience. A highly successful individual with APD will not only have an intellectual under-standing of how others will respond to the deceit but also sufficient skill to select an audience which will at least appear to be impressed by the boast-ing. Less successful individuals may be able to deceive effectively (having practised this routine and received feedback) but may not have such realistic appraisals of their self-efficacy when it comes to bragging about the lies to others. Therefore those with APD are concerned with others' feedback but only in terms of direct behaviour and only as it affects them. Further to this wide-ranging deceitfulness is the requirement for instant gratification and the seizing of opportunities as they present, whether positive or, more likely, negative (towards others). Impulsivity or failure to plan ahead is parti-cularly relevant when considering spontaneous behaviour linked to irrit-ability and aggressiveness which is illustrated through repeated violent altercations within and outside the family arena.

Similarly and in parallel to conduct disorder, the behaviours exhibited incorporate irritability and aggressiveness, repeated involvement in physical altercations and assaults whether intra- and/or extra-familial. There is a further general disregard for the safety of self and others around them with a sense of invincibility characterizing the behaviours displayed. Ultimately this recklessness is dangerous and includes risking life and limb in activities where damage could be fatally sustained but the sense of concern is gener-ally negligible. The lifestyle of individuals living in this antisocial world is further characterized by repeated failures to sustain consistent work or maintain financial obligations including non-payment of bills, a lack of compliance in any working environment and the avoidance of parental responsibilities such as child support. The outlook is a generalized lack of remorse for actions that negatively impact on those around them and an indifference or range of external rationalizations for victimizing others. This leads to a failure to accept responsibility and a general perspective which heightens the potential for interactions to be challenging and nega-tive. Whilst individuals exhibiting antisocial characteristics can admit to behaving in a certain manner and committing offences, they can maintain deception even when presented with a logical and evidenced explanation. This supports the discussion in Chapter 2 about realistic self-efficacy appraisals not always being applicable to deception.

To identify the true nature of the antisocial perspective held by young people, it is important to interpret as a belief system free from psychoticism and delusional thinking – this view of the world incorporates wider attitudes, beliefs and behaviours. The society or community (the exo- and macro-systems) in which individuals live can further reinforce such perspectives. Any capacity for guilt and a moral code is therefore likely to be specific to the confines of the world in which they live, with views being passed on through generations. This suggests the development of self-defined boundaries leading to acceptable and unacceptable behaviours – hence a likelihood of internal policing within the community in which individuals live.

Borderline Personality Disorder

Borderline Personality Disorder (BPD) is characterized by especially challenging and complex beliefs and behaviours which can result in deceptive behaviour. Although particularly prevalent in terms of diagnosis in female mental health populations, BPD characteristics and behaviours should not be excluded from male general or forensic mental health populations. A misconception of BPD is that it is not a true personality disorder but describes individuals who are possibly or possibly not disordered. However, a diagnosis of BPD is mutually exclusive and forms a distinct personality disorder as described in *DSM-IV-TR* (APA, 1994). Accordingly, the characteristics of individuals presenting with BPD require interpretation and insight to fully respond and understand their interpersonal style and likely engagement in deceptive activity. It is crucial to note that such characteristics are often undiagnosed and interpreted in different ways. Hence it is vital that practitioners have knowledge of BPD in order to identify and refer young people for appropriate intervention.

In adolescence, the characteristics of BPD are largely emerging and in some cases will not be fully apparent without in-depth knowledge of an individual. Therefore the relevance of our discussion is to identify the pertinent issues to consider, and to highlight why it is that this personality disorder is so important to identify in young people. The major considerations with BPD are the residual effects of past experiences that influence the current behaviour of individuals. Those diagnosed with BPD tend to report a history of abandonment, whether through family life (e.g. parental) or intimate relationships. Often there is evidence of sexual, physical or psychological victimization. To regain control over future relationships, individuals have a tendency to overcompensate and can become involved in new relationships at a faster pace than would most. There is a further problem with intimacy and trust, with casual sexual encounters being a source of intimacy and even perceived as loving. As a result of multiple let-downs across a range of intra- and extra-familial relationships, and particularly with regard to parental relationships, individuals can "collect" caregivers, whether other responsible adults within a family unit or elsewhere in their community. The intensity of relationships is correspondingly the outcome of the lack of resources which would have been generated through stable, positive relationship experiences and results in perceptions of real or imagined abandonment – illustrated by incidents of possessiveness, jealousy and violence. Therefore the individual may create preventative strategies in order to maintain the "relationship" regardless of whether it has any legitimate future which in some extreme cases could include becoming pregnant. Relationships are characterized as intense and unstable and individuals with BPD alternate between poles of idealization and devaluation. This can occur within minutes, hours or days and is largely dependent on the extent to which their needs are being met by the other party. Therefore, those on the receiving end can feel as though they have lurched from being on a pedestal to being in the gutter within a very truncated time period, often with little knowledge of why this has occurred. This is accompanied by affective instability with the reactivity of mood with expressed anger, depression and anxiety with chronic feelings of emptiness. Furthermore the presence of inappropriate and intense anger or general irascibility is expressed in planned and spontaneous ways.

As a result of the personal experiences of those with BPD, there is a tendency towards some form of identity disturbance and a search for belonging – this can manifest through activities such as joining groups (positive or negative) in order to feel a sense of attachment. The vulnerability that accompanies this can draw individuals towards behaviours and activities that are potentially self-destructive including extreme promiscuity, binge eating and purging, substance misuse, reckless driving and spending. This can include lying to parents about eating behaviours, drug usage or money problems. However, with the excess and vulnerability there can be an additional factor of suicidal ideation, gestures and threats, and self-harming behaviour. In order to manage their worldview and successfully interact with others, there can be a necessity for BPD individuals to engage in subtle and overt manipulation. The likely objective of the deception, however, will be that which meets their particular goals at that point in time. Although this can be compared with normal goal directed deception, in the case of individuals with BPD, the deceit is all encompassing within their lives and includes a level of self-deception where individuals actually believe what they are saying. This can make the deceit all the more convincing as a result. In terms of intervention and support, individuals can present with pseudo attempts at improvement and associated narrative in order to provide some impression of change, or threats of suicide where no overt intentions underpin the actions, e.g. setting fire to a property with a false intent to commit suicide but lying adjacent to the front door which is left unlocked and ajar for the arrival of the fire service. However, the challenge for the practitioners and family members dealing with such myriad characteristics is to communicate with each other in order that the "true" version of events is identified. Although the descriptions and discussion of BPD might appear to paint a picture that would lead practitioners to despair, the more awareness there is, the more effectively young people exhibiting such characteristics and behaviours can be helped.

Histrionic Personality Disorder

Histrionic Personality Disorder is commonly associated with characteristics of BPD, although our consideration here moves to individuals who are uncomfortable when they find themselves in situations where they are not the centre of attention. Their overriding need is to be involved and central to all events which ultimately is underpinned by low self-esteem and a "need to be needed". Hence they can interact with others, including total strangers, in inappropriate and at times a sexually seductive manner, interpreting the behaviour of third parties as overtly romantic or sexually inviting. The exhibition of emotions rapidly shifts and the feelings expressed change and fluctuate according to the environment and those around them. Appearance can be utilized as an effective way in which to gain attention. In some instances this will involve non-conformity although this is over and above that expected with the development of identity during adolescence. Therefore individuals might routinely wear sexually provocative clothing, despite any potential risks to personal safety, or alter their appearance purely in order to receive reactions from those around them. In everyday interactions and when with practitioners there is a danger that individuals exhibiting characteristics of HPD experience and perceive an often unjustified close bond with people they have just met. This can include the sharing of intimate personal information or an increased focus towards one person if they believe it will result in increased attention.

When considering the assessment of credibility during any interactions, it must be borne in mind that the dominant motivation of individuals is attention. Identification and knowledge of histrionic characteristics will ultimately assist in an overall assessment of an individual and aid in any accompanying deceptive actions. Deception is most likely to be associated with a requirement to perpetuate and maintain a particular image to others. When related to offending behaviour, attention seeking through false claims or allegations will result in the need to deceive. The level of deceptive activity will likely relate to the severity of the deception, e.g. in the case of false allegations of rape and sexual assault which in certain cases can result in highly elaborate fabrication of events such as feigned abductions. Hence the requirement for focused interviewing in such cases is vital to identify the veracity of any allegation made. This is not to say that all allegations will be false. However, there is a need to distinguish between those that are legitimate and those where third parties are innocent but accused of a serious offence.

It is important to acknowledge that during interactions, histrionic individuals can present as incredibly impressionistic, altering their attitudes and beliefs according to the topic of conversation and the views of peers or practitioners. Their behaviour can appear overly dramatic and theatrical and emotions are expressed in the same manner. As a result, interactions with such individuals can be draining, and for practitioners result in less focus on the pertinent issues due to distractions in interview and topic avoidance. Ultimately therefore it is important that practitioners are aware of the difficulties in interactions and how this could impact on their ability to accurately assess credibility. Again, as with BPD discussed earlier, it is crucial that practitioners communicate to ensure that each gains a full understanding of the latest set of circumstances in the young person's life and any potential problems on the horizon.

Narcissism in adolescence

When it comes to the development of challenging adolescent behaviour, one crucial aspect is that of narcissism. During adolescence there is a heightened likelihood of egocentrism as young people develop their sense of identity and struggle with a greater sense of independence. Hence the ability of some young people to take the views, beliefs and attitudes of others into account can be significantly lacking. However, this is in relation to the challenges of heightened egocentricity and grandiosity rather than those adolescents who exhibit high self-esteem and are socially competent. In the context of offending behaviour, this can become a serious problem when combined with a lack of empathy for others. This phase of self-centredness within adolescence is perceived as more or less problematic depending on the extent to which third parties become the focus of negative reactions or behaviours. Overall the egocentrism exhibited during adolescence is an internal perspective in which individuals regard themselves as more socially significant than they really are. This brings with it potential drawbacks and limitations when exhibited in more extreme ways. One perspective in understanding heightened levels of egocentrism is presented by Berger (2008) and illustrates the following beliefs held during adolescence: the invincibility fable; the personal fable; the imaginary audience.

The invincibility fable

This is the perception held by young people that they will never fall victim – as others might and do – to dangerous behavioural exploits. Such illustrations of this level of adolescent risk taking can be seen in pastimes such as recklessly jumping from cliffs into the sea despite warning signs of fast currents or rocks; engaging in multiple impersonal sexual liaisons without the necessary protection from pregnancy or sexually transmitted diseases; consuming excessive quantities of alcohol and/or drugs with no consideration of the consequences; and high risk driving (e.g. without seatbelts, whilst intoxicated, at excessive speeds, or under chase by the police). There is empirical support for the uptake in adolescence of the invincibility fable with regard to sexual behaviour (e.g. Wickman, Anderson, & Smith-Greenberg, 2008). However, for some individuals invincibility further becomes a dominant aspect of adulthood and defines much of their view of the world and actions towards others. Depending on the sanctions invoked as a result of risk-taking behaviour, there will be some requirement for adolescents to deny or minimize the extent of their actions, possibly inclining more towards deception. Therefore the choice of deception may be influenced by how much relevant adults and peers are willing to accept some risk taking and the degree to which a young person's risky behaviour could be considered a normative or non-normative process (Hendry & Kloep, 2002). The outcome of such lies will vary hugely and the decision to lie impacting on the potential ramifications. However, the nature of invincibility will often be evidenced in the deceptive acts undertaken, with a perception of success and even a delight gained from such interactions.

The personal fable

This relates to the outcome of adolescent egocentrism being a perception that an individual's own life is unique and special in some way – this difference from others being distinguished by unusual experiences, perspectives and values. The quest for a truly individual identity is ultimately unobtainable, particularly when viewed through the eyes of adults who have "seen it all before" the phase of adolescence is often perceived as transitional. However, a need to express oneself in a number of ways can ultimately result in punitive consequences, e.g. being convicted for offences.

The imaginary audience

This is the assumption that during adolescence (and for some continuing into adulthood) individuals consider that other people around them are as intensely interested in them as they themselves are. The imaginary audience can turn into reality if young people present themselves as a leader in some regard, for example, in a "gang", and require others to behave in a manner that supports their position and enhances their status. The potential for illegal activity here becomes greater, particularly if more than one individual vies for the status of leader of a group. In common with the other two considerations, this need for adoration and attention has the potential to continue into adulthood, not to be an exclusive part of adolescent development. When detecting deceit, this perspective should be acknowledged because it can assist in the interpersonal strategies taken by practitioners or others when interacting with such young people.

Narcissistic Personality Disorder

Narcissistic Personality Disorder (NPD) is one of the more challenging disorders for the practitioner to respond to while maintaining the specific objective and focus. The grandiose self-importance exhibited is highly exaggerated, as are reported achievements and talents, which might include a propensity for a range of offending or boasting sexual prowess. Such individuals are focused on a fantasy and attempt to fulfil a reality of huge success, power and brilliance, and a belief that the only people who have any insight into who they are will be those with a correspondingly high status – this has accompanying implications for the practitioners engaging in assessments including credibility. These individuals demand excessive admiration from others and when slighted or perceiving a threat to their status and power can react with an overcompensatory response to exert control over the situation. One strategy to deal with this would be for the young person to select associates who do not threaten their view of themselves. However, this only works for challenges completely within the young person's control. A lack of additional resources to meet different types of challenges would lead to further problems in interactions and ultimately to developmental decay. In relation to "gangs" and young offenders, narcissism can increase the danger to others when weapons are used as a way to manage situations. Of particular note is that NPD involves a significant deficit in perspective taking (both cognitive and emotional), including empathy towards others, whether peers, victims or relatives. This can have major implications for understanding or interpreting offending behaviour and relevant issues surrounding intent toward victims. This is further discussed in Chapter 6 with the Chameleon Interview Approach.

PSYCHOPATHY

An understanding of psychopathy is relevant to practitioners working with young people exhibiting a range of challenging personality and behavioural characteristics. One concern with psychopathy relates to the implications for future development and involvement in forensic/psychiatric services. The term "fledgling psychopath" was coined by Lynam (1996) in attempting to identify and understand chronic offenders in adolescence who might develop into more severe and concerning individuals in adulthood. Practitioners are, perhaps unsurprisingly, reticent to label young offenders as psychopaths, particularly as a result of the general lack of research on the long-term stability of the construct over time into adulthood. However, when considering the interpersonal interactions of young people in forensic settings and accompanying assessments, it is important to focus on the here and now in terms of the presentation of behaviour and the manifestation of the elements of psychopathy. Offences committed by individuals assessed as psychopathic can at times defy rational explanation. Such people often experience a world devoid of emotion, empathy and love and are more likely to commit serious offences and reoffend because their capacity for concern towards victims is limited or absent. Hare (2005) describes such individuals as having "the ability to sing the lyrics but not respond to the melody".

The Psychopathy Checklist – Youth Version (PCL-YV; Forth, Kosson, & Hare, 2004) comprises 20 items that taken together develop a picture of the personality of individuals through the co-occurrence of the behaviours and actions. The scoring of the items is achieved through examination of collateral file based information concerning a young person, discussions with multidisciplinary practitioners and a structured clinical interview. Therefore decisions made relate to whether the item is absent, possibly present or definitely present result in a score of 0, 1, or 2 respectively. Ultimately the overall score (up to a total of 40) provides the levels of psychopathic characteristics present and further scrutiny enables a profile of an individual in terms of items that are particularly relevant. This is especially important in terms of a consideration of risk factors.

Forth and Burke (1998) administered the PCL-YV using a cut-off score of >30 and found prevalence rates 3.5% in young people in community care, 12% in those on probation and 28.3% in incarcerated youth. However, the prevalence following assessments appears to increase when a slight reduction (to >28) is made to the cut-off score, where Brandt *et al.* (1997) reported a rate of 37% in incarcerated youth. Although there are discrepancies in the appropriate cut-off score for psychopathy, it is crucial to identify the profile of scores and interpret these in light of the individual being assessed. Any ability to identify and interpret the behaviours of young people who score around or above the cut-off can hugely assist in increasing the effectiveness of interactions.

The following outlines the combination of 20 items taken from the PCL-YV as presented by Cooke and Michie (2001) who present a three-factor model of psychopathy: (1) *arrogant and deceitful interpersonal style*; (2) *deficient affective experience*; (3) *impulsive and irresponsible behavioural style*. This considers 13 of the original items, the remaining seven being related to generally observable criminal behaviours that are argued to be less directly relevant to the concept of psychopathy. The various items are described in more detail in relation to the three factors in order to consider implications for interviewing and the assessment of credibility in young offenders who exhibit such characteristics.

The initial overall impression on meeting an individual who exhibits the above characteristics is perhaps the most relevant to a discussion of deception and adolescence. At a basic level, the ability to engage easily in deceit and manipulation is further exacerbated when wider characteristics are considered. The deceit can be very easily masked by those who are adept at a seductive and charming presentation and is further disguised by an ability to deflect and avoid responding to questions. However, the interviewer needs to be prepared for such interactions and to be flexible in their responses – it is all too easy to be oblivious to the deception lying underneath the charm.

As was illustrated in Chapter 4, the initial accounts provided by young suspects of crime in police interviews provide an opportunity for interviewers to initially assess how individuals will present themselves interpersonally and verbally. This is not only relevant for the identification of complex personality characteristics, but also for the likely strategies or tactics that young people might employ during police interviews. One consideration with the *arrogant and deceitful interpersonal style* is that it can result in diverse responses depending on how the individual chooses to portray themselves (Box 5.1). In one instance it might only be upon reflection following an initial encounter that any concerns will be raised. In another, an individual's presentation can evoke incredibly strong emotions from practitioners due to the arrogance and aloofness displayed. Hence, the main requirement for practitioners engaging with young offenders who initially appear to present with these characteristics is to consider the way in which they can co-occur with the *deficient affective experience* and the *impulsive and irresponsible behavioural style*.

Box 5.1

Arrogant and deceitful interpersonal style

Impression management. The individual exhibits pseudo-conformity to notions of social desirability and therefore can present themselves in a good light with accompanying superficial charm. Hence individuals can present as helpful and behaviourally appropriate and can put practitioners at ease which can impede the concern for the behavioural presentation.

Grandiose sense of self-worth. The individual is dominating, opinionated, and has an inflated view of their ability with assumed grandiosity and superiority over others. They present as vertically aloof and intellectually arrogant regardless of actual skills and qualifications.

Pathological lying. The individual exhibits pervasive lying, and during all interpersonal interactions can lie readily, easily and obviously. Therefore the deceptive persona is a part of their communication strategy but occurs with little regard for the consequences and the potential impact on themselves or others. On being challenged or found out, the individual will easily rework their story to bring it into line with what is expected from the target of the deception.

Manipulation for personal gain. The individual engages in deceitful manipulating actions and dishonest or fraudulent schemes that can result in criminal activity. This can further relate to criminal activity specifically targeting vulnerable victims in order to more fully exploit a potential opportunity for a con, e.g. lone elderly victims.

Source: Based on Cooke and Michie (2001).

The overall presentation when considering the *deficient affective experience* (Box 5.2) is that primarily there is no legitimate emotional reaction to the offending behaviour and the associated consequences. Furthermore, the offender portrays little empathy towards victims and is able verbally to avoid all responsibility for their actions regardless of ultimate reality. Ultimately these young people do not give the impression that they are concerned nor have the capacity to fret about their criminal actions.

Box 5.2

Deficient affective experience

Lack of remorse. The individual has no capacity to experience guilt for their negative actions and can experience duping delight with successful cons and offences. They lack concern about the impact of their actions on others and will easily exhibit justifications and rationalizations for their abuse of others, most notably externalizing blame.

Shallow affect. The individual has only superficial bonds with others and lacks a capacity to express true emotions or to exhibit true intimacy to others. Although well able to feign emotion, this is akin to role play where the behaviour and exhibited verbal affect will not correspond. Emotions are presented on a surface level and although the affective presentation appears convincing, the depth of experience is lacking.

Callous or lacking empathy. The individual expresses a profound lack of empathy, perceives others as objects to be exploited and lacks the ability to perspective take with little appreciation of the needs or feelings of others.

Failure to accept responsibility. The individual blames others for any problems they have, claim that allegations are malicious, that they have been "set up" and is incapable of and unwilling to accept personal responsibility for their actions. Therefore, blame for all actions that are linked to negative consequences is externally projected with excuses for behaviour and rationalizations.

Source: Based on Cooke and Michie (2001).

Generally the lifestyle of the offender with the *impulsive and irresponsible behavioural style* lacks future goals, and the person is reliant on others for financial needs, using strategies including intimidation, stealing and claiming benefits (Box 5.3). In addition, these individuals have a need for stimulation which is gained through excessive behaviours bordering on the self-destructive or violent towards third parties. The reactions and behaviours are spontaneous, illustrating high levels of impulsivity and widely irresponsible behaviour across a number of life domains.

Box 5.3

Impulsive and irresponsible behavioural style

Stimulation-seeking. The individual requires novelty and excitement in life and becomes easily bored with routine. Hence there is an increased likelihood of risk-taking behaviour which includes sexual promiscuity, drug taking, dangerous and/or drunk driving.

Parasitic orientation. The individual depends on others in order to achieve specific goals through exploitation of family and friends to meet financial obligations and through intimidation and threats to get others to complete schoolwork. This can include a heavier reliance on government benefits with the knowledge on how to play the system to maximize income.

Lacks goals. The individual has little interest or understanding of the need for education or skills, lives life day to day with little or no thought for the future or the consequences of their actions and has unrealistic aspirations for the future. This is linked with the parasitic orientation and the knowledge that conning and manipulation can be employed in order to achieve any required objectives.

Impulsivity. The individual will have a history of acting out frequently, dropping out of formal schooling, leaving home on a whim, reacting and making decisions on the spur of the moment and does not consider the consequences of their impulsive actions. Generally there is a lack of thought in criminal actions to the potential outcome particularly when coupled with poor anger controls.

Irresponsibility. The individual regularly fails to meet obligations or pay debts and exhibits reckless and irresponsible behaviour across a range of settings, including school and home environments.

Source: Based on Cooke and Michie (2001).

Cooke and Michie (2001) argue that the associated behaviours concerned with general observable criminal behaviour are not directly related to an understanding of psychopathy. However, they are important in conceptualizing the entire set of behaviours that would be evaluated using the PCL-YV (Forth, Kosson, & Hare, 2004) and hence will be discussed in order to maintain a complete view of this as exhibited by young offenders.

The *observable criminal behaviour* items (Box 5.4) that incorporate criminality and relationships within the concept of psychopathy cannot be considered in isolation of the remaining items contained within the other three groupings of arrogant and deceitful interpersonal style, deficient affective experience and impulsive and irresponsible behavioural style. This provides further support for an interactionist approach to development. In isolation, the criminal versatility and impersonal and volatile interpersonal relationships and sexual interactions are applicable to many young persons who experience a generally chaotic and inconsistent lifestyle within and outside the home environment. In particular, it can be challenging for practitioners to interpret the personality characteristics and offending behaviour, particularly when young offenders exhibit a lack of affective ties with family and peers and a general disregard for others. Interactions with young offenders can be especially difficult when they appear "walled off" or show a coldness and contempt for their victims.

Box 5.4

Observable criminal behaviour

Poor anger control. The individual is prone to hotheadedness and is easily offended, reacting with verbal or physical aggression to real or perceived slights from others. They will be easily provoked to exhibit violence although will externalize blame for their actions.

Impersonal sexual behaviour. The individual engages in excessive and casual sexual encounters, maintains multiple indiscriminate sexual relationships using deception and employs coercion and threats to get what they want. This also links to sexual offending.

Early behavioural problems. The individual has engaged in a behavioural pattern of lying, thieving and fire setting before ten years of age. It is likely that the behaviour will have been prominent in a range of settings within and outside the home and that the young person will have records on file that relate to this.

Unstable interpersonal relationships. The individual engages in turbulent relationships (extra-familial) which are characterized by a lack of commitment and loyalty. Relationships are volatile and fluctuate with periods of aggression and violence and movement from person to person. This mirrors the nature of the actions and behaviours in the home environment which tend to be chaotic and inconsistent.

Serious criminal behaviour. The individual has multiple charges or convictions for criminal activity which includes high volume and serious criminal activity from an early age.

Serious violations of conditional release. The individual has successfully attempted to escape from containment with security or has breached the particular conditions of probation or community sentencing options. This is characterized with a range of actions to avoid attendance or to drop out of specific programmes.

Source: Based on Cooke and Michie (2001).

Research on the bigger picture of adolescent psychopathy shows that individuals who exhibit many psychopathic traits are more likely than not to have a history of maladaptive family environments (Forth, 1996, cited in Gretton, Hare, & Catchpole, 2004), a lack of attachment to parents (Kosson *et al.*, 2002), and a wide range of antisocial and violent behaviours (Forth, 1996; Kosson *et al.*, 2002). Although there is debate about the classification of the characteristics (e.g. Cooke, Michie, & Skeem, 2007; Hare, 2003) and whether two or three factors should be used, it is clear that psychopathy is associated with a high degree of manipulativeness combined with a lack of empathy for the victims of deceit, a failure to take responsibility for actions and a high level of impulsivity. Their shallow experience of emotions should make them more effective deceivers as they are unlikely to experience strong affect, guilt or fear of being caught, three features which Ekman (e.g. Ekman, 2009) identifies as being associated with lies failing. This reduction in fear responses was found in a study by Patrick, Cuthbert, and Lang (1994). Participants with high and low psychopathy scores were asked to engage in a mental imagery task with a neutral and a fear-arousing sentence and were asked to process each stimulus four times. They then repeated this for five further pairs of neutral and fear-arousing sentences. Physiological measures such as heart rate and skin conductance were taken during this procedure. Those low in psychopathy showed stronger fear responses during the processing of fear-arousing sentences than the high psychopathy group did, thus supporting the notion of shallow affect.

However, despite the evidence for reduced affective responses, when tested directly outside of the context of malingering, the evidence that psychopaths are more effective deceivers is equivocal. Cogburn (1993) found that those who scored more highly on the Psychopathy Checklist Revised (PCL-R) were more likely to be regarded as untruthful even when they were actually telling the truth, a finding supported by more recent research (Lee, Klaver, & Hart, 2008). This may be because psychopaths use their verbal and non-verbal behaviours to dominate interpersonal interactions, rather than showing the level of interpersonal awareness. For example, Louth, Williamson, Alpert, Pouget, and Hare (1998) asked psychopaths and non-psychopaths to speak about a range of different topics, including neutral and emotionally affective material, and recorded the mean amplitude of the speech. Their results indicated that psychopaths' speech had lower amplitude than non-psychopaths. This effect applied to all types of spontaneous speech as well as emotionally neutral and affectively laden sentence completion tasks. Speaking more quietly could suggest an attempt to engage attention by forcing the audience to listen more carefully.

Two papers by Klaver and colleagues (Klaver, Lee, & Hart, 2007; Lee, Klaver, & Hart, 2008) provide more comprehensive evidence of how psychopaths' verbal and non-verbal behaviour may differ from non-psychopaths'. Klaver, Lee, and Hart (2007) asked participants to provide self-report data about frequency of lying, experience of fear, guilt and excitement during deception and to rate their own deception abilities. They then asked psychopaths and non-psychopaths to describe an offence they had committed (truthful) and one which they had not (false). The non-verbal behaviour was then coded in each condition. High scores on the "arrogant and deceitful interpersonal style" scale were positively associated with self-reports of lying ability. Additionally those who scored higher on the PCL-R used more illustrators, took longer to respond and spoke for longer. Lee, Klaver, and Hart (2008) found psychopathic offenders produced less coherent narratives but made more spontaneous corrections (indicative of truth) and gave more appropriate details when lying. Although these results demonstrate superiority for some verbal indicators of credibility, the overall pattern fits with previous research. However, it is possible that because the presentation of psychopaths is perceived as dominant, this hinders their believability. Ultimately there are many factors that influence the perception of psychopaths by an observer, not least their profile of scores on the PCL-R and whether this results in heightened interpersonal communicative skills or a perceived overcompensation which is deemed suspicious in some way. Hence, in adolescence it is important to consider the development of a range of factors including social skills, empathy, insight and perspective taking in parallel to psychopathy. Depending on the individuals concerned, some adolescents may well suffer from both the inability to appear credible and to learn from this experience to improve their behaviour in the future.

CASE EXAMPLES

Examining the range of serious offending actions that have been committed by adolescents highlights relevant examples for discussion. The following examples have been chosen as illustrative of especially challenging and complex individuals and particularly sadistic and violent offences. The first example relates to the murder of a young man who was incredibly vulnerable due to the excessive consumption of alcohol (Box 5.5).

Box 5.5

Case study

In January 2008 two young offenders were convicted of manslaughter after an attack on a 25-year-old male, Toby Atkin, who was under the influence of alcohol at the time of the attack. The assault included kicking the victim and the offenders, Quantrill (16 yrs) and Orme (14 yrs) filmed each other using a lighter to brand and burn the face and neck of the victim although subsequently tried to delete the evidence. The burn marks were in the shape of 'smilies' – a pattern to look like a smiling face. The offenders set the clothes of the victim alight and urinated on him. Quantrill jeered and cajoled Orme to assist in pushing the unconscious victim into the river to drown. The investigating officer DS Davison described the offence: "Overall the victim was subjected to having his clothing burned in at least 11 places, having a heated lighter placed directly on his face on no less than four occasions and burning one set of his eyelashes. They also kicked him about the body, pushed sticks up his nose and urinated on him. Finally the two offenders jointly pushed him into the river, where Toby never regained consciousness and drowned."

The prosecutor stated that "Mr Atkin didn't sink immediately. They stood and watched him float. They could have pulled him out, but they chose not to. It was obvious to them that Mr Atkin had remained unconscious. The older boy in particular seemed very satisfied about what he had done."

Offenders' behaviour

There was no exhibited remorse shown for the actions of the offenders when they were sentenced at Nottingham Crown Court. The disclosure of the offenders' previous convictions was many and varied. Quantrill had 24 previous convictions of offences including battery, possessing an offensive weapon, burglary and handling stolen goods and his most serious sentence was a four-month detention and training order. Orme had 13 prior convictions including harassment, battery, arson, burglary and theft but had never received a custodial sentence. The offenders were described in court as acting with "unpleasantness" which quickly escalated to "callous disregard" towards the victim.

Outcome of case

The offenders were described as "totally out of control" by the Judge in court. Quantrill, who was 16 at the time of the incident, was sentenced to five years' detention while Orme, who was 14, was given three-and-a-half years. DS Davison said: "The boys told lies to the police, which has been proven, and while Orme has shown some measure of remorse, neither has had the decency to admit his responsibility towards Mr Atkin's death." The offenders had claimed they had looked on helplessly as the victim fell into the river.

Source: K. Nicolson, *Peterborough Today* (2008).

Callous disregard for life

Although the nature of offending can be more fully understood with awareness of particular personality and mental health factors, interactions between adolescents during an offence can also provide valuable insight. In particular when considering major crime offences, the level of violence committed against victims appears to be excessive and more than required to cause death, for example. It is important therefore not only to understand the dynamics of such offences and exhibited callousness towards victims but also the aftermath where the external projection of blame and lack of responsibility has implications for assessing credibility and interpreting the young person's views of the world and their perspective of offending.

One case of murder and attempted murder (BBC, 2000) committed by six young people aged 15 to 22 years outlines how such situations can occur and result in hugely negative and disastrous consequences. In a brutal event that turned from a relatively minor offence of street robbery into murder, two students were assaulted and beaten unconscious before their bodies were thrown from a bridge into the river Thames by the offenders. One victim, Timothy Baxter, failed to regain consciousness and drowned; his friend Gabriel Cornish was rescued and survived. On hearing the case, Trial Judge Ann Goddard of the Old Bailey described the offender as having engaged in "heartless, gratuitous violence".

On arrest and throughout the trial, the six offenders attempted to blame each other for the murder and attempted murder and pleaded "not guilty" – taking no responsibility for their actions in the offences. However, the jury found them guilty of the offences – three receiving adult life sentences and three juvenile life sentences. This resulted in 20-year-old Sonni Reid being ordered to be detained for life for the murder with a concurrent sentence of 16 years for attempted murder; 22-year-old John Riches to be detained for life with a concurrent 14 years for attempted murder; and 19-year-old Cameron Cyrus to be detained for life with a concurrent 16 years in a youth attendance institution for attempted murder. Two further male offenders aged 15 and 17 and a female aged 16 years were ordered to be detained for murder with concurrent sentences for attempted murder of 16, 12, and 12 years respectively. Although there was no evidence to show that the 16-year-old female had played a physical part in the offence, she and her boyfriend were captured on CCTV exchanging a kiss and laughing and joking with a third member of the group.

Initially three of the group had attempted to rob the two victims as they walked home from a night out in the West End of London. Further evidence showed that the remaining three of the group had approached the victims from the opposite end of the Thames bridge walking towards them. One victim, Mr Cornish, appealed to them for assistance, not realizing that they were part of the same group of offenders. Instead of helping the victims, they joined in the assault and assisted in throwing the unconscious victims from the bridge. Alarmingly for the victims, one of the group had called out that it would be "fun" to throw the students into the river having beaten and kicked them unconscious.

The callousness of the act committed by this group was extreme. Indeed, the pleasure experienced by the group in beating and ditching the bodies into the river for some will be beyond comprehension. However, when considering the most challenging spectrum of disordered personalities, such individuals can be capable of heinous acts of violence, dehumanizing victims into mere objects for their pleasure. However, whatever one's view as to the nature of such offences and the motivations of the offenders concerned, the reality for forensic practitioners is that such individuals require immense understanding in order to be managed within the criminal justice system. The natural decision to deceive on arrest and to maintain the deception despite evidence to the contrary is indicative of an antisocial perspective, but the evidence of callousness and enjoyment derived from such extreme acts creates huge challenges for practitioners working with such young people. This offender perspective that lacks remorse and maintains an egocentric view of self, blaming others and diminishing personal responsibility, can be potentially mirrored within forensic settings. Attempting to detect when individuals with a predisposition to lie are pulling the wool over your eyes is a challenge and will be discussed further in Chapter 6.

CHAPTER SUMMARY

This chapter has presented mental health issues that we consider relevant to the detection of deception or the interpersonal presentation of young people who might be inclined to deceive. Therefore the inclusion of material on conduct disorder, personality disorder and psychopathy all allow practitioners to approach assessments of credibility with young people in an informed and focused manner. Again, as stated earlier in the chapter, it is crucial to avoid pathologizing young people. Although we have included consideration of young offenders and individuals who would be potentially diagnosed with challenging personality characteristics, this is provided to inform the approach to the detection of deceit. Ultimately practitioners should have awareness of a range of relevant knowledge in order to be able to approach this challenge and be effective in so doing.

6 Techniques in detecting deceit

The detection of deception and the assessment of credibility are crucial aspects of practitioner work in the forensic domain and in our interactions in everyday life. Although we move our focus here to the detection of adolescents' lies, what we are interested in is the interpretation of different types of interpersonal communication through the implementation of a holistic and bespoke approach. The holistic element we refer to here involves consideration of the range of factors that leads to the young person's choice to engage in deception and by their very nature are multifaceted. Hence we have moved away from a piecemeal approach where only certain elements of communication are considered and are drawn instead on a multitude of issues. This is in part because, as we have argued earlier, detection as with the choice to engage in deception is concerned with the communication context and the variety of resources presented in Chapter 2. Therefore in line with our approach to understanding and interpreting deception in adolescence, we will not be suggesting specific verbal or non-verbal cues to look out for. We further propose that it is crucial for the identification of deception to be developed via a thorough understanding of the individual being assessed. This requires a broader and deeper perspective than mere behavioural movements or speech utterances considered in isolation of a larger picture. This reflects emerging evidence from, for example, the use of the process of sketching locations as a technique for detecting deception (e.g. Vrij, Leal, Mann, Warmelink, Granhag, & Fisher, 2010; Vrij, Mann, Leal, & Fisher, 2010) where a crucial aspect seems to be the triangulation of information across multiple forms of presentation.

Furthermore, this chapter considers our own ability to detect deception and on a wider scale assess the overall credibility of what an individual is saying to us. It is also important to consider those skills and techniques that effective lie detectors require. The interaction between deceiver and target is therefore an important one and needs further focus in order to ensure that the knowledge of adolescent deception and its detection are not confined to this text. Therefore it is the responsibility of those engaging in the detection of adolescent deception to develop a range of crucial skills to enable the identification of 'red flags' which could be indicative of deceit and require further focus during current and/or subsequent interactions.

Drawing a distinction between adolescent social/lifestyle lies that are inherently low in impact and deception which relates to "at risk" situations or is criminally motivated, it is helpful to consider how such behaviours can be identified and responded to. If someone is motivated to conceal information or an action, then it might be possible that they will maintain this over time. However, once a direct or unequivocal question is asked of them that is directly relevant to what is being hidden, the potential for deception occurs. It is therefore the identification of deception potential that is key. This could relate to a trivial issue that a young person wishes to hide from their parents, avoidance of punishment in the school environment, concealing "at risk" behaviour such as self-harm, or committing a range of criminal acts. Hence the context in which any discussions takes place will assist with the identification of such instances.

INITIAL CONSIDERATIONS

Prior to a focus on detecting deceit in young persons, it is important to consider the circumstances, skills and methods required to undertake this challenge. Practitioners need a tutored eye in order to negotiate successfully the interactions they have with young people, some of whom can present in especially challenging ways.

Diverse deceptive opportunities

The nature of deception detection varies across forensic cases and the context and objectives of the deceiver. For example, in certain police investigations the involvement of a particular young person as a suspect may be identified although with a lack of credible evidence. In such cases where deception is overt in police investigations, for example through the provision of an alibi, the challenge is to prove that a certain course of events has occurred. Hence the detection occurs through the development of an argument and evidence against a particular individual to illustrate how they committed a particular offence and ultimately to present a case for the prosecution to pursue.

To consider the various ways in which deception can manifest itself, it is necessary to think about typical adolescent lies told to a range of individuals and, when cases are most challenging, to focus on a multidisciplinary response and the options available once we have become the target of deceit. However, in some instances, the deceit exhibited is multifaceted and focused on a range of practitioners in order to enable the perpetuation of particular behaviour. This was illustrated in the case of a teenage couple who tortured their baby over a period of 50 days. The child sustained fractures to his thigh bones, wrists, above and below his knees and above his left ankle, multiple rib fractures, right hand index finger fracture, fractures to the spine, haemorrhages to the eyes and cuts to the tongue. Aspects of the substantial injuries were identified by a range of practitioners, although the couple lied to social workers, police and medical personnel and in one instance stated the injuries had been caused when the child caught his hand and poked himself in the eyes. Although such cases are rare, they require significant intervention and communication across relevant agencies in order that the detection of deceit and level of risk can be fully ascertained. Given that selective sharing of information can be a highly skilled way of deceiving and even parents in a strong relationship can be caught out (Chapter 3; Taylor & Rolfe, 2005), practitioners need to ensure that they do not end up at the wrong end of such skill when applied to antisocial behaviours. Hence wider communication across and between multidisciplinary teams is of paramount importance to identify inconsistencies in accounts and to respond to risk that is being concealed.

Acknowledging the lie

As discussed in Chapters 2 and 3, the outcome of discovering and accusing someone of deception can be a loss of trust and damage to interpersonal relationships. It is generally a consideration of the lie detector, in circumstances where there is an established interpersonal relationship, to respond to an identified suspicion of deceit. However, the potential harm from accurately detecting and confronting an individual has to be weighed up against the consequences of getting it wrong and making a false allegation of deceit. A challenging situation can ensue if a mistake is made and deception is incorrectly alleged, although as we saw in Chapter 3, people can play on such instances, resulting in targets of suspected deceit feeling chary of making the accusation. Research by Taylor and Nash (2006) identified detectors' use of the "alternative explanation" for unusual behaviour. In other words, detectors often suggested that anything other than deception could explain inconsistent emotion and non-verbal behaviour indicative of nerves or cognitive load. They simply did not want to accuse the senders. Similarly, the young people we interviewed and discussed in Chapter 3 made it very clear that they would only confront someone suspected of lying if they had incontrovertible evidence (e.g. a copy of a text message), and even then they would initially ask for an explanation before making an accusation.

The reticence that appears to exist in relation to accusations surrounding deception highlights the challenges faced in interpersonal interactions. Ultimately there is a difficulty in accepting that we might be the target of a lie, whether parents, peers or teachers. However, in such circumstances consideration of why an individual has a need to deceive is a further factor in the assessment of credibility. The motivation to keep information from others for some form of benefit, whether personal or altruistic, is something that as lie detectors we need to understand. Hence, although there appears to be an assumption that the identification of any deceit should be overtly acknowledged and the means by which it was discovered disclosed, there are benefits and drawbacks involved. Ultimately if we are suspicious of another person and the veracity of the information they divulge, this is not always the appropriate response. When working professionally with young people, this will not always assist in longer term interactions where particularly challenging behaviour is exhibited and when individuals lie in a sophisticated manner. One example could be during interactions where it is beneficial to know when a young person is engaging in deceit but the identification of the lie has little or no impact on the objective of the interaction. This can ultimately assist in gathering information on the various levels of deception exhibited in order to become more effective in the identification of deceit that is crucial to an investigation or assessment. Young people requiring considerable intervention from criminal justice and other agencies have the potential to become experienced and adept at knowing what is required when interacting with practitioners, whether for positive or negative agendas. This can include manipulation and deceit, interpersonal game playing and obstructiveness – all challenges in need of an appropriate response. Therefore in situations with interpersonally flexible young people, identifying knowledge of being a target of deceit can put practitioners at a disadvantage. However, this becomes a side issue were a young person to conceal information that might put themselves or a third party at risk. Avoidance of openly asserting that you know someone has deceived you will be appropriate in certain instances through adopting an approach of "slowly slowly catchy monkey" – knowing that time will enable wider interpersonal intelligence to be gained. This will increase the challenge for a young person and may put additional demands on their existing resource pool.

Establishing credibility – detecting the truth

Our personal experience of engaging in deception and being targeted by others who deceive, whether in general or forensic settings, will likely influence the manner in which we approach the detection of credibility assessment in the future. There are times when experience can assist us in identifying deception. However, it can also make us more suspicious of others and on occasion prone to making incorrect allegations of deception. Hence, although there will be generic assumptions that individuals will make about their own methods for detecting deceit, there is still a requirement to consider individuals as just that – and approach such situations in a tailored focused way.

When we consider everyday lies, we should bear in mind the importance of reputation. As assessors of credibility we need to be careful not to be overly influenced by positive or negative reputations. For example, when we spoke to a group of 11 and 12 year olds (reported in Chapter 3) they cited an occasion where one of their group (the youngest and most innocent looking) had transgressed in class but had blamed it on another member of the group. The projection of blame on to the peer was easily believed because the accuser was adept at adopting a cherubic presentation to authority and because of the second boy's reputation (he had already disclosed that he had been in detention a dozen times that term). The outcome of being wrongly blamed for an incident he was not involved in did not concern the accused because this helped the second boy and had simply meant another detention (and another made-up excuse to his mother for being late home). He was content to take the blame and retain his reputation within the classroom setting.

Although we discuss in this chapter the considerations for the detection of deception, it is vital to make accurate judgements when we detect whether a young person is being truthful. This can relate to incidents where young people make false allegations about being a victim of crime or who are themselves accused wrongly of committing an offence. Unfortunately the identification of the truth can be negatively affected by a range of factors that can result in young people being wrongly believed or discriminated against. This involves understanding our preconceived ideas about how victims or suspects behave – expectations and perceptions which inform our judgements and can ultimately lead us to make wrong accusations, blaming individuals who are innocent of deceit. Therefore the decision to accuse can have higher stakes than the lie itself.

The case of 18-year-old Rosie Waggett illustrates how this can occur. She made a false allegation of sexual assault against a taxi driver, claiming that he had grabbed her thigh during the journey back to her home and had made overtly sexual remarks. Waggett had told the police that the taxi driver had grabbed her leg and said "If I don't get my money off you, I don't get sex off my wife. If I don't get sex off her then I have to get it somewhere." However, she had also told an acquaintance that she did not have enough money for the taxi ride home and that if she was made to pay the full fare she would say the driver had tried to rape her. On arrival at Waggett's address, the young woman screamed and shouted to her mother that she had been assaulted and as a result the taxi driver was attacked by two men from the property before being arrested by the police and remaining in custody for nine hours. During the case, the judge described Waggett as "callous, clinical, warped and wicked". Her lack of concern for the taxi driver and the implications of her allegations highlighted her perspective of externalizing blame towards others in order to solve her own short-term personal circumstance. In the case of the taxi driver, the false allegation was quickly identified. However, in some cases this type of deceit can perpetuate a string of events within the criminal justice system, particularly in offences of a sexual nature when the challenge is in determining one person's account against another. This is clearly an instance where the macro-system has an influence on an individual and how they are perceived and where an individual's actions may be misinterpreted in a stereotyped context. This increases the pressure on those required to detect deceit and although many instances involve physical evidence the onus is on establishing consent. Cases involving alleged sexual offences require practitioners to have an increased focus on the detection of deception and to maintain an open mind about the nature of events being investigated. This can be especially difficult when juries can form the belief that the victim meets the criteria that enable their account of an offence to be discredited.

An example relates to the case of 18-year-old Ricky Younger who, although convicted of raping a woman working as a prostitute in Aberdeen, Scotland, had an alibi that could have resulted in a "not guilty" verdict. The suspect developed an alibi where he claimed the victim had consented to sexual intercourse and stated that he had not been aware that she was a prostitute until she demanded cash; during the row that ensued he had hit her. The victim's injuries and DNA evidence supported that sexual intercourse had taken place and that it had been violent. The provision of an alternative version of events can lead to challenges for the prosecution and the availability of negative information concerning the credibility of a victim who is a prostitute, single mother and ex-heroin user. Such cases can require additional evidence in order that the true version of events is fully identified. However, in cases where collateral information is not relevant to the case, the detection of deception can be difficult to achieve.

Denial

Denial of events can occur for a range of reasons whether in forensic or non-forensic domains. There is sometimes difficulty for practitioners in interpreting the motivation for denial of offences when there is evidence that they have been committed. Lord and Wilmot (2004) identified two overall levels of denial – outright and partial. Such denial can be in relation to (a) denial at being at the scene of the crime; (b) denial of the veracity of the victim or witness evidence; (c) denial of criminality of a certain activity (e.g. sexual consent).

Partial denial is perhaps where there is more room for interpretation in the type of communication that is presented from an individual attempting to reduce the amount of information they disclose. However, it is important to acknowledge that denial can occur within the narratives of truthful and deceptive young people. The following are examples of the ways in which denial can be presented in interactions and should be considered in terms of credibility assessment:

1   *Denial of certain offences* – "I did break into the house but I never hurt the people in there."
2   *Denial of key details* – "I used no violence." "I reminded her that I'd missed her while I was away and that I'd phoned her every week. I just didn't tell her who I was with."

3   *Denial of responsibility* – "I was hearing voices, depressed, off my head on speed." "If she hadn't been going on about my doing my coursework, I wouldn't have had to lie to her."

4   *Denial of harm* – "She smiled and so must've enjoyed it."

5   *Denial of planning/fantasy* – "I didn't plan to do that to them – it just happened."

6   *Partial or total denial of memory* – "If they said I did it, then it must have been me. I have no recollection of it." "I suppose I must have got off with someone but I was too drunk to remember."

7   *Denial of enduring risk/need for relapse prevention* – "It was a one-off."

The important aspect of responding to denial is to understand what is being said, the motivation of the young person choosing to present events in this manner and the implications of their narrative if it is to be believed. The context of the interaction will hugely impact on the interpretation of credibility in this case and some of the strategies employed to deny parallel those illustrated in Chapter 3 with the descriptions of interpersonal lies that young people tell and in Chapter 4 with the first accounts of young suspects in a police interview.

Hearing and seeing

For an assessor of credibility, it is important to remember that failure to really listen to what the sender is saying can lead to difficulties. This applies particularly in interpersonal lies where individuals can easily engage in distraction/deflection techniques. Hence the need to attend to the content of what is said and to ensure that the question posed is answered. If there is already a level of familiarity between the deceiver and the target of the deceit, it will be based on prior knowledge of the target and what will be effective.

The young people we spoke to talked about the importance of using different strategies with different teachers to get out of work or to cover up for not doing homework and the way that parental anxiety over their well-being could sometimes be used to their advantage. As mentioned by one of our participants from Chapter 3, difficult situations can sometimes be avoided by saying that "something" had happened and that they were not ready to talk about it. As she pointed out, "Something has always happened . . . even if it's just that you've cleaned your teeth" and this can provide an opportunity to lie without falsifying information.

In a study by Taylor and Rolfe (2005), this manipulation of expectations was seen in the lies that participants reported they told and those who were attempting to assess credibility sometimes made this situation easier for the liar by not listening. For example, one young person described the lies he told to his mother, making these extremely detailed and long-winded. This was because he knew she would bore easily and would stop listening very quickly. This failure to listen carefully would ultimately lead to difficulties for a detector.

Our ability to listen to what others say to us has to be heightened if we are to optimize the detection of deceit. Many conversational interactions, particularly those where we do not attend to the discussion directly or "tune out" because of a lengthy response, can make us vulnerable to missing important indicators. The breadth and depth of the communication is crucial to understand, hence listening fully to what someone says, why they say it and how they choose to portray it can yield immense information. Initially this might seem like a road to the impossible – to attend too greatly to interpersonal interactions – but with experience and knowledge of how to "separate the wheat from the chaff" it can be achieved with relative ease. For practitioners who routinely interview such as police officers, suspect inter-actions can become routine and therefore lacking in need to attend. The tape or video recording of interviews allows the opportunity to revisit the inter-action and the paperwork provides the option of paraphrasing the content of the questioning. Generally though, in order to detect deceit accurately, one must experience and practise listening, attending and responding to the detail contained within individuals' responses to questions. This is relevant for those of us who wish to identify adolescent deception in general interactions and for those working within the criminal justice systems, regardless of discipline.

Identifying patterns

For much of the research on actual deception cues, these results are obtained by asking people to lie and to tell the truth and then coding individual behaviours to receive final overall scores for the truthful and deceptive sections. This can be a frequency count or a measure of the duration and can be corrected for the overall response length. Disappoint-ingly, this research has indicated very few differences between deceptive and truthful behaviour (DePaulo *et al.*, 2003). However, this is perhaps not surprising when behavioural characteristics are taken in isolation or when people are asked to tell the truth or deceive with little acknowledgement of other permutations. Although some differences were found when looking at variables requiring a more general rating (e.g. how evasive, co-operative or tense the person appears to be). It appears that when viewing behavioural characteristics occurring together, there is much more in the way of credi-bility assessment. It is important to consider the patterns of behaviour, and this can be linked to the Chameleon Interview Approach discussed later in this chapter and wider factors that impact on the overall impression gained about an individual. It is vital to be flexible in our approach in order to assess credibility and to understand motivation to deceive, the subtleties of language used and the various methods of presenting different versions of events.

Perception of proof and evidence

Perception of proof can also be important in interpersonal everyday lies told by adolescents. For example, one of our students cited a situation where he was in a relationship with a girl who was "attached". This continued for about a year and was successfully concealed. When questioned about how he had achieved this continued deception as far as all of his (and her) friends were concerned, his answer was simple; as long as neither of them said anything, they were safe because no proof existed that there was a relationship at all. This situation had the potential to be exposed depending on the level of awareness of the couple having the affair and whether they became complacent. He commented that many of his friends had been suspicious but there was nothing they could do. This illustrates the difficulty in assessing credibility – it appears that observers sensed something was not quite right but had no concrete examples to pursue in order to gain some proof. As is also the case for our interactions with young offenders, sensing that there is more to a particular situation or that we are not being told the full story can result in suspicions which require further investigation.

PRACTITIONER INTERPERSONAL CONSIDERATIONS

The myriad factors to consider when interviewing young offenders and attempting to assess credibility may seem overwhelming. However, the reality is that if practitioners are appropriately trained and understand the different strategies and tactics employed by young offenders engaging in deceit, this can greatly enhance the interaction. There may be occasions when the entire interaction with a young person will seem stilted, difficult and challenging. The perceived objectives of the young person should always be assessed initially prior to immersing oneself in the interaction and, by association, the detection of deceit.

It is important not to enter each interaction with young people holding the view that the individual is likely to engage in deceit. Obviously some interactions and assessments require the overt detection of deceit through the processes that are employed, e.g. risk assessments and police interviewing. However, there are numerous other communication situations where assessing credibility will be important but the outcome will lead to different responses from the target of the deceit. This can be discussions within the home, at school or amongst peers.

Wall of resistance

The range of challenging interpersonal presentations of young offenders when interviewed by the police can lead to difficulties on the part of the interviewer in that the negative and obstructive behavioural responses may evoke strong emotions and require practitioners to maintain a calm and professional response to provocation. The wall of resistance that young offenders can put up may be very difficult for practitioners to respond to. It is a natural reaction when faced with resistance during an interview for the practitioner to experience a reduced ability to communicate effectively. This can result in a different perspective being taken where there could potentially be less benefit from the interaction as a result of a reduction in communication within the dyadic interaction.

THE CHAMELEON INTERVIEW APPROACH

In order more fully to utilize knowledge of the various characteristics and to react appropriately within interviews where deception is a potential consideration, it is necessary to consider the ways in which young people can present as chameleon. The Chameleon Interview Approach (Gozna & Boon, 2009, 2010) is a framework for understanding and assessing challenging and diverse individuals and can assist in the detection of deception as a result of the holistic perspective that is taken by practitioners. Consideration of young people who are able to present a flexible demeanour to family, peers and practitioners can result in heightened difficulties in establishing the credibility and intent of a young person. Gozna and Boon (2009, 2010) developed an approach to dealing specifically with individuals who commit offences and subsequently display chameleon style qualities. This approach can also be considered helpful for individuals interacting with and reacting to more challenging non-offending adolescents.

Primarily this approach will be most useful to practitioners because its widespread applicability is possible due to the flexible and holistic approach adopted and is again supportive of systems approaches to development and behaviour. Although some of the descriptions may appear to err towards the more serious end of the scale in terms of challenges with young people, we have included some everyday examples of young people in non-offending situations. This approach, along with the material discussed in Chapter 4, will assist in the development of a healthy practitioner scepticism to the potential of young people whose intention it is to be disingenuous. Whilst some disciplines working with youth will rarely be exposed to such behaviours, others will be only too knowledgeable.

As has been emphasized in earlier chapters, it is crucial to develop a bespoke strategy to any credibility assessment – particularly with young people who exhibit chameleon characteristics and have the potential to manipulate those who interact with them. This perspective is more likely to be helpful with challenging and complex young people, although chameleon characteristics may be less apparent when dealing with younger individuals whose personality and identity are emerging and not exhibited fully until later adolescence. Although we are acknowledging here that young people can exhibit challenging interpersonal behaviours, there is also a need to consider that such interactions are a positive skill which in many situations have been honed over time and used as an effective means of communication, despite the external view that might be portrayed. Hence, hostility, anger, obstructiveness and other overtly difficult interpersonal styles can be a learned response to manage and deal with other interactions and ultimately result in what develops into normative behaviour.

Therefore knowledge of how such characteristics can manifest may assist in practitioner responsiveness to the challenge of interactions with those who are difficult yet diverse. This allows for the consideration that young people can present in a chameleon manner during interactions and over time across different situations. This difference in presentation can create problems in the interpretation of behaviour. In order to illustrate this we have developed some descriptive cases to highlight the differences that can occur with a range of young people and hope this allows practitioners to identify and react to the overriding impressions they receive when working with young people. Let us consider a number of interpersonal presentation styles and how practitioners might respond.

Our first style is of an individual who generally presents in an entirely unapologetic manner with regard to their offences, so much so that one might feel there is no likelihood of deception occurring due to the appearance of such interpersonal transparency. This may not necessarily be a young person with an offending history; it can also refer to those who have venomous views on those whom they perceive to have slighted or wronged them in some way – parents, siblings, teachers, other individuals in authority, or when various types of abuse are considered. Therefore, depending on the context in which such beliefs are held, one might be in entire agreement with the young person or could feel that such strong views might result in problems later down the line.

However, any exhibited lack of remorse, regret and repentance for their beliefs and/or actions does not mean that the young person will not engage in deceit – depending on their agenda, there might still be a need to conceal certain beliefs or intentions if they perceive this could be detrimental to meeting particular objectives within an interaction. Outright lies might be less prevalent and replaced by concealment – hence the requirement to listen to what is not being said as much as what is. If it is an offence that the young person refers to with this perspective, then it is possible that deception has occurred during the commission of the crime, towards victims or prior to being arrested or making an admission of guilt.

It is possible that any pride in their offending that is exuded will instil negative feelings in those who are trying to understand or assess what has happened. Young people with this interpersonal style can present with an unguarded willingness to say what they think or have done. If they are approached with quasi-respect/interest, they can be more than pleased to explain the rationale for their actions. It is as important to know when the deception has occurred as it is to know why it has occurred. Therefore, practitioners should facilitate this communication but be aware that any perception of an interpersonal threat towards the young person through direct questioning or hostility will likely result in game-playing or clamming up. If such young people are interviewed with this is mind, they can be more than pleased to give detailed accounts – sometimes ultra-detailed – of their modus operandi (MO). Their objectives are invariably vengeful and demonstrative of contempt for their victim or potential victim (e.g. partner) – or, just as likely, victim group/s (e.g. opposing gangs, racial minorities, homosexuals, social economic status, etc.). Any sense in which they minimize their actions (criminal or not) is interesting in that it will be presented in such a way as to reduce the consequences in terms of the victim/s lack of worth or by emphasizing that the said individual/s are worthy victims.

However, in other self-serving respects it can be possible for a young person to diversely maximize the significance of their activity with unqualified, high-ground justifications, statements of personal bravery and risk taking and a stance of conviction that what they did was and is right. Accordingly, it is possible to be met with surly and volatile responses to any criticism from those whom they perceive to judge their actions. It is therefore necessary to consider that there is room for "clamming up" during interactions if they perceive that there has been such a "misunder-standing" or alternatively to refocus discussions towards their own agenda. The young person's perspective might be that the practitioner will be ignorant of their problems and hence not worth speaking to. This can relate to a lack of understanding of their cause or rationale (e.g. territory and associated risk with gangs) or knowledge about their offences.

Our second interpersonal style considers those young people who can appear to have a similar venomous stance as mentioned above, that is, with the surface certainty that they are right in what they did and/or do – yet there are some subtle differences apparent in their underlying psychology. For example, both types of individual can appear arrogant and with total conviction in support of their behaviour. The key difference is that the former does not care what anyone thinks while the latter – in need of personal recognition for his or her deeds – does care. With that in mind it becomes easier to understand how a young person can appear cocky, overconfident and full of bravado, intellectually arrogant and aloof – particularly when interacting with a range of practitioners.

Again though there is a surface and underlying distinction to be drawn between the two ways of interpersonal presentation. On the surface young people displaying such interpersonal styles regard themselves as "knowing better" than anyone else their personal agenda and rationale. However, beneath the surface it is only the young person whose interpersonal style is characterized by overt venom who will be concerned with others' regard of them and their actions – picking up on same and reacting accordingly. In contrast, the second interpersonal style is almost completely self-contained and detached from others' points of view. Since the young person does not care what others think of them – they are more likely to be consistent when interacting with different practitioners – the deception may at times be incredibly overt and at others the interpersonal presentation may be wilfully obstructive and game playing. The perspective of the young person tends towards the antisocial and anti-authority although with some level of collaboration or co-operation where they perceive their needs are being met. There is the potential for interactions with certain practitioners to be perceived by young people as a means to an end by appearing to meet objectives set, saying the right things and behaving accordingly, all for their longer term objective. Therefore the likelihood of deceit is dependent on the objectives held by the young person and whether it is in their interest to lie for greater gain.

Although the third style of presentation we discuss focuses much more on a young person who exudes charm, as with the previous two there are some overlaps in terms of the young person's respective qualities. However, it is in the differences that the real worth of judging an individual with a tutored eye materializes; differences which once identified allow for informed insight into how to interact with such young people at any given time. The self-confidence that is exhibited with the third interpersonal style might also be identified in others, but young people in this instance will be much more aware of the impact they have on others and will be very adept at reading the responses of practitioners to their behaviours.

Whilst some practitioners might be met with an arrogant or venomous interpersonal style, charm can be equally as beneficial to a young person if it is used in a conscious way to meet their objectives. Again this is a learned response from a multitude of interactions where charm has been most positively reinforced. It also illustrates the ability to read others and when used for negative means is a cynical, self-congratulatory attempt to manipulate for their own gain. Hence this type of young person has a wealth of experience in saying the right things in the right way and deceives effortlessly. Practitioners and others should challenge them on the veracity of the information they provide, although it is very likely that they will be adept at reworking it into something equally plausible. If involved in criminal activity, it will be those crimes requiring polished deceit and disingenuous charm – e.g. coercive sexual activity including night-club rape, confidence tricking and fraud. However, when the charming façade diminishes, they are also well able to engage in excessive violence, usually within the home environment, but present as the victim or with an innocent demeanour to those who might question events. In interview too they use these social skills to pursue their objectives, carefully weighing up which buttons to press to be most successful.

Those young people who perceive themselves as highly successful sexually and physically attractive would be very likely to use charm via flirtation – verbally and sexually – with any practitioners if they thought it might serve their objectives. It is vital to make no mistake here in the assessment and interaction with young people who use charm for manipulation; for all their pseudo-helpfulness, humour and reasonableness, they are entirely superficial and mask a cold persona very effectively. It is therefore possible that narcissistic and psychopathic characteristics will be in evidence during interactions if practitioners and others are observing and listening carefully. Hence the focus of the interaction is to see whether the charm and accompanying characteristics are superficial or genuine and this will assist in credibility assessment.

In evidence with some especially interpersonally challenging young people is a presentation of utter chaos, that is, their demeanour, circumstances and psychology are all in a state of disarray. This manifestation of behaviour is the result of a complex number of difficulties and can be missed unless the individual is involved with multidisciplinary teams who have gained knowledge over time and across a range of situations. Underpinning such a psychology in the main are the characteristics of borderline and histrionic personality and can present a very formidable task to deal with.

Although there is debate as to the relevance and prevalence of personality disorders with onset during adolescence, such characteristics can be emerging and vary vastly across individuals as to the severity and challenge posed. This is because these young people are constantly changing to serve their personal needs, which in the main are attention driven, rather than to get themselves out of trouble. Hence this young person is likely to create as much mayhem as possible and abhor a vacuum of attention – only really existing by creating a stir. Critically they present as being highly convincing because they not only lie to others but also to themselves. As a consequence life becomes one long act and as with "method acting" they actually believe what they are saying when they say it. Accordingly, when they say it they convey all the emotional corollaries to accompany the role they are playing to themselves and others, which results in huge challenges to detect when deceit is occurring. By turns they can idolize any given individual only to despise them seemingly without reason shortly afterwards. They can present and be characterized by roller-coaster switches, moving from depths of pseudo-depression and/or substance abuse through to apparent normality. This fluctuation has the potential to draw others into their cycle and provides such individuals with grounds to appear the victim. In serious cases, this could lead to allegations of rape or other boundary issues towards practitioners or other people in their lives.

All of this means they can be extremely convincing and as such can very easily manipulate others – not just practitioners but other people in their lives who would almost certainly have become embroiled in their machinations and games. Experienced practitioners will easily be able to recall such individuals who have presented in this way. Within the forensic context all agencies concerned need to keep each other informed about these young people. In consideration of young offenders, such a perception can seem highly negative towards a "vulnerable" individual. However, with specific focus and identification of behaviours and actions practitioners can gain some level of insight and respond accordingly. If it has been identified that a young person is presenting in this manner, it is beneficial for practitioners to increase their awareness and insight by speaking with those who have dealt with them previously. Armed with this information, the practitioner will not only be aware of the young person's capacity to attention seek, deceive and distort, but can also gain as thorough knowledge as possible of the specific relevant issues in order to confront and manage the young person.

The emphasis of the four distinct interpersonal presentations discussed above is that they create a chameleon-like manifestation and therefore as such cannot be considered mutually exclusive – one or more can occur within or across interactions with young people who are deemed challenging for a variety of reasons. There are further considerations when interacting with young people that can be transient rather than enduring over time and focused to meet a particular agenda. One such presentation is that of individuals who are eager to please via a one-size-fits-all approach. This style is entirely unsophisticated when compared with those who use overt charm successfully. The presentation is characterized by a blanket admiring obsequiousness towards practitioners. In this respect the young person will at times behave in a grovelling manner that others would not be able to contemplate, partly due to a lack of confidence and self-esteem. The statements made will be laced not only with awe for the practitioners but also self-pity, self-deprecation, wallowing in negative circumstances and personal victimization. This can be further emphasized by a catastrophizing of events which can be motivated by attention seeking – as with chaotic individuals – or to emphasize the victim stance and hence warrant pity. It is therefore crucial that practitioners are able to distinguish between a case worthy of sympathy and one where the agenda is disingenuous and manipulative and brought in from a lifetime's experience despite the youthfulness of the individual. The knowledge that such individuals' lives are traded in the currency of sympathy and manipulation can therefore be helpful to practitioners who can use it accurately to interpret the underlying motivation of certain interactions.

A further relevant consideration is the avoidance of responsibility or participation in specific situations – whether criminal or non-criminal – to meet a certain agenda or need. It is helpful from the outset to distinguish between young persons who have bona fide difficulties and disabilities and those who feign such incapacity in a bid to gain self-advantage. It is not difficult to envisage a wide array of qualities that an individual could try to affect in order to obtain their objectives including feigning illness to avoid examinations at school or minimizing involvement in crimes of which they have been accused by laying blame on others with a demonstration of mental inability to have understood what was going to happen in the offences. Alternative presentations can include adopting a dazed state and an inability to comprehend and/or answer questions in interviews or court. Typically such attempts involve trying to look "dim", "fake bad" or appearing unintelligent, unduly pliant and/or suggestible, or through drink/drugs unable to recall key details material to a successful prosecution. Therefore it is paramount that any practitioners who are assessing a young person should consider feigning as an option that forms an aspect of the assessment of credibility.

To effectively identify the extent of such behaviour, it is crucial for practitioners to have an ability to determine feigned from fabricated trauma (e.g. in cases of sexual abuse), or genuine vs. false intellectual or learning disabilities, suggestibility or compliance. In some instances, collateral independent information will enable objective verification such as educational or medical records. In contrast, determining this in the seemingly intelligent young person can be rather more difficult and such assessment involves careful analyses of inconsistencies and incorporates the ability to provide evidence that can back up a perspective either way. Practitioners should therefore look for a history of deception, e.g. not accepting responsibility where clearly they are to blame, grossly lying about qualifications to obtain jobs, anything in fact which shows a capacity for low guile.

One final aspect to consider in relation to a chameleon interpersonal presentation in young people is perhaps the most challenging of all and requires substantial effort and observation on the part of the practitioner drawing on all of their resources. Although this is a rare occurrence, young people such as this can and do exist and if one does not expect such a challenging individual the outcome can be catastrophic in terms of their ability to leave you and others feeling psychologically stunned and dazed. It is crucial to move forward from the view that young people, and more commonly young offenders, can be challenging but ultimately unsophisticated in their interpersonal abilities. This is potentially dangerous from an interpersonal perspective. The ability for some young people to appear unfathomable highlights just how accomplished they are. Every bit as convincing in their acting as someone who is self-deceptive, this individual utilizes a full spectrum of skills and psychological awareness of others in a very focused and pre-prepared manner. This is not about attention seeking, to fill a void of their personal inadequacies, to exact revenge or to emphasize their mark on the world; in criminal circles, this individual will be planes above such facile perspectives. They will have planned their offences, developed a pseudo respectable (even noble) persona in public, cultivated a sham relationship with their unsuspecting partner, have a false alibi in place, etc. Chance is kept to the absolute minimum and as such these individuals can all too easily be taken at face value. They are the masters of disguise, psychologically morphing not in a reactive but proactive and calculated way.

Although many young people have to a greater or lesser degree the capacity to present in a chameleon manner, depending on the situation and any accompanying agenda, the most accomplished individual is the last word in adeptness at switching due to their astounding ability to be one step ahead of those they move amongst and exploit. The most effective way to manage interactions with young offenders who are suspected as presenting in such a way is to take nothing at face value. Furthermore, it is paramount that any practitioners engaging in credibility assessment should not exhibit signs of suspicion. Although there are unlikely to be many, any mistakes, inconsistencies and weaknesses in the young person's account should be kept back unused until absolutely necessary to disclose. It is therefore more beneficial to give the most challenging young person the confidence that he or she is dealing with practitioners who are not as clever, leading to further mistakes through overconfidence. This individual remains the ultimate challenge throughout all points of criminal activity and encounter with the judicial system.

Although such interpersonal interactions will be more commonly observed in young people who have difficult backgrounds or circumstances where they have developed a range of methods to manage and react to their own perceived threats, elements of the behaviours and interactions above will also be found in largely problem-free adolescents who are experiencing transient issues or problems. There will be occasions when the presentation is enduring over time and also when there are peaks and troughs of problematic or challenging behaviour where deception can occur as one aspect of a holistic consideration.

Our understanding and responses to the various chameleon interpersonal presentations can be challenging and stretch our skills in interpreting and responding to behaviours. In order to assist practitioners in the implementation of the interactive dimensions of the various chameleon presentations, a mnemonic developed by Gozna and Boon (2007) can assist in recalling the pertinent factors. The CHAMELEON presentation of individuals is useful in determining the particular perspective taken during an interaction where credibility assessment is important to undertake, and is particularly relevant to forensic settings, whether pre- or post-conviction.

C HARACTERIZED BY CHANGE
H EALTH (PERSONALITY & MENTAL DISORDERS/PHYSICAL)
A TTITUDES, ALLEGIANCES & AFFILIATIONS
M INDSET & MOTIVATION & MALIGN INTENT
E YES (INTERACTIONS, INTERVIEWS & INTERVIEWERS)
L IES & LIMITATIONS
E NVIRONMENT
O FFENCES & OPPORTUNITIES
N UANCES, NEGATIVITY & NEEDS

Practitioner preparation

This section of the chapter is more relevant for those working in domains requiring a range of credibility assessments rather than for the detection of everyday deception and would include social work, education and forensic settings. Preparing strategies for interviewing challenging individuals is vital in order to increase the effectiveness of interactions. Having discussed the approaches used to attempt to detect deceit, the personality characteristics of more challenging and complex young offenders and factors concerning exhibited disorders, there are important ways in which practitioners can adapt their behavioural interactions accordingly.

The German proverb *Über seinen eigenen Schatten springen* when translated means "to jump over one's own shadow", which aptly describes the skill required when dealing with individuals who are chameleon in their presentation. Practitioners routinely become used to working in a particular way with clients, although this proverb emphasizes the need to break away from conventional patterns in order to adapt reactions and behaviour to the situation. Hence it is sometimes appropriate for practitioners to become chameleon themselves in order to increase the effectiveness of an interview situation. This to an extent already occurs in situations such as police interviews where there is initially a relaxed atmosphere in gaining general information that moves into a challenge phase where specific evidence or questions are put to a suspect. There is a similar saying that you actually cannot jump over your own shadow, which we know to be true given the physical impossibility of doing this. However, in the figurative sense we need to respond to such a proverb when working in challenging situations with forensic clients.

Ultimately, the assessment of credibility with adolescents will be increasingly effective when the deceiver is understood in terms of their motivation, the content of their narratives and the wider context in which deception could occur. Equally, potential targets of deceit can be forewarned and to an extent will have some level of awareness of the range of factors that could increase the likelihood that they will be deceived, whilst maintaining an open mind and considering all the evidence prior to making decisions.

CHAPTER SUMMARY

This chapter has considered the challenges of detecting deception in adolescents and has proposed that, rather than relying on traditional deception approaches such as the focus on non-verbal behaviours, there needs to be a holistic and bespoke approach to working with young people. Hence there is a need to focus on the individual rather than a consideration of generic factors that have the potential to bias the focus of decision making.

Questions to consider

- What is the motivation behind the young person's deceit?
- What is the purpose of deception for the young person?
- How is the deception manifesting and how does this impact on your general perspective of the young person?
- Is it appropriate to make an allegation of deceit or do you want to wait until you have increased evidence?
- Is the young person or a third party put in danger as a result of deceit taking place?
- Do you have particular preconceived ideas about the young person and how does this impact on your decisions about credibility?

7 Conclusions, thoughts and future directions

As seen in the six previous chapters, deception in adolescence has a number of interesting features. However, most importantly it cannot be taken in isolation and should be considered within a holistic bespoke approach to interpersonal interactions with young people. This final chapter reinforces our main message and presents some general conclusions and suggestions for researchers and practitioners to consider.

DECEPTION IS NOT AN ISOLATED BEHAVIOUR

We argued at the beginning of the book that deception was one of a set of potential communication strategies and needed to be considered alongside truthful behaviour. We have seen evidence from offending and non-offending adolescents that this is the case. In the majority of cases, clear lies are not observed. Instead we see a variety of minimizations, deflections and topic avoidances. We see "liars" blaming other people – the targets of their deceptions, co-offenders, society in general – and we see the use of different versions of truth to divert attention from a difficult conversational topic. However, what we very rarely see is the use of complete falsification often found in deception research. Occasionally we do see elaborate lies under-taken with a high degree of planning and enacted with the help of others. However, these are definitely in the minority of lies which people report. Even in forensic settings, the prevalent pattern of behaviour is of strategic evasion, deflection and minimization in order to present a particular impression to the target of the deceit.

Evasion, deflection and concealment are regarded by researchers in the field as forms of deception. However, there is a general contention that these are different from truthtelling in terms of process, motivation and outcome. This is not supported by our discussions with young people in different settings. Moreover, our interviews show that young people may engage in the same processes of planning, may experience the same emotions and may produce the same behaviours and outcomes when deciding to be completely honest. They recognize that both honesty and deception have consequences. For this reason, we suggest that researchers and practitioners widen their focus to give a greater emphasis to different types of truthful as well as deceptive communication in order that the detection of truthful behaviour is also considered when assessing credibility.

COMMUNICATION IS NOT AN ISOLATED PROCESS

In this book we have reviewed literature and discussed data that address the communication behaviour of adolescents who offend, those who do not offend and those who are "at risk" in some way. This latter category can be those with chaotic family circumstances, who exhibit signs of psychopathology or who are simply "at risk" of staying on an offending trajectory rather than limiting delinquent behaviour to adolescence. In order to understand the similarities and differences of their communication, we need to consider the surrounding variables as a package.

For example, consider the situation of a 16 year old who is being interviewed by the police. His communication patterns may be influenced by his internal state (beliefs about the police, perceptions of the strength of evidence against him, physiological arousal, presence of alcohol and drugs), his prior experience of dealing with the police, his experiences during arrest and while in custody awaiting interview, the presence of a solicitor, choice of appropriate adult (he may be happy to tell the police what happened but may not want his father to find out), the offence type, existence of co-suspects, existence of a victim (and victim type) and his first impressions of the officers conducting the interview. He may also be influenced by the physical environment in the interview room, the questions asked by the officers and their immediate reactions to his replies. All these variables will have an interactive rather than an additive effect.

Real-world communication is not created in the laboratory and single variables cannot be manipulated in isolation. This has been argued elsewhere (Boon & Gozna, 2009; Gozna & Boon, 2010) and is supported by the data presented in earlier chapters. Communication has a minimum of two participants, each with a unique perspective and a context that stretches far beyond the interaction itself. To adequately deal with this broader context, we will be required to use multimethod approaches and multivariate analyses. More daunting for researchers and practitioners is the fact that time and patience will be needed as well as an increased tolerance for blurred boundaries. However, it is essential to adopt this approach to conducting real-world research and will reap rewards in the long term as regards our psychological understanding of diverse and challenging individuals.

FURTHER INTERACTION BETWEEN RESEARCHERS AND PRACTITIONERS IS NECESSARY

One of the most challenging things about credibility and communication at any stage of the lifecourse is the complex range of associated factors that underpin any interaction. As argued above, this complexity needs to be addressed in new research agendas. However, this should go further and the following is a useful starting point. First, existing laboratory based research needs to be re-evaluated to ensure that findings or their real-world utility are not being over-interpreted. If research indicates that, for example, participants display a greater (or lesser) frequency of blinking when providing deceptive accounts to fellow students about their course information, this may not reflect the blink rate displayed by a suspected terrorist or informant interviewed by the intelligence or military community. We therefore need to be careful as researchers about suggesting such quick fixes without focused, appropriate and realistic real-world evaluation. Second, we should remember that researchers cannot do this without the support of those in practice. If we are required to present a simple solution to gain the support of practitioners and policymakers or are not able to conduct real-world research, then we will have to retreat to the lab. Hence those whose roles are to act as gatekeepers need to be cognizant of the benefits of collaboration with the academic community. The solution is an increased dialogue between those working with and those researching the credibility of young people to ensure that research and practice are conducted to the benefit of both parties.

EVEN "EVERYDAY" LIES HAVE A WIDER CONTEXT

The argument is made here and elsewhere (Boon & Gozna, 2009) that laboratory research and forensic relevance do not go hand in hand. Our understanding of how suspects behave in police interviews or in risk assessments post-conviction will be imperfect if we try to model this behaviour in the laboratory. This is because the "police interview context" or the "young offender institution scenario" is missing, and however we may try to re-create it we will fail. Further, neither communicator will use the same resources in a laboratory as in the real-life setting. Therefore, at best laboratory research is useful for generating lines of enquiry or testing theoretical approaches that can then be followed up in real-world forensic research. This applies equally to everyday lies. In general, even when the question of forensic relevance is raised, it is considered with regard to stakes and amount of cognitive effort (e.g. Vrij *et al.*, 2006). It is assumed that there is a smaller gap between lying in the laboratory and lying in everyday contexts. However, clearly the points we raise with regard to context and complexity can apply to trivial everyday lies as well as complex forensic ones. It is also necessary to consider the extent to which lies have been mentally rehearsed by individuals and the number of times such "stories" have been imparted to practitioners. This has huge implications for level and coping mechanisms for cognitive load, the experience of emotions and impression management.

For example, a 12 year old deciding whether or not to ask for permission to go to a party (or whether to pretend she is studying elsewhere) may be influenced by knowledge about her parents, the quality of their relationship, stereotypes of what parents are likely to get upset about, feedback from her friends and siblings about how they handled similar situations in the past, or her beliefs about the appropriateness of the behaviour and its likely success. The likelihood of getting permission may be influenced by parental perceptions of risk (affected by the media), parental judgements about what behaviours are appropriate for someone of 12 (as opposed to 8, 16 or 18), the degree of trust that the parents place in their daughter, her previous behaviour when given additional freedom, or even the parents' own behaviour as adolescents and the reactions of their parents. All these considerations are beyond the control of our 12-year-old partygoer but she needs to second guess them in order to get the communication right. Further, our 12 year old needs to understand why her parents' reaction might be different if the party were in a local church hall or at the house of someone they have never met. Taking a single variable out of this list (e.g. the quality of the parent–child relationship) means we are underestimating the complexity of the situation and will poorly predict the outcome of the interaction. Therefore we need to consider the system in order to understand the communication.

UNDERSTANDING THE "SYSTEM" WILL HELP THOSE WORKING WITHIN IT

Chapters 4 and 5 in particular focused on the way in which practitioners might approach interviews with young people in a range of different settings. These included young offenders and those with relevant mental health problems or chaotic lifestyles which created risks of offending. The importance of these chapters is not just in highlighting such lying behaviour but in showing the practical application of a dynamic systems approach. After all, there is little utility in taking such a perspective unless this also provides useful insights and signposts for practitioners. Therefore this book is as much about the way that a systems approach could work in real-life interview settings with young people as the theoretical contribution that this approach could make to deception research. The conceptualization of the chameleon offender presented by Gozna and Boon (2009, 2010) illustrates the importance of a bespoke and flexible approach to these interviews and demonstrates how a range of systemic factors can actually work in specific case situations. This was also seen when examining the suspect strategy work in Chapter 4 which demonstrates that (a) a dynamic systems approach can be useful for practitioners and (b) future research in this area should assess the application of this flexible and holistic perspective to interviewing and credibility assessment in a range of settings.

NOT ALL ADOLESCENTS' LIES ARE NEGATIVE, RISKY OR PATHOLOGICAL

A large portion of previous research on adolescents' lies has been interpreted to indicate wider negative or pathological behaviour. Despite this, evidence from interviews in Chapter 3 shows that some lies are necessary to protect the person themselves or someone close to them; some are justifiable in the context of maintaining privacy or gaining autonomy; and some, while they cannot be described as "good", certainly do not indicate evidence of psychopathology, delinquency or poor parental relations. In fact some of the lies (and non-lies) are actually more indicative of interpersonal sensitivity and social skill. Furthermore, young people have boundaries. There are things they will not lie about and people they will not lie to. They understand the nature of trust and lying is not something they always feel good about. This reflects the types of lies in adult populations and applies even to some lies told by offenders and "at risk" youth. Researchers and practitioners need to be cautious in "pathologizing" deceptions which do not deserve that label. Failure to do so could potentially result in a judgemental attitude towards more appropriate deceptions and could cause problems in discriminating those situations where pathological lying really is occurring. The findings from Chapter 3 make it clear that young people can experience a strong sense of injustice when they are wrongly accused and this can change their perceptions of the people involved. This would be damaging in a setting where communications with "at risk" youth are essential to ensure full investigations or appropriate care and intervention. Chapter 6 provides guidance on the communication behaviours of concern and those which are more "normal" than pathological. However, we would like to see researchers underlining this difference in their future endeavours.

ADOLESCENT COMMUNICATION (DECEPTIVE AND TRUTHFUL) IS PART OF A LIFELONG PROCESS

As with all skilled behaviour, it is possible to improve in making appropriate communication choices and carrying them off successfully. We have provided evidence to show that adolescent communication is a process of continual development and refinement of new skills as well as the exercise of existing ones in novel situations. However, this depends on a large and varied resource pool and on the challenge being presented to the young person. While we have focused on the resources and challenges available to adolescents, we see no reason why such an approach cannot be taken across the lifecourse. As argued earlier in this chapter, context is crucial and understanding the historical background of a communication setting will significantly add to our ability to predict the outcome. A study of adult offenders and the credibility of adults in general can be informed by our knowledge of adolescent behaviour. When working with adult offenders, an understanding of their life history can often provide useful information to explain patterns of behaviour, particularly in the consideration of risk which invariably incorporates an understanding of adolescence (e.g. the Psychopathy Checklist Revised). This applies particularly when there are issues of maturation or early life experiences that generate stereotyped patterns of responding to adult situations. However, understanding how adolescents make communication choices can also often illuminate everyday adult interactions. For example, we may communicate in an adult fashion in the majority of our interactions with our chosen partner but may resort to childlike or adolescent communication strategies when challenged in certain ways.

Additionally, taking a developmental perspective can be a way of seeing changes in the process of communication. This gives further scope to the understanding of communication and credibility as skilled behaviours. Indeed, we have already applied our perspective to adult as well as young offenders (Gozna & Boon, 2009) and are working towards understanding deception choice and success in older adults (Stuart-Hamilton, Taylor, & Nash, in prep). Therefore, if the challenge requires it, we would argue that deception is not just a young person's life skill, but one which applies to people of all ages.

CHAPTER SUMMARY

The current chapter highlights some key recommendations and directions arising from the research presented in the book as a whole. It emphasizes the importance of communication skills and a flexible holistic approach for both parents and practitioners. The dynamic systems perspective outlined in Chapter 1 has been shown to be a useful addition to this area of research. Specifically it highlights key questions for practitioners and researchers to consider about their own perspectives and assumptions as well as emphasizing that communication is a strategic and skilled process.

References

Abrams, D., & Hogg, M. A. (1988). Comments on the motivational status of self-esteem in social identity and intergroup discrimination. *European Journal of Social Psychology, 18*, 317–334.

Abrams, L. S., Anderson-Nathe, B., & Aguilar, J. (2008). Constructing masculinities in juvenile corrections. *Men and Masculinities, 11*, 22–41.

Akehurst, L., Köhnken, G., Vrij, A., & Bull, R. (1996). Lay persons' and police officers' beliefs regarding deceptive behaviour. *Applied Cognitive Psychology, 10*, 461–471.

American Psychiatric Association (APA, 1994). *Diagnostic and Statistical Manual of Mental Disorders* (4th ed). Washington, DC: American Psychiatric Association.

Anderson, J. R. (1982). Acquisition of cognitive skill. *Psychological Review, 89*, 369–406.

Anderson, J. R. (1987). Skill acquisition: Compilation of weak method problem solutions. *Psychological Review, 94*, 192–210.

Anolli, L., Balconi, M., & Ciceri, R. (2003a). Deceptive miscommunication theory (DeMiT): A new model for the analysis of deceptive communication. In L. Anolli, R. Ciceri, & G. Riva (Eds.), *Say not to say: New perspectives on miscommunication*. Amsterdam: IOS Press.

Anolli, L., Ciceri, R., & Riva, G. (Eds.). (2003b) *Say not to say: New perspectives on miscommunication*. Amsterdam: IOS Press.

Arnett-Jensen, L., Arnett, J. J., Feldman, S. S., & Cauffman, E. (2004). The right to do wrong: Lying to parents among adolescents and emerging adults. *Journal of Youth and Adolescence, 33*, 101–112.

Aune, R. K., & Waters, L. L. (1994). Cultural differences in deception: Motivations to deceive in Samoans and North Americans. *International Journal of Intercultural Relations, 18*, 159–172.

Bandura, A. (1986). *Social foundations of thought and action: A social cognitive theory*. Englewood Cliffs, NJ: Prentice-Hall.

Bandura, A. (1997). *Self-efficacy: The exercise of control*. New York: W H Freeman.

Barry, L. M., & Burlew, S. B. (2004). Using social skills to teach choice and playskills to children with autism. *Focus on Autism and Other Developmental Disabilities, 19*, 45–51.

Bavelas, J. B., Black, A., Chovil, N., & Mullett, J. (1990). *Equivocal communication*. Newbury Park, CA: Sage.

BBC News online (2000, May 19). Bridge murder gang get life. Retrieved June 1, 2010, from http://news.bbc.co.uk/1/hi/uk/755081.stm

Berger, K. S. (2008). *The Developing Person Through Childhood and Adolescence.* New York: Worth.

Berndt, T. J. (2002). Friendship quality and social development. *Current Directions in Psychological Science, 11,* 7–10.

Berndt, T. J., & Hoyle, S. G. (1985). Stability and change in childhood and adolescent friendships. *Developmental Psychology, 21,* 1007–1015.

Berry, D. S. (1991). Accuracy in social perception: Contributions of facial and vocal information. *Journal of Personality and Social Psychology, 61,* 298–307.

Blair, J. R. (2007). Empathic dysfunction in psychopathic individuals. In T. Farrow, & P. Woodruff (Eds.), *Empathy in mental illness.* New York: Cambridge University Press.

Bogart, L. M., Benotsch, E. G., & Pavlovic, J. D. (2004). Feeling superior but threatened: The relation of narcissism to social comparison. *Basic and Applied Social Psychology, 26,* 35–44.

Boon, J. C. W., & Gozna, L. F. (2008, July). *The Chameleon offender: A new look at our interactions with offenders.* Paper presented at the 18th Conference of the European Association of Psychology and Law, Maastricht.

Boon, J. C. W., & Gozna, L. F. (2009). Firing pea-shooters at elephants. *Psychologist, 22,* 762–765.

Brandt, J. R., Kennedy, W. A., Patrick, C. J., & Curtin, J. J. (1997). Assessment of psychopathy in a population of adolescent incarcerated offenders. *Psychological Assessment, 9,* 429–435.

Branscombe, N. R., Ellemers, N., Spears, R., & Doosje, B. (1999). The context and content of social identity threat. In N. Ellemers, R. Spears, & B. Doosje (Eds.), *Social identity: Context, commitment, content.* Oxford: Blackwell.

Braun, V., & Clarke, V. (2006). Using thematic analysis in psychology. *Qualitative Research in Psychology, 3,* 77–101.

Bronfenbrenner, U. (1979). *The ecology of human development.* Cambridge, MA: Harvard University Press.

Bull, P. (2006). Invited and uninvited applause in political speeches. *British Journal of Social Psychology, 45*(3), 563–578.

Buller D. B., & Burgoon J. K. (1996). Interpersonal deception theory. *Communication Theory, 6,* 203–242.

Buller, D. B., Comstock, J., Aune, R. K., & Strzyzewski, K. D. (1989). The effect of probing on deceivers and truthtellers. *Journal of Non-verbal Behaviour, 13,* 155–170.

Burgoon, J. K., Buller, D. B., Dillman, L., & Walther, J. B. (1995). Interpersonal deception IV: Effects of suspicion on perceived communication and nonverbal behaviour dynamics. *Human Communication Research, 22,* 163–196.

Burleson, K., Leach, C. W., & Harrington, D. M. (2005). Upward social comparison and self-concept: Inspiration and inferiority among art students in an advanced programme. *British Journal of Social Psychology, 44,* 109–123.

Carlson, J. R., George, J. F., Burgoon, J. K., Adkins, M., & White, C. H. (2004). Deception in computer-mediated communication. *Group Decision and Negotiation, 13,* 5–28.

Ceschi, G., & Scherer, K. R. (2003). Children's ability to control the facial expression of laughter and smiling: Knowledge and behaviour. *Cognition and Emotion, 17,* 385–411.

Chan, A., & Poulin, F. (2007). Monthly changes in the composition of friendship networks in early adolescence. *Merrill-Palmer Quarterly, 53*, 578–602.

Chi, M. T. H. (2006). Two approaches to the study of experts' characteristics. In K. A. Ericsson, N. Charness, P. J. Feltovich, & R. R. Hoffman (Eds.), *The Cambridge handbook of expertise and expert performance*. New York: Cambridge University Press.

Christie, R. F., & Geis, F. L. (1970). *Studies in Machiavellianism*. New York: Academic Press.

Clark, A. (2007). A sense of presence. *Pragmatics and Cognition, 15*, 413–433.

Cogburn, K. R.-A. (1993). A study of psychopathy and its relation to success in interpersonal deception. *Dissertation Abstracts International, 54*, 2191.

Coie, J. D., Belding, M., & Underwood, M. (1988). Aggression and peer rejection in childhood. In B. B. Lahey, & A. E. Kazdin (Eds.), *Advances in Clinical Child Psychology, 11*, 125–158.

Colby, A., & Kohlberg, L. (1987). *The measurement of moral judgment, Vol. 1: Theoretical foundations and research validation; Vol. 2: Standard issue scoring manual*. New York: Cambridge University Press.

Cooke, D. J., & Michie, C. (2001). Refining the construct of psychopath: Towards a hierarchical model. *Psychological Assessment, 13*, 171–188.

Cooke, D. J., Michie, C., & Skeem, J. (2007). Understanding the structure of the Psychopathy Checklist Revised: An exploration of methodological confusion. *British Journal of Psychiatry, 190*, s39–s50.

Crosnoe, R., Riegle-Crumb, C., Field, S., Frank, K., & Muller, C. (2008). Peer group contexts of girls' and boys' academic experiences. *Child Development, 79*, 139–155.

Decker, S. H., & Curry, G. D. (2000). Addressing key features of gang membership: Measuring the involvement of young members. *Journal of Criminal Justice, 28*, 473–482.

DePaulo, B. M., Ansfield, M. E., & Bell, K. L. (1996). Theories about deception and paradigms for studying it: A critical appraisal of Buller and Burgoon's interpersonal deception theory and research. *Communication Theory, 6*, 297–310.

DePaulo, B. M., Charlton, K., Cooper, H., Lindsay, J. J., & Muhlenbruck, L. (1997). The accuracy–confidence correlation in the detection of deception. *Personality and Social Psychology Review, 1*, 346–357.

DePaulo, B. M., Kashy, D. A., Kirkendol, S. E., Wyer, M. M., & Epstein, J. A. (1996). Lying in everyday life. *Journal of Personality and Social Psychology, 70*, 979–995.

DePaulo, B. M., Lindsay, J. L., Malone, B. E., Muhlenbruck, L., Charlton, K., & Cooper, H. (2003). Cues to deception. *Psychological Review, 129*, 74–118.

DePaulo, B. M., Wetzel, C., Sternglanz, R. W., & Wilson, M. J. W. (2003). Verbal and non-verbal dynamics of privacy, secrecy and deceit. *Journal of Social Issues, 59*, 391–410.

Derks, B., van Laar, C., & Ellemers, N. (2009). Working for the self or working for the group: How self- versus group affirmation affects collective behaviour in low-status groups. *Journal of Personality and Social Psychology, 96*, 183–202.

DeWall, C. N., Baumeister, R. F., & Vohs, K. D. (2008). Satiated with belongingness? Effects of acceptance, rejection, and task framing on self-regulatory performance. *Journal of Personality and Social Psychology, 95*, 1367–1382.

Drury, J., & Reicher, S. (2000). Collective action and psychological change: The emergence of new social identities. *British Journal of Social Psychology, 39,* 579–604.

Ekman, P. (2001). *Telling lies: Clues to deceit in the marketplace, politics and marriage.* New York: Norton.

Ekman, P. (2009). *Telling lies: Clues to deceit in the marketplace, politics and marriage.* (2nd ed.). New York: Norton.

Ekman, P., Roper, G., & Hager, J. C. (1980). Deliberate facial movement. *Child Development, 51,* 886–891.

Elaad, E. (2003). Effects of feedback on the overestimated capacity to detect lies and the underestimated ability to tell lies. *Applied Cognitive Psychology, 17,* 349–363.

Elliott, D. S., & Menard, S. (1996). Delinquent friends and delinquent behaviour: Temporal and developmental patterns. In J. D. Hawkins (Ed.), *Delinquency and crime: Current theories.* New York: Cambridge University Press.

Emler, N., & Reicher, S. (1995). *Adolescence and delinquency: The collective management of reputation.* Malden: Blackwell Publishing.

Engels, R. C. M. E., Finkenhauer, C., & van Kooten, D. C. (2006). Lying behaviour, family functioning and adjustment in early adolescence. *Journal of Youth and Adolescence, 35,* 949–958.

Ennis, E., Vrij, A., & Chance, C. (2008). Individual differences and lying in everyday life. *Journal of Social and Personal Relationships, 25,* 105–118.

Evans, T., & Wallace, P. (2008). A prison within a prison? The masculinity narratives of male prisoners. *Men and Masculinities, 10,* 484–507.

Farrington, D. P. (2003). British randomised experiments on crime and justice. *Annals of the American Academy of Political and Social Science, 589,* 150–167.

Farrington, D. P. (2005). The integrated cognitive antisocial potential (ICAP) theory. In D. P. Farrington (Ed.), *Integrated developmental and life-course theories of offending* (pp. 73–92). New Brunswick, NJ: Transaction.

Feldman, R. S., Forrest, J. A., & Happ, B. R. (2002). Self-presentation and verbal deception: Do self-presenters lie more? *Basic and Applied Social Psychology, 24,* 163–170.

Feldman, R. S., Jenkins, L., & Popoola, O. (1979). Detection of deception in adults and children via facial expressions. *Child Development, 50,* 350–355.

Feldman, R. S., Tomasian, J. C., & Coates, E. J. (1999). Nonverbal deception abilities and adolescents' social competence: Adolescents with higher social skills are better liars. *Journal of Non-verbal Behaviour, 23,* 237–249.

Fenigstein, A., Scheier, M. F., & Buss, A. H. (1975). Public and private self-consciousness: Assessment and theory. *Journal of Consulting and Clinical Psychology, 43,* 522–527.

Festinger, L. (1954). A theory of social comparison processes. *Human Relations, 7,* 117–140.

Finkenhauer, C., Engels, C. M. E., & Meeus, W. (2002). Keeping secrets from parents: Advantages and disadvantages of secrecy in adolescence. *Journal of Youth and Adolescence, 31,* 123–136.

Fishbein, M., & Ajzen, I. (1974). Attitudes towards objects as predictors of single and multiple behavioural criteria. *Psychological Review, 81,* 59–74.

Forgas, J. P., & East, R. (2008a). On being happy and being gullible: Mood effects on scepticism and the detection of deception. *Journal of Experimental Social Psychology, 44,* 1362–1367.

Forgas, J. P., & East, R. (2008b). How real is that smile? Mood effects on accepting or rejecting the veracity of emotional judgements. *Journal of Non-verbal Behaviour, 32*, 157–171.

Forth, A. E. (1996). *Psychopathy and young offenders: Prevalence, family background, and violence.* Unpublished manuscript. Carleton University, Ottawa, Canada. Cited in Gretton, H. M., Hare, R. D., & Catchpole, R. E. H. (2004). Psychopathy and offending from adolescence to adulthood: A 10-year follow-up. *Journal of Consulting and Clinical Psychology, 72*(4), 636–645.

Forth, A. E., & Burke H. C. (1998). Psychopathy in adolescence: Assessment, violence and developmental precursors. In D. Cooke, A. Forth, & R. Hare (Eds.), *Psychopathy: Theory, Research and Implications for Society* (pp. 205–230). Dordrecht: Kluwer.

Forth, A. E., Kosson, D. S., & Hare, R. D. (2004). *The Hare Psychopathy Checklist: Youth Version Manual.* Toronto: Multi-Health Systems.

Gabriel, S., Renaud, J. M., & Tippin, B. (2007). When I think of you, I feel more confident about me: The relational self and self-confidence. *Journal of Experimental Social Psychology, 43*, 772–779.

Gangestad, S. W., & Snyder, M. (2000). Self-monitoring: Appraisal and reappraisal. *Psychological Bulletin, 126*, 530–555.

Gardner, M., & Steinberg, L. (2005). Peer influence on risk taking, risk preference, and risky decision making in adolescence and adulthood: An experimental study. *Developmental Psychology, 41*, 625–635.

Ge, X., Donnellan M. B., & Wenk, E. (2001). The development of persistent criminal offending in males. *Criminal Justice and Behaviour, 28*, 731–755.

Global Deception Research Team (2006). A world of lies. *Journal of Cross-Cultural Psychology, 37*, 60–74.

Gozna, L. F. (2002). Individual differences in telling lies, detecting lies and the consequences of getting caught. Unpublished PhD thesis, University of Portsmouth.

Gozna, L. F. (2007). Tackling ecological validity: Conducting observations in a police suspect interview. *Issues in Forensic Psychology, 6*, 57–63.

Gozna, L. F. (2008). Interviewing and deception techniques. In K. Fritzon, & P. Wilson (Eds.), *Forensic and criminal psychology: An Australian perspective* (pp. 151–164). Sydney: McGraw-Hill.

Gozna, L. F., & Boon, J. C. W. (2007, May). *The Chameleon offender: The synergising of psychology and psychiatry to meet the challenge.* Paper presented at the Conference of Research in Forensic Psychiatry, Regensburg, Germany.

Gozna, L. F., & Boon, J. C. W. (2009, March). *The development of a bespoke approach to interviewing in forensic settings: Introducing the Chameleon offender.* Paper presented at the American Psychology and Law Society Annual Conference, San Antonio.

Gozna, L. F., & Boon, J. C. W. (2010). Interpersonal deception detection. In J. Brown, & E. Campbell (Eds.), *The Cambridge handbook of forensic psychology* (pp. 484–491). Cambridge: Cambridge University Press.

Gozna. L. F., Gray, H., & Boon, J. C. W. (under review). Trouble on the streets: Exploring the offence supportive beliefs of prolific young offenders. Submitted to *Journal of Adolescence Research.*

Gozna, L. F., & Taylor, R. (2011). *Unpacking the deception resource pool.* Manuscript in preparation.

Gozna, L. F., Teicher, S., & Boon, J. C. W. (2009, April). *First impressions:*

Strategies used by suspects during initial accounts in real life police interviews. Paper presented at the International Investigative Interviewing Research Group Annual Conference, Teesside.

Gozna, L. F., Teicher, S., & Boon, J. C. W. (2010, June). *Chameleon suspects: Gaining a psychological understanding from interviews with criminally versatile major crime offenders.* Paper presented at the 4th International Investigative Interviewing Conference, Brussels, Belgium.

Gray, H., & Gozna, L. F. (2010, July). *Exploring the offence supportive beliefs used by young offenders.* Paper presented at the Youth 2010 Conference, Surrey, UK.

Gross, E. F., & Hardin, C. D. (2007). Implicit and explicit stereotyping of adolescents. *Social Justice Research, 20,* 140–160.

Gudjonsson, G. H., & Sigurdsson, J. F. (1999). The Gudjonsson confession questionnaire-revised (GCQ-R): Factor structure and its relationship with personality. *Personality and Individual Differences, 27,* 953–968.

Hall, J. A., & Mast, M. S. (2008). Are women always more interpersonally sensitive than men? Impact of goals and content domain. *Personality and Social Psychology Bulletin, 34,* 144–155.

Hare, R. D. (2003). *Manual for the Revised Psychopathy Checklist* (2nd ed.). Toronto: Multi-Health Systems.

Hare, R. D. (2005, August). *Training course for the Psychopathy Checklist – Revised Version.* Darkstone Research Group Koobra OY (The Finnish Psychiatric Association and The Finnish Psychological Association), Helsinki, Finland.

Hare, R. D. (2006). Psychopathy: A clinical and forensic overview. *Psychiatric Clinics of North America, 29,* 709–724.

Hart, J. L., O' Toole, S. K., Price-Sharps, J. L., & Schaffer, T. W. (2007). The risk and protective factors of violent juvenile offending: An examination of gender differences. *Youth Violence and Juvenile Justice, 5,* 367–384.

Hartwig, M., Granhag, P. A., & Strömwall, L. A. (2007). Guilty and innocent suspects' strategies during police interrogations. *Psychology, Crime and Law, 13,* 213–227.

Hasebe, Y., Nucci, L., & Nucci, M. S. (2004). Parental control of the personal domain and adolescent symptoms of psychopathology: A cross-national study in the United States and Japan. *Child Development, 75,* 815–828.

Hendry, L. B., & Kloep, M. (2002). *Lifespan development: Resources, challenges and risks.* London: Cengage Learning.

Henning, K., Jones, A. R., & Holdford, R. (2005). "I didn't do it, but if I did I had good reason": Minimization, denial, and attributions of blame among male and female domestic violence offenders. *Journal of Family Violence, 20,* 131–139.

Hoffman, M. L. (2000). *Empathy and moral development: Implications for caring and justice.* New York: Cambridge University Press.

Hogg, M. A., & Mullin, B. A. (1999). Joining groups to reduce uncertainty: Subjective uncertainty reduction and group identification. In D. Abrams, & M. A. Hogg (Eds.), *Social identity and social cognition.* Malden: Blackwell Publishing.

HMIP (2007). Independent inspection of probation and youth offending work. Her Majesty's Inspectorate of Probation. [Electronic version]. Retrieved March 16, 2009, from http://inspectorates.homeoffice.gov.uk/hmiprobation/docs/HMIP_Annual_Report_2006/HMIP_06_07.pdf

Howard League for Penal Reform (2009). Weekly prison watch – March 2009. Retrieved March 16, 2009, from http://www.howardleague.org/index.php?id=775

Huesmann, L. R., Eron, L. D., Lefkowitz, M. M., & Walder, L. O. (1984). Stability of aggression over time and generations. *Developmental Psychology, 20,* 1120–1134.

Hughes, C., & Leekham, S. (2004). What are the links between theory of mind and social relations? Review, reflections and new directions for studies of typical and atypical development. *Social Development, 13,* 590–619.

Jackupeak, M., Tull, M. T., & Roemer, L. (2005). Masculinity, shame, and fear or emotions as predictors of men's expressions of anger and hostility. *Psychology of Men and Masculinity, 6,* 27–284.

Johnson, B. T., Maio, G. R., & Smith-McLallen, A. (2005). Communication and attitude change: Causes, processes and effects. In D. Albacarrin, B. T. Johnson, & M. P. Zanna (Eds.), *The handbook of attitudes.* Mahwah, NJ: Lawrence Erlbaum Associates, Inc.

Josephson Institute (2008). The ethics of American youth. Retrieved October 9, 2009, from www.charactercounts.org

Kashy, D. A., & DePaulo, B. M. (1996). Who lies? *Journal of Personality and Social Psychology, 70,* 1037–1051.

Kawabata, Y., & Crick, N. R. (2008). The role of cross-racial/ethnic friendships in social adjustment. *Developmental Psychology, 44,* 1177–1183.

Klaver, J. R., Lee, Z., & Hart, S. (2007). Psychopathy and non-verbal indicators of deception in offenders. *Law and Human Behaviour, 31,* 337–351.

Kloep, M., & Hendry, L. B. (in press). A systemic approach to the transitions to adulthood. In J. J. Arnett, M. Kloep, L. B. Hendry, & J. L. Tanner, *Emerging adulthood: Stage or process? A debate.* Oxford: Oxford University Press.

Knowles, E. D., Lowery, B. S., & Schaumberg, R. L. (2010). Racial prejudice predicts opposition to Obama and his health care reform plan. *Journal of Experimental Social Psychology, 46,* 420–423.

Knox, D., Zusman, M. E., McGinty, K., & Gescheidler, J. (2001). Deception of parents during adolescence. *Adolescence, 36,* 611–614.

Kohlberg, L. (1984). *Essays on moral development: Vol. 2. The psychology of moral development.* New York: Harper.

Kosson, D. S., Cyerski, T. D., Steuerwald, B. L., Neumann, C. G., & Walker-Mathews, S. (2002). The reliability and validity of the Psychopathy Checklist:Youth Version (PCL:YV) in non-incarcerated adolescent males. *Psychological Assessment, 14,* 97–109.

Larochette, A., Chambers, C. T., & Craig, K. D. (2006). Genuine, suppressed and faked facial expressions of pain in children. *Pain, 126,* 64–71.

Larson, R., & Csikszentmihalyi, M. (1978). Experiential correlates of time alone in adolescence. *Journal of Personality, 46,* 677–693.

Larrick, R. P., Burson, K. A., & Soll, J. B. (2007). Social comparison and confidence: When thinking you're better than average predicts overconfidence (and when it does not). *Organisational Behaviour and Human Decision Processes, 102,* 76–94.

Laursen, B., Furman, W., & Mooney, K. S. (2006). Predicting interpersonal competence and self-worth from adolescent relationships and relationship networks: Variable-centred and person-centred perspectives. *Merrill-Palmer Quarterly, 52,* 572–600.

Lee, Z., Klaver, J. R., & Hart, S. (2008). Psychopathy and verbal indicators of deception in offenders. *Psychology, Crime and Law, 14,* 73–84.

Lenhart, A., & Madden, M. (2007, January 7). Social networking websites and terms: An overview (memo). *Pew Internet and American Life Project*. Retrieved June 1, 2009, from www.pewInternet.org

Lehman, D. R., & Hemphill, K. J. (1990). Recipients' perceptions of support attempts and attributions for support attempts that fail. *Journal of Social and Personal Relationships, 7*, 563–574.

Lerner, R. M. (2006). Developmental science, developmental systems, and contemporary theories of human development. In R. M. Lerner, & W. Damon (Eds.), *Handbook of Child Psychology* (6th ed.). Hoboken, NJ: Wiley.

Lord, A., & Willmot, P. (2004). The process of overcoming denial in sexual offenders. *Journal of Sexual Aggression, 10*, 51–61.

Livingston, M., Stewart, A., Allard, T., & Ogilvie, J. (2008). Juvenile offending trajectories. *Australian and New Zealand Journal of Criminology, 41*, 345–363.

Lopez, V. A., & Emmer, E. T. (2002). Influences of beliefs and values on male adolescents' decisions to commit violent offences. *Psychology of Men and Masculinity, 3*, 28–40.

Louth, S. M., Williamson, S., Alpert, M., Pouget, E. R., & Hare, R. D. (1998). Acoustic distinctions in the speech of male psychopaths. *Journal of Psycholinguistic Research, 27*, 375–384.

Lynam, D. R. (1996). Early identification of chronic offenders: Who is the fledgling psychopath? *Psychological Bulletin, 120*(2), 209–234.

Maas, F. K. (2008). Children's understanding of promise, lying and false belief. *Journal of General Psychology, 135*, 301–321.

Massey, E. K., Gebhardt, W. A., & Garnefski, N. (2008). Adolescent goal content and pursuit: A review of the literature from the past 16 years. *Developmental Review, 28*, 421–460.

Masip, J., Garrido, E., & Herrero, C. (2003). Facial appearance and judgments of credibility: The effects of facial babyishness and age on statement credibility. *Genetic, Social, and General Psychology Monographs, 129*, 269–311.

Masip, J., Garrido, E., & Herrero, C. (2004). Facial appearance and impressions of credibility: The effects of facial babyishness and age on person perception. *International Journal of Psychology, 39*, 276–289.

Mayer, J. D., & Salovey, P. (1997). What is emotional intelligence? In P. Salovey, & D. J. Sluyter (Eds.), *Emotional development and emotional intelligence: Educational implications*. New York: Basic Books.

Mayer, J. D., Salovey, P., & Caruso, D. R. (2008). Emotional intelligence: New ability or eclectic traits? *American Psychologist, 63*, 503–517.

Mayer, J. D., Salovey, P., Caruso, D. R., & Sitarenios, G. (2003). Measuring emotional intelligence with the MSCEIT V2.0. *Emotion, 3*, 97–105.

Mazur, E. (2005). Online and writing: Teen blogs as mines of adolescent data. *Teaching of Psychology, 32*, 180–182.

Mazur, M. A., & Hubbard, A. S. E. (2004). "Is there something I should know?" Topic avoidant responses in parent–adolescent communication. *Communication Reports, 17*, 27–37.

McCarthy, A., & Lee, K. (2009). Children's knowledge of deceptive gaze cues and its relation to their actual lying behaviour. *Journal of Experimental Child Psychology, 103*, 117–134.

McCornack, S. A., & Levine, T. R. (1990a). When lovers become leery: The relationship between suspicion and accuracy in detecting deception. *Communication Monographs, 57,* 219–230.

McCornack, S. A., & Levine, T. R. (1990b). When lies are uncovered: Emotional and relational outcomes of discovered deception. *Communication Monographs, 57,* 119–138.

Ministry of Justice (2008). *Reoffending in juveniles: Results for the 2006 cohort.* Ministry of Justice Statistics Bulletin. Retrieved 16 March, 2009, from http://www.justice.gov.uk/docs/re-offending-juveniles-2006.pdf

Moffitt, T. E. (1997). Adolescence-limited and life-course-persistent offending: A complementary pair of developmental theories. In T. P. Thornberry (Ed.), *Developmental theories of crime and delinquency.* New Brunswick, NJ: Transaction Publishers.

Mullins, C. W. (2006). *Holding your square: Masculinities, streetlife and violence.* Abingdon: Willan Publishing.

Mussweiler, T., & Rüter, K. (2003). What friends are for! The use of routine standards in social comparison. *Journal of Personality and Social Psychology, 85,* 467–481.

Nicolson, K. (2008). Just a few years inside for teenage killers. [Electronic version] *Peterborough Today.* Retrieved April 20, 2009, from http://www.peterborough today.co.uk/news/Just-a-few-years-in.3643187.jp

Nisbett, R. E., & Wilson, T. D. (1977). The halo effect: Evidence for unconscious alteration of judgments. *Journal of Personality and Social Psychology, 35,* 250–256.

Nucci, L. P. (1996). Morality and the personal sphere of actions. In E. S. Reed, E. Turiel, & T. Brown (Eds.), *Values and knowledge.* Hillsdale, NJ: Lawrence Erlbaum Associates, Inc.

Office of National Statistics (ONS, 2007). General household survey, 2007 [Electronic version]. Retrieved July 30, 2009, from http://www.statistics.gov.uk/STATBASE/Product.asp?vlnk=5756

O'Sullivan, M. (2005). Emotional intelligence and deception detection: Why most people can't "read" others, but a few can. In R. E. Riggio, & R. S. Feldman (Eds.), *Applications of nonverbal communication.* Mahwah, NJ: Lawrence Erlbaum Associates, Inc.

O'Sullivan, P. B. (2000). What you don't know won't hurt me: Impression management functions of communication channels in relationships. *Human Communication Research, 26,* 403–431.

Patrick, C. J., Cuthbert, B. N., & Lang, P. J. (1994). Emotion in the criminal psychopath: Fear image processing. *Journal of Abnormal Psychology, 103,* 523–534.

Perkins, S. A., & Turiel, E. (2007). To lie or not to lie: To whom and under what circumstances. *Child Development, 78,* 609–621.

Petty, R. E., Cacioppo, J. T., Strathman, A. J., & Priester, J. R. (1994). To think or not to think: Exploring two routes to persuasion. In S. Shavitt, & T. C. Brock (Eds.), *Persuasion: Psychological insights and perspectives.* Needham Heights: Allyn and Bacon.

Plowman, J. (2008). *Relationships between emotional intelligence and accuracy of detecting deceit.* Unpublished dissertation, University of Glamorgan.

Porter, H., & Hirsch, A. (2009). Taking liberties: The live show. Liberty Central blog post 26 February 2009. Retrieved June 1, 2010, from http://www.guardian.co.uk/commentisfree/henryporter/2009/feb/25/police-civil-liberties

Pretty, G. M. H., Conroy, C., Dugay, J., & Fowler, K. (1996). Sense of community and its relevance to adolescents of all ages. *Journal of Community Psychology*, *24*, 365–379.

Prison Service (2009a). Young adult offenders. Retrieved August 29, 2009, from http://www.hmprisonservice.gov.uk/adviceandsupport/prison_life/youngoffenders/

Prison Service (2009b). Young people (juvenile offenders). Retrieved August 29, 2009, from http://www.hmprisonservice.gov.uk/adviceandsupport/prison_life/juvenileoffenders/

Raine, A. (1991). The SPQ: A scale for the assessment of schizotypal personality based on DSM-III-R criteria. *Schizophrenia Bulletin*, *17*, 555–564.

Raja, N. S., McGee, R., & Stanton, W. R. (1992). Perceived attachments to parents and peers and psychological well-being in adolescence. *Journal of Youth and Adolescence*, *21*, 471–485.

Reicher, S., Levine, R. M., & Gordijn, E. (1998). More on deindividuation, power relations between groups and the expression of social identity: Three studies on the effects of visibility to the in-group. *British Journal of Social Psychology*, *37*, 15–40.

Reicher, S., Spears, R., & Postmes, T. (1995). A social identity model of deindividuation phenomena. In W. Stroebe, & M. Hewstone (Eds.), *European review of social psychology* (Vol. 6). Chichester: Wiley.

Reinhard, M., & Sporer, S. L. (2008). Verbal and nonverbal behaviour as a basis for credibility attribution: The impact of task involvement and cognitive capacity. *Journal of Experimental Social Psychology*, *44*, 477–488.

Riggio, R. E. (1986). Assessment of basic social skills. *Journal of Personality and Social Psychology*, *51*, 649–660.

Riggio, R. E., Salinas, C., & Tucker, J. (1988). Personality and deception ability. *Personality and Individual Differences*, *9*, 189–191.

Riggio, R. E., Tucker, J., & Throckmorton, B. (1987). Social skills and deception ability. *Personality and Social Psychology Bulletin*, *13*, 568–577.

Riggio, R. E., Tucker, J., & Widaman, K. F. (1987). Verbal and nonverbal cues as mediators of deception ability. *Journal of Nonverbal Behaviour*, *11*, 126–145.

Rotter, J. B. (1954). *General principles for a social learning framework of personality study*. Englewood Cliffs, NJ: Prentice-Hall.

Rotter, J. B. (1971). External control and internal control. *Psychology Today*, *5*, 37–42, 58–59.

Sabourin, M. (2007). The assessment of credibility: An analysis of truth and deception in a multiethnic environment. *Canadian Psychology*, *48*, 24–31.

Schlenker, B. R., Pontari, B. A., & Christopher, A. N. (2001). Excuses and character: Personal and social implications of excuses. *Personality and Social Psychology Review*, *5*, 15–32.

Simpson, P. A., & Stroh, L. K. (2004). Gender differences: Emotional expression and feelings of personal inauthenticity. *Journal of Applied Psychology*, *89*, 715–721.

Smetana, J. G. (1995). Parenting styles and conceptions of parental authority during adolescence. *Child Development*, *66*, 299–316.

Smetana, J. G., Metzger, A., Gettman, D. C., & Campione-Barr, N. (2006).

Disclosure and secrecy in adolescent–parent relationships. *Child Development, 77*, 201–217.

Smith, J. A. (Ed.). (2008). *Qualitative psychology: A practical guide to research methods* (2nd ed.). London: Sage.

Stott, C., & Drury, J. (2000). Crowds, context and identity: Dynamic categorization processes in the "poll tax riot". *Human Relations, 53*, 247–273.

Strömwall, L. A., Hartwig, M., & Granhag, P. A. (2006). To act truthfully: Nonverbal behaviour and strategies during a police interrogation. *Psychology, Crime and Law, 12*, 207–219.

Stuart-Hamilton, I., Taylor, R., & Nash, P. (in preparation). Perceptions of credibility of younger and older adults. Manuscript in preparation.

Sullivan, C. J. (2006). Early adolescent delinquency: Assessing the role of childhood problems, family environment and peer pressure. *Youth Violence and Juvenile Justice, 4*, 291–313.

Tajfel, H. (1972). *Experiments in a vacuum. The context of social psychology: A critical assessment.* Oxford: Academic Press.

Tajfel, H., & Turner, J. C. (1979). An integrative theory of group conflict. In W. G. Austin, & S. Worchel (Eds.), *The social psychology of intergroup relations.* Monterey, CA: Brooks-Cole.

Tarrant, M., & Campbell, E. (2007). Responses to within-group criticism: Does past adherence to group norms matter? *European Journal of Social Psychology, 37*, 1187–1202.

Taylor, R., & Gozna, L. F. (2010, July). *Adolescent deception: Boundaries, strategies and blame.* Paper presented at 20th Annual Conference of the European Association of Psychology and Law, Gothenburg, Sweden.

Taylor, R., & Hick, R. F. (2007). Believed cues to deception: Judgments in self-generated trivial and serious situations. *Legal and Criminological Psychology, 12*, 321–331.

Taylor, R., & Nash, P. (2006). Decision-making during deceptive interactions: Sender and receiver perspectives. In L. Goodwin (Ed.), *Psychological correlates of criminality.* London: IA-IP Press.

Taylor, R., Nicholls, J., & Fisher, H. (under review). *Excuses, strategies and evasion: Differences between high and low self-monitors.* Manuscript submitted for publication.

Taylor, R., & Rolfe, C. (2005, July). *Believed cues to deception: A qualitative investigation.* Paper presented at the 15th Conference of the European Association of Psychology and Law. Vilnius, Lithuania.

Taylor, R., & Rolfe, C. (2009). "Well you made me do it!" Perceptions of the targets and perpetrators of everyday deceptions. *Social Psychology Review, 11*, 51–56.

Taylor, R., & Rolfe, C. (under review). *Beliefs about the cues to deception: Distraction, deflection and impression management.* Manuscript submitted for publication.

Thomas, M. (2009). Stop and search? Carry the card [Electronic version]. *The Guardian*, 10 February 2009. Retrieved June 1, 2010, from http://www.guardian.co.uk/commentisfree/2009/feb/09/liberty-central-stop-and-search-police

Turner, J. C. (1985). Social categorization and the self-concept: a social cognitive theory of group behaviour. *Advances in Group Processes: Theory and Research, 2*, 77–122.

Twenge, J. M., Baumeister, R. F., Tice, D. M., & Stucke, T. S. (2001). If you can't join them, beat them: Effects of social exclusion on aggressive behaviour. *Journal of Personality and Social Psychology, 81,* 1058–1069.

Tyler, J. M., & Feldman, R. S. (2007). The double-edged sword of excuses: When do they help, when do they hurt. *Journal of Social and Clinical Psychology, 26,* 659–688.

Vrij, A. (2004). Why professionals fail to catch liars and how they can improve. *Legal and Criminological Psychology, 9,* 159–181.

Vrij, A. (2008). *Detecting lies and deceit: Pitfalls and opportunities* (2nd ed.). New York: Wiley.

Vrij, A., Akehurst, L., Brown, L., & Mann, S. (2006). Detecting lies in young children, adolescents and adults. *Applied Cognitive Psychology, 20,* 1225–1237.

Vrij, A., & Holland, M. (1998). Individual differences in persistence in lying and experiences while deceiving. *Communication Research Reports, 3,* 299–308.

Vrij, A., Leal, S., Mann, S., Warmelink, L., Granhag, P. A., & Fisher, R. P. (2010). Drawings as an innovative and successful lie detection tool. *Applied Cognitive Psychology, 24,* 587–594.

Vrij, A., Mann, S., Leal, S., & Fisher, R. P. (2010, July). *Drawings as a tool to detect deceit in occupation interviews.* Paper presented at the 20th Annual Conference of the European Association of Psychology and Law, Gothenburg, Sweden.

Vrij, A., Mann, S., Robbins, E., & Robinson, M. (2006). Police officers' ability to detect deception in high stakes situations and in repeated lie detection tests. *Applied Cognitive Psychology, 20,* 741–755.

Vrij, A., Semin, G. R., & Bull, R. (1996). Insight into behaviour displayed during deception. *Human Communication Research, 22,* 544–562.

Vygotsky, L. S. (1978). *Mind in society.* Cambridge, MA: Harvard University Press.

Wickman, M., Anderson, N., & Smith-Greenberg, C. (2008). The adolescent perception of invincibility and its influence on teen acceptance of health promotion strategies. *Journal of Paediatric Nursing, 23,* 460–468.

Wilkowski, B. M., Robinson, M. D., Gordon, R. D., & Troop-Gordon, W. (2007). Tracking the evil eye: Trait anger and selective attention within ambiguously hostile scenes. *Journal of Research in Personality, 41,* 650–666.

Wilson, A. E., Smith, M. D., & Ross, H. S. (2003). The nature and effects of young children's lies. *Social Development, 12,* 21–45.

Wolak, J., Mitchell, K. J., & Finkelhor, D. (2002). Close online relationships in a national sample of adolescents. *Adolescence, 37,* 441–455.

Wong, Y. J., Pituch, K. A., & Rochlen, A. B. (2006). Men's restrictive emotionality: An investigation of associations with other emotion related constructs, anxiety, and underlying dimensions. *Psychology of Men and Masculinity, 7,* 113–126.

Youth Justice Board (2009). About the Youth Justice Board. Retrieved February 1, 2009 and August 15, 2009, from http://www.yjb.gov.uk/en-gb/yjs/

Zebrowitz, L. A., Voinescu, L., & Collins, M. A. (1996). "Wide eyed" and "crooked-faced": Determinants of perceived and real honesty across the life span. *Personality and Social Psychology Bulletin, 22,* 1258–1269.

Author index

Subject index